Routledge Library Editions

THE ECONOMICS OF A DECLINING POPULATION

ECONOMICS

Routledge Library Editions – Economics

WELFARE ECONOMICS AND ECONOMIC POLICY

In 8 Volumes

I	Essays in Economic Management	*Cairncross*
II	Keynes, Beveridge and Beyond	*Cutler et al*
III	Some Aspects of the Inequality of Incomes in Modern Communities	*Dalton*
IV	National Income and Social Accounting	*Edey et al*
V	Political Arithmetic	*Hogben*
VI	The Economics of a Declining Population	*Reddaway*
VII	Welfare and Competition	*Scitovsky*
VIII	Papers on Welfare and Growth	*Scitovsky*

THE ECONOMICS OF A DECLINING POPULATION

W B REDDAWAY

Routledge
Taylor & Francis Group
LONDON AND NEW YORK

First published in 1939
Published 2014 by Routledge

2 Park Square, Milton Park, Abingdon, Oxfordshire OX14 4RN
711 Third Avenue, New York, NY 10017

First issued in paperback 2014

Transferred to Digital Printing 2007

Routledge is an imprint of the Taylor & Francis Group, an informa business

British Library Cataloguing in Publication Data
A CIP catalogue record for this book
is available from the British Library

The Economics of a Declining Population

ISBN 978-0-415-31408-4 (hbk)
ISBN 978-1-138-87864-8 (pbk)

Miniset: Welfare Economics and Economic Policy

Series: Routledge Library Editions – Economics

THE ECONOMICS OF A DECLINING POPULATION

BY

W. B. REDDAWAY

M.A.

Clare College, Cambridge

Routledge
Taylor & Francis Group
LONDON AND NEW YORK

FIRST PUBLISHED IN 1939
SECOND IMPRESSION 1946

PREFACE TO THE SECOND IMPRESSION

THIS book has been out of print since 1941, when the remaining stock was destroyed by enemy action. In view of the current interest in population questions the publishers have allotted a part of their paper ration to the production of a new edition.

Several factors have combined to make this new edition simply a reproduction of the old. Firstly, as a member of the Economics Committee of the Royal Commission on Population I feel it would be inappropriate for me to publish anything fresh on the subject until the Commission has presented its report. Secondly, there is in fact nothing which I want to alter in the fundamental analysis, whilst any attempt to bring the illustrative statistics up-to-date would be of little value until the war is over. Finally, the war-time shortage of printing facilities encouraged the use of a photographic method to give, literally, a reproduction of the first edition. As a consequence, of course, all statements which appear in the present tense must be read as referring to 1939.

One point does, however, seem to deserve even more emphasis than it receives in the text, because the war has made it more important. On pages 218–19 the point is made that if our population were still increasing at the old rate, then we should be perpetually having to find more outlets for our exports in order to pay for our increased import requirements. The difficulty of doing this on satisfactory terms seemed great enough even before the war to make the absence of population increase a real relief. We are now officially told that such factors as the sale of our international assets and the piling-up of international debts call for a 50% increase in our pre-war exports even with our present population. We can indeed be thankful that this formidable task is not rendered ever more difficult by the necessity for a further increase to cover the needs of a rapidly rising population.

W.B.R.

Cambridge,
February, 1945.

PREFACE TO THE FIRST EDITION

THE economic consequences of our changing population are matters in which many classes of people take a lively interest. To the aspiring writer on the subject this is both a great encouragement and a great difficulty. For some of the topics to be discussed lend themselves readily to a "popular" treatment, whereas a proper analysis of others really requires an extensive use of advanced economics. (It is almost impossible, for example, to examine the effect of a declining population on unemployment unless one has a clear idea of what determines its level *now.*) Consequently any single book is in danger of falling between at least half a dozen stools.

Nevertheless, this one is frankly a compromise, designed as far as possible to fill all the gaps which undoubtedly exist. Thus I have tried to avoid the use of difficult technical terms, and to include enough preliminary explanations to enable the lay reader to follow at least the main points. I have also designed my bibliographies primarily for him, confining them to short lists of works which really should be helpful, instead of compiling a book catalogue to impress the critics. I make no apology, however, for saying that if he wants to derive the full benefit from his reading, then he must be prepared to work hard; a novice cannot expect to do advanced figure-skating without a real effort, even though he can omit many of the initial exercises included in the ordinary curriculum.

The professional economist, on the other hand, may want to skip the parts primarily designed for the beginner. Such a procedure would be quite natural, and I have tried to facilitate it by providing summaries of two chapters. But I must confess that I hope he will not do so. The lay reader often serves as a useful excuse for dealing carefully with points which are not really as simple as they seem; I have personally learnt a great deal by reading other people's "elementary" treatments which contained more than appeared on the surface.

The plan of the book really needs no explanation. Part I describes briefly how estimates of future populations are made, and what the position is in this country; it contains little which is new, but is required as a basis for Part II. This examines in turn the probable developments in each of the more important parts of our economic life; where appropriate I have suggested measures which would help to maximize the advantages and minimize the disadvantages. On all issues I have tried to preserve a sense of proportion, and not to exaggerate the influence of the population factor. Where it seems impossible to give an answer, except by hedging it around with so many limitations as to make it useless, I have not been afraid to say so.

One word of warning seems to be necessary. The words "Declining Population" in the title have been used to cover all the coming changes in its size and age-composition. This has the sanction of much current usage; but some of the changes are really due to factors which cannot possibly be included in the word "declining"—e.g. the increased expectation of life, which actually serves to postpone the fall in numbers. Where the distinction is important—above all when we are discussing the advisability of trying to raise the birth-rate—the effects of the two factors have been separated out.

Mr. D. V. Glass has given me valuable assistance on some statistical points, but must not be held responsible for the use I have made of his material; various essays written by my pupils have been helpful in more ways than one.

W. B. REDDAWAY

CLARE COLLEGE, CAMBRIDGE
March 1939

CONTENTS

Part I

INTRODUCTION

Economists are sometimes accused of inventing imaginary worlds quite unrelated to reality, and then wasting their own and their students' time in laborious analysis of these creations.

In the nineteenth century, a proposal to write a book about the economic consequences of a declining population would have been regarded as a typical instance of this perverse habit. At the beginning of the century, Malthus had written at great length about the tendency of populations to increase up to the limits set by the means of subsistence. His original doctrine had been whittled down somewhat by qualifications and exceptions, both by himself and by others. But the general impressions remained—that for practical purposes one could assume an increasing population in all cases which were likely to arise, and that the object of policy should be to restrict this increase to manageable proportions.

Moreover, this impression was confirmed and strengthened by recorded facts—always far more convincing than the most plausible reasoning. Successive censuses showed the following results for England and Wales (to the nearest million).

1801 ..	8 millions	1861 ..	20 millions
1811 ..	10 ,,	1871 ..	23 ,,
1821 ..	12 ,,	1881 ..	26 ,,
1831 ..	14 ,,	1891 ..	29 ,,
1841 ..	16 ,,	1901 ..	33 ,,
1851 ..	18 ,,		

This persistent increase, secured despite a considerable amount of emigration, seemed to most people conclusive. Sensationalists drew terrible pictures of a world in which there would be standing room only. The apostles of birth control regarded themselves as performing a public duty.

Moreover, the phenomenon was in no way peculiar to England; similar results were being shown in almost all countries. Even in 1911 the possibility of a declining population was considered to be of little more than theoretical interest, if we may judge by the following quotation from the eleventh edition of the *Encyclopaedia Britannica:*—

"Population is continually in a state of motion, and in large aggregates the direction is *invariably* towards increase. The forces underlying the movement may differ from time to time in their respective intensity, and, in *highly exceptional* cases, may approach equilibrium, their natural tendencies being interrupted by special causes, but the instances of general decline are confined to wild and comparatively small communities brought into contact with alien and more civilized races."[1]

Yet now the picture is completely changed. In all countries for which we have reliable statistics, the natural rate of increase (i.e. the rate ignoring migration) has fallen substantially, and in many of the most "civilized," it is now almost negligible. In the case of England and Wales, for example, the rates in the last five years have all been below 3·5 per 1,000, whereas for 1876–80 the average was 14·5.[2]

But this is only part, and not even the most important part of the story. The rate at which a population is changing at any time depends on the difference between what are known as the crude birth-rate and the crude death-rate. These are the figures which are most easily calculated from the recorded statistics, being simply the proportions of births and deaths to the total population. For a study of population trends, however, they are of very little value, because they do not measure any of the fundamental factors, but are greatly influenced by one which may be purely temporary—the age-composition of the existing population.

[1] Article on Population; my italics.

[2] See the Registrar-General's *Statistical Review* for 1936 (Part II, Civil), p. 70.

The importance of this point will be readily appreciated with the aid of a single example. We have seen that the records of births and deaths for England and Wales show a small excess of births for all recent years, and it might be thought that the population is likely to stabilize itself at about the present level "unless there is some fundamental change in social habits." Yet nothing could be further from the truth. If we give the most natural meaning to the proviso about "social habits," then each future generation is likely to be at least 20 per cent smaller than the one before.

The object of this book is to deal with the consequences of a declining population, not the technical methods of forecasting it; those readers who are interested in the details of the latter problem should consult the works of Dr. Charles, Professor Carr-Saunders, Dr. Kuczynski, and others. But the fundamental principles of the method adopted are not difficult to understand, and it is important that the reader should appreciate the strength of the evidence on which various estimates of future population have been made. Chapter I, therefore, describes the technique in broad outline. Readers who are already familiar with it will find a summary at the end, which should suffice to remind them of the essential points.

CHAPTER I

POPULATION FORECASTING

THIS subject falls naturally into two parts, a study of births and a study of deaths. In defiance of nature we shall begin with the latter, partly because it simplifies the exposition, partly on the schoolboy's principle of shirking the more difficult subjects until they can be avoided no longer.

The first thing to be noted is that the probability of a person's dying within a year varies very considerably with his (or her) age.[1] It is comparatively high (6–7 per cent in England and Wales) for newly-born infants; but if they survive the perils of the first year, then the chance of their dying in the next is much reduced. It sinks to an almost negligible figure (0·1 per cent) in the years of childhood, and then slowly rises. At about 50 it reaches 1 per cent again, and thereafter its increase is more rapid, until for very old people it becomes almost a certainty.

The whole question has been very carefully studied by life insurance companies, who base their rates on "life tables." These set out how much longer the average man (or woman) can expect to live if he has already reached a certain age; they are prepared by estimating the chance of his dying this year, next year, the year after and so on, on the basis of past experience. Needless to say, the result may be wildly wrong in individual cases, but the business of life insurance would be almost impossible if the tables were not reasonably accurate when the results are averaged over a large number of people.

It follows from the above argument that we shall expect far more deaths in a given year, if the population is composed

[1] It is also somewhat different for the two sexes, but we shall not deal with this (comparatively unimportant) complication.

largely of old people or babies, than we would with an equally healthy population made up mainly of adolescents. We have an excellent illustration of this in the figures for different towns; some of the most healthy towns in the country show a high death-rate because old people settle down there when they retire. Thus Bournemouth has a figure (1936) of 13·9 per 1,000, and Bath one of 15·2, against a national average of 12·1. To secure some sort of comparability, the Registrar-General publishes also a correcting factor designed to allow for the difference between the age- and sex-composition of each town, and that of the whole country. The adjusted figures for Bournemouth and Bath are 10·4 and 11·2 respectively.[1]

The crude death-rate is, therefore, of little use for making population forecasts, because there is no reason to suppose it will remain at all constant if the age-composition is changing. The fundamental factors are the mortality-rates, which give the probability of people of different ages dying within a year, or the life-table, which gives the same information in a different form. Experience shows that these change only slowly, though any one year may show results materially different from the normal on account of an unusual epidemic. Such a disturbance will generally not have much lasting effect, because a life-table based on experience automatically allows for a "normal" frequency of epidemics; the bad year will therefore be balanced by a number of relatively good ones. The general trend of mortality-rates is downwards, on account of improved hygiene and higher incomes; but the movement is gradual, and a reasonable allowance can be made for its continuance. The only factor which is likely to cause a serious error in estimates of future mortality-rates is a major war.

With the aid of our mortality-rates we can calculate the number of deaths to be expected in a population of given age-composition, and so the crude death-rate. Such a

[1] Figures from Registrar-General, op. cit., Table E.

statement, however, is not in itself very helpful for forecasting population changes. It rather resembles the statement by the mice that if they could discover a way of tying a bell to the cat, then they would know when the cat was coming. Mortality-rates will tell us the future death-rate if we can find out the future age-composition; but how are we to find out the latter?

Unlike the mice however we have a fairly easy way of solving our problems. We know the age-composition of the population in 1931 from the census and, neglecting minor technicalities about migration, we can bring this up to date with the records of subsequent births and deaths. (In fact the Registrar-General does this each year.) The principle of the method is, then, as follows. Suppose we want to estimate the number of people who will be aged 27 a year hence; still ignoring migration, these can only come from the people who are now 26. Some of the latter will however, have died within the year; our mortality table tells us the most probable number. We have only to subtract these, and our problem is solved; and similarly for the numbers at all ages above one year. The number aged less than one can only be calculated if we know, or can estimate, the number of births which will take place in the next twelve months, and the subject must therefore be postponed.

Having thus obtained the figures for next year's population, we can repeat the process for as many years as we desire. At each stage we calculate from the mortality-rates how many people aged (say) 23 will survive to constitute the number aged 24 for next year. We need not continue to use the same mortality-rates for future years as we did for the first; if we consider it likely that these will continue to fall, then we can steadily reduce them by a small amount. Clearly opinions may differ as to the appropriate amount—pessimists might even want to raise them on the grounds that the political situation suggests frequent wars. But few responsible estimators would want to make alterations so large as to make much difference except over a very long period.

The careful reader will have observed that for each year that we carry such a forecast into the future, we leave one more blank in our table. For the first year we had no figure for people under twelve months; for the second we could similarly say nothing about people aged one year, but not yet two; and so on. These age-groups can only be filled in when we have found out how many people will be born in the various years between now and the date for which the estimate is required.

Nevertheless we can answer a fair number of important questions on the basis of mortality-rates alone, without any knowledge of births. Suppose for example we want to know how many old-age pensioners there will be in 1979, assuming that everybody over 65 is eligible. All the potential candidates must already be alive and over 25, and we know how many there are of each age. We can, therefore, calculate how many survivors there will still be 40 years hence by the method described. The only difficulties are to allow for migration and for changes in mortality-rates, though it must be admitted in this case, the uncertainty about the latter may be rather important.

Or take another example, the importance of which will be apparent when we discuss births. We shall then want to know how many women of child-bearing age will be alive at different dates. It is usually assumed that the limits of this period are 15 to 45, so that we can calculate the answer for any year up to 1954 without any knowledge of birth-rates. We may, perhaps, anticipate subsequent arguments somewhat by putting this conclusion in another way. Nothing that may happen to the birth-rate now can affect the number of "potential mothers" in the slightest for fifteen years; and its full effect will not be secured for forty-five years.

Other possible uses for calculations based on mortality-rates alone would be to estimate the number of people of working age at future dates, for use in preparing a scheme of unemployment insurance; or the number of potential soldiers; or the number of children of school age. The last calculation can, however, only be made for a very few years without some estimate of births, because it is concerned with age-groups for which blanks soon appear in the table.

It is worth noticing that in making these forecasts we have never actually calculated the crude death-rate for future years. Our concern has been with the survivors in each age-group, and for this the separate mortality-rates have always been used. This need not surprise us, for we saw at the start that the death-rate is not itself a fundamental factor, but a sort of statistical accident—a compound of the mortality-rates, which may be said to measure the healthiness or "long-livedness" of the people, and the current age-composition. Of course, we *can* calculate it quite simply—or rather we shall be able to as soon as we have filled in the blanks in the table by making our estimates of births. For all we have to do is to add up the number of deaths in the various age-groups, and divide by the total population. The answer will doubtless be "interesting" in a vague way to people who have seen the annual figures derived from official records. But the only people who ought to regard it as really *important* are the undertakers.[1] If for the moment we may be allowed to anticipate subsequent work for their benefit, we can assure them that the English rate is almost certain to rise in the near future, even if improved hygiene reduces mortality-rates; for the proportion of old people in the community is steadily increasing.

Having broken the glad news of a coming boom to the undertakers we must now turn our attention to the question of births. How are we to estimate the number of

[1] Perhaps one should add the Chancellor of the Exchequer, who is concerned with the number of people who will pay death-duties.

births to be expected in future years, so as to fill in our blanks?

One thing may be said straight away. The crude birth-rate is of no more use for this purpose than the crude death-rate was for estimating deaths. And the reason is the same; it does not correspond with any single fundamental factor, such as the number of children in the average family, or the proportion of women who have no family, nor even to a simple combination of these. Once more it is vitally affected by the age-composition of the population, which can (and does) change greatly.

The simplest method of estimating births is as follows. We know for many years past the number of women in the population who were of child-bearing age, as defined above. We also know the number of births recorded in each of these years. From these two we calculate a "fertility-rate," measuring the number of children born per thousand "potential mothers." We then study these rates, perhaps plotting them on a graph, and decide what rates we shall assume to hold for future years. (We might, for example, assume that the rate will remain the same in future as in the latest year, or that the downward trend which has persisted, with minor interruptions, for many years will continue.) We can then calculate the number of births to be expected this year (since we know the number of "potential mothers"), apply the mortality table to allow for babies dying before the end of it, and fill in the first blank in our table. By continuing the process, we can complete the entire table, since for each year we can estimate the number of potential mothers, and so the number of births.

To what extent does the use of the fertility-rate avoid the objection which we levelled against the use of the crude birth-rate as a means of estimating the number of births? It is clearly an improvement, for the number of births is more directly connected with the number of potential mothers than with the size of the total population, irrespective of age or sex. In effect, the method assumes that the number of births in any year depends on two factors —the number of "potential mothers," and what we may term "the attitude towards child-bearing," which we measure by the fertility-rate. We shall examine the difficulties inherent in the second factor in a moment; for the present we shall consider only the first.

If a woman were equally likely to bear a child at any age between 15 and 45, then there would be nothing more to be said. But this is not the case. In England we have no records which throw any light on the subject, because the mother's age is not recorded when a birth is registered. (As I write this a Bill is before Parliament which would provide for this to be done.) But common observation tells us that the chance of a girl of 15 bearing a child is far smaller than it is for a woman of 25; and also that few women bear children when they are 45. If we call the chance of a woman bearing a child at any given age the "specific fertility-rate" for that age, then we shall expect it to be small at both ends of the range and highest somewhere in the twenties.

If this is so (and the statistics of countries such as Sweden and Australia show that it is), then we should clearly make some allowance for it in calculating the probable number of births. It is quite true that a woman of 45 and one of 25 are both "potential mothers," in the sense that they might bear a child. But they obviously should not be counted as of equal importance for population forecasting.

The matter is essentially similar to the problem of estimating deaths. Any individual may die within a year, whatever his age; he is, if you like, a "potential corpse." But the undertaker who wanted to estimate the probable demand for his services would never reckon a man in the prime of life and a centenarian as of equal value. Our first approximation in forecasting the number of births was to divide the women in the community into "possibles" and "impossibles," just as the undertaker might decide that people under 40 could be ignored, and reckon all above that age equally as "prospects." We now have to subdivide the possibles into their component age-groups, just as the undertaker might.

The procedure is also very similar. We assume for each age a specific fertility-rate (corresponding with the mortality-rate), and multiply this by the number of women of that age. (The omission of women outside the range 15 to 45 simply amounts to assuming the rate to be zero for those ages.) In this manner we make full allowance for the age-composition of the population in the year under discussion; our first method was an approximation which would be accurate if the age-composition of the potential mothers remained the same, and reasonably so if it did not vary much. By eliminating the factor of age-composition we have now cleared the way for the more difficult task of forecasting any change in what we called "the attitude towards child-bearing"; this is now represented by a complete table of mortality-rates.[1]

We have now arrived at the really crucial question for any long-range forecast of population. How confidently can we predict future levels of specific fertility-rates? Changes in these are far more important than changes in mortality-rates, because the latter mainly affect people who can no longer influence the size of future generations. It is of comparatively little importance whether or not the doctors find ways of making old people live longer; it is of absolutely vital importance to know whether the average woman will bear more or fewer children, because these will also have children, so that the effect is cumulative. The mortality-rates for people under 40 are already so low that even a reduction

[1] It may be asked how this technique can be applied in England, since the records do not tell us the initial value of the specific fertility-rates. This difficulty is avoided with the aid of Swedish figures. These show very similar results for the general fertility-rate, and we assume that the English specific rates will be proportional to the Swedish. The possible errors involved in this assumption are very small.

by 50 per cent would not greatly affect the size of the next generation.

If we look at past records, we find a continuous fall in fertility-rates. This has not been uniform for the different ages, but this fact is not for the moment so important as its enormous size. The official figures for the birth-rate show a fall which is big enough in all conscience; in England and Wales it has declined from 33·5 in 1881–85 to 14·7 in 1933–36. Yet the fall in fertility has been decidedly greater, the birth-rate being kept up by the increased proportion of potential mothers in a population with relatively fewer children.

Where a rate has proved so variable in the past it is obviously unwise to speak dogmatically of its future behaviour, even though the general trend has been always in the downward direction. With mortality we could be reasonably confident in our estimates; changes in the past have been far less sensational, and the factors affecting it are reasonably well understood. Moreover, they are ones in which the influence of human decisions can (apart from wars) be assumed to operate only in one direction—we all approve of efforts to improve the health and well-being of the community. Medicine may have some surprises in store for us, but they will have to be veritable sensations if they are seriously to upset our estimates.

Fertility on the other hand depends on very complex factors, and is particularly subject to changes arising out of human decisions, the nature of which cannot be predicted. We must therefore confess that any single estimate of future population must be subject to a very considerable margin of error, because it may be based on a false assumption about fertility-rates. This does not, however, mean that all our laborious calculations are futile and that nothing can be said about future trends. In the first place we have already seen that a great many questions can be answered, particularly about the next fifteen years or so, without knowing anything about fertility at all. In the second we can say with confidence that fertility-rates are most unlikely to change violently in a short period, except for such reasons as the ending of a war, and even then the movement is generally a temporary one; hence we can estimate the number of births for the next ten years or so with *reasonable* confidence. And in the third we can make alternative assumptions about future fertility-rates which we regard as setting the upper and lower limits to any changes which are sufficiently likely to be worth considering. Opinions may of course differ greatly about these limits, and it might well be expected that no significant conclusions would be established with any certainty. It so happens, however, that for England and Wales (and many other countries) this is not the case. Even putting fertility-rates at the highest figures which any responsible person would consider reasonable (failing a deliberate and determined social policy to raise them), the future population is certain both to be smaller and to have an older age-composition. We shall examine this question more fully in Chapter II.

There is one more piece of statistical technique which must be briefly described. We have seen how to prepare a complete table showing the size and age-composition of the population in future years. But it would obviously be useful to have a short-cut method of telling whether the fundamental factors in the situation—the fertility- and mortality-rates—are making for a larger or smaller population, and how rapid the movement is likely to be. How much larger or smaller will future generations be than the present ones? This question is most quickly answered by calculating what is known as the "net reproductive rate."

The broad principle involved in this concept is that we should calculate how many girl children will be born on the average to each girl born this year. The procedure may best be understood by following the probable life-history of one thousand of the latter until they are past child-bearing age.

In each year the mortality-rates tell us what proportion will probably die, and so we can calculate the probable number of survivors at any age. For the ages between 15 and 45 the specific fertility-rates tell us what proportion of these survivors will probably bear a child, and so we can find out the number of children born in each year, and hence the total number that these mothers will bear during their lives. For really accurate work we should then allow for the ratio of baby girls to baby boys, but in general it will suffice to calculate the number of girls by dividing by two; to obtain the net reproductive rate we then divide by 1,000.

If the net reproductive rate is less than one, then the number of girls in the next generation will be smaller than that in the present one, and the fundamental factors are making for a decline in population. Unless they change, this decline is certain to come fairly soon, even if (as is now the case) a favourable age-composition may *temporarily* outweigh them and produce an increase. Hence the great usefulness of the net reproductive rate as a means of summing up the really important factors in the situation. Hence also the considerable amount of work which has been devoted to making it as reliable an instrument as possible. The technical details of this are outside the scope of this book, but one warning is perhaps necessary. Net reproductive rates are frequently calculated on the basis of the birth statistics for a single year. Such a procedure is open to serious criticism, because the number of births in any one year may well be abnormally reduced, say through the postponement of marriages in a depression; provided the depression is not permanent, this deficiency will be at least partially offset by a subsequent excess. No insurance company would use mortality tables based on a single year, which might have witnessed a violent epidemic; and there is even less justification for calculating net reproduction rates with the aid of fertility tables so compiled.

To repeat, the net reproductive rate tells us how much

larger or smaller the next generation will be than the present one, assuming fertility- and mortality-rates to remain unchanged. It is not an adequate substitute for the full calculation, because in general we should not regard this assumption as the most likely one. Provided we state clearly what we are doing, we can of course interpret the assumption about fertility and mortality as meaning that the rates experienced in a single year (generally the latest) will persist. But this is not really a very sensible procedure, since almost every year is peculiar in some respect. Fertility-rates are meant to represent "the current attitude towards child-bearing," and since marriages and births can be postponed, this is essentially a thing which should be estimated from results spread over a period.

I hope the reader will also have concluded that there is no point in recording net reproduction rates to several places of decimals. This gives an appearance of great accuracy which is highly misleading. It is doubtful whether the data are sufficiently accurate to make such calculations reliable, even when we define our assumptions precisely. It is certain that no useful conclusions can be drawn from the numerous decimals because, as we have seen, the rate tells us what will happen *on assumptions that we know to be subject to large errors.* In my opinion, the most useful statement that can now be made about the present position in England and Wales is that the rate is between 0·7 and 0·8. This is true on all reasonable interpretations of the definition, and it tells us as much as a summary should.

One final word about the crude birth-rate. Its position is essentially similar to that of the crude death-rate—it has acquired an "interest value" quite disproportionate to its real importance. It does not appear anywhere in our calculations, but we can estimate it quite simply from them. And we can then not only satisfy our idle curiosity, but also issue a warning to manufacturers of cradles, baby food, and the like that the birth-rate will fall further, even if fertility-rates are maintained. If the reader cannot work out the reason for himself, he had better re-read this chapter.

SUMMARY

1. Population forecasts are based on knowledge about the size and age-composition of the present population, derived from the census and records of subsequent births, deaths, and migration.
2. Neglecting future migration, the number of people aged, say, 25 in 1940 must be equal to the number who are aged 24 in 1939, less the ones who have died. Mortality tables tell us, with considerable accuracy, what proportion of the people of any age will die within a year. Hence we calculate the size of all the age-groups in 1940 except the lowest.
3. This process is continued into the future. At each stage we should allow for expected changes in mortality-rates, which have slowly declined in the past. This introduces some uncertainty into our estimates but, apart from the risk of a possible major war, it is not very serious. We can regard estimates of those parts of future populations, which consist of the survivors of people already born, with some confidence.
4. The number of births in the first year is estimated by multiplying the number of women in each age-group between 15 and 45 by the "specific fertility-rate" for that age. (This measures the proportion of women of that age who will probably bear a child, and is based on past experience.)
5. Allowance is then made for the number of these babies who will die before the end of the year, and so the complete age-composition for 1940 is known. And the population for all future years is similarly derived from that of the year before.
6. The uncertain element is the future movement of fertility-rates. These have declined very rapidly in the past, and it must be confessed that no confident prediction can be made about their future behaviour.
7. Since the influence of changes in fertility is cumulative, estimates extending beyond one or two generations are subject to a very wide margin of error indeed. But two important results do, nevertheless, emerge; in the case of many countries, including England and Wales, the highest estimate of fertility which anyone would consider reasonable,

failing a deliberate social policy aimed at raising it very greatly, still makes a fairly rapid decline inevitable; and there will also be a greatly increased proportion of people in the higher age-groups.

8. A convenient summary of the fundamental trend of population is provided by the net reproductive rate. This tells us the ratio of the size of the next generation to the size of this one, assuming fertility- and mortality-rates to remain unchanged. It is calculated by following the probable history of a thousand girls born this year and seeing how many girl children they may be expected to bear.
9. The net reproductive rate should be used with some caution and a full appreciation of the assumptions involved. In particular the rates assumed for fertility should not be based on a single year's experience, and the result should not be given to more than two places of decimals as an absolute maximum. The present rate for England and Wales is between 0·7 and 0·8.

BIBLIOGRAPHY

I have deliberately avoided the more difficult and technical points, such as the problem of allowing for the number of recent marriages to improve the usefulness of fertility-rates, distinction between legitimate and illegitimate births, the treatment of deaths below the age of one, and so on. None of these are really important for a book of this kind. For a more extended treatment of the whole subject the reader should consult:—

R. R. KUCZYNSKI: *The Balance of Births and Deaths*
Fertility and Reproduction
The Measurement of Population Growth

E. CHARLES: *The Menace of Under-population* (Chapter 2)

D. V. GLASS AND C. P. BLACKER: *Population and Fertility*

CHAPTER II

THE PRESENT POSITION IN GREAT BRITAIN

THE object of Chapter I was to explain the method of population forecasting; now we have to see what results are obtained by applying this technique to the present situation in this country. The reader will then be able to appreciate the relevance of this book; he will find that many of the more important conclusions have already been mentioned as incidental illustrations. In particular he will already be aware of the fact that the net reproductive rate for England and Wales is between 0·7 and 0·8, and of what that implies.

There is one point which may be usefully cleared out of the way before we begin. Official statistics are generally published separately for England and Wales, and for Scotland. The position in the two regions is somewhat different, for Scotland has consistently shown higher birth- and fertility-rates. In the years before the depression, however, there was considerable emigration from Scotland, both to other parts of this island and overseas; so that the population in 1931 was actually slightly lower than in 1921. With emigration replaced by a small return flow of Scots the population has recently increased at a faster rate than that of England and Wales. And, what is more important for our purpose, there is no reason to expect a decline for many years, unless fertility falls or emigration is resumed, for her net reproductive rate is not much below unity. In the discussion which follows we shall be concerned almost exclusively with England and Wales. To some extent, of course, this means that the problems will be exaggerated; but the population of Scotland is only about a ninth of the whole, and so its exclusion makes comparatively little difference.

The classic study of the position in England and Wales

was made by Dr. Charles, and originally published in 1935 as Special Memorandum No. 40 of the London and Cambridge Economic Service; it has since been republished in slightly amended form (including a treatment of the Scotch position) in *Political Arithmetic*.[1] My treatment of the subject will be based mainly on this work. The actual conclusions will be given very briefly, and those who want greater detail should consult the original. I shall make one or two comments which seem to be necessary.

Dr. Charles made three estimates, based respectively on the following assumptions:—

(*a*) That fertility- and mortality-rates would remain the same as in 1933 (the latest year then available).

(*b*) That both rates would continue to decline in much the same way as they had done in the past.

(*c*) That mortality-rates would fall, but that fertility would rise by about 10 per cent to the 1931 level and remain constant. (This was regarded as a purely theoretical "outside limit," and was not treated in such detail.)

In each case migration was ignored, and the starting-point was the population on January 1, 1935. We must first consider the legitimacy of adopting these estimates as guides to the future. In the first place, should we not take a more recent starting-point, since later information is now available?

On paper we can make out quite a good case for revising at least the second estimate in this way. It assumed that fertility in the years 1935–38 would fall progressively further below that of 1933. Such an assumption was inherently most improbable even when made, for some short-period *rise* from the slump level was virtually certain as postponed marriages took place. And in fact the number of births in those years (and so the number of people in the lowest age-groups on say January 1, 1939) were very materially higher than those given in this estimate.

[1] *A Symposium of Population Studies*, edited by Lancelot Hogben, published by George Allen & Unwin, 1938.

Quite apart, however, from the enormous labour of preparing a revised table, we must consider what we want the estimates for. They are to serve as limits, between which we feel reasonably sure the answer must lie. We shall only use the results as a basis for broad conclusions, most of which will hold good wherever the answer may lie within this range. For such a purpose there is no point whatever in giving the limits in anything but round numbers. What do we gain, for example, by including the decimals in a statement that the population in 1965 will be 38·504 millions on estimate (*a*), 35·799 on estimate (*b*), and 43·744 on estimate (*c*)? In point of fact we shall make little use of the lower limit given by estimate (*b*).

We shall, therefore, do no more than make a note that Dr. Charles's figures on the second estimate are too low for the youngest people in the early years, and the corresponding age-groups later on. This chapter does not pretend to give an elaborate statistical treatment, and a small difference in the age-distribution for the bare year would not influence the results sufficiently to affect our conclusions. What is much more important is the question of whether we can accept Dr. Charles's assumptions about the future, or rather, which ones should be given most weight.

Dr. Charles herself has clearly shown her opinion of the relevance of estimate (*c*) by making no mention of it whatsoever in her revised version. In this she treats estimate (*a*) as setting an upper limit "unless unforeseen social agencies are brought to bear." Can we accept such a conclusion?

For the very near future the answer is clearly No. The recorded number of births has each year been in excess of the estimates, since these assumed no rise in fertility above the 1933 level. Hence if we use her figures to estimate the size of the school population in (say) 1942, our answer would certainly be too low—at any rate we cannot regard an estimate which will even probably be exceeded as setting a maximum.

However, we must not make too much of this discrepancy. In the first place it is small—the excess is less than 5 per cent for the ages affected. But more important is the fact that it is easily explained and shown to be a temporary phenomenon. The explanation is simply that the years in question had the benefit not only of the "normal" number of births, but also of the arrears accumulated during the depression. The most important aspect of this is the extra number of first births following marriages delayed by the depression.[1] The significant fact is that even with this temporary aid the fertility-rate rose so little, and did not nearly reach the 1931 level.

We may conclude that throughout the period of slump and recovery there was a continuing decline in the basic or trend level of fertility, with a cyclical fluctuation superimposed. For a purely short-term forecast it would have been fantastic to take the 1933 figure as a maximum; a critic might justly accuse Dr. Charles of neglect in failing to point this out in *Political Arithmetic*. An ideal forecast would have allowed for some temporary rise followed by a relapse, and also for a fall in future mortality-rates. But over a moderate period it seems safe, "unless unforeseen social agencies are brought to bear," to regard estimate (*a*) as giving a maximum figure for the total population—though one which may well be closely approached; over a long period (say thirty years or more) this last presumption weakens. So as not to overstate the case we shall lay more emphasis on this set of results than on the minimum figures. There is no reason to challenge Dr. Charles's rejection of her original third estimate; fertility has not recovered to the 1931 level, even with the temporary aid of the "arrears."[2]

[1] See *Political Arithmetic*, pp. 69 ff, for a discussion of the similar German experience, accentuated by the granting of marriage loans.

[2] The reader should realize that Dr. Charles's under-estimate of births in the past few years does not mean that her figures exaggerate the future trend of the population. The "arrears" phenomenon will probably be a thing of the past by the time this book is published. Hence the main

With these observations to help us, let us now examine Dr. Charles's results. It is natural to begin with the estimates of the total population, which can be summarized in this diagram, reproduced by kind permission from *Political Arithmetic*, p. 83.

Starting from 1935, we find that each estimate suggested

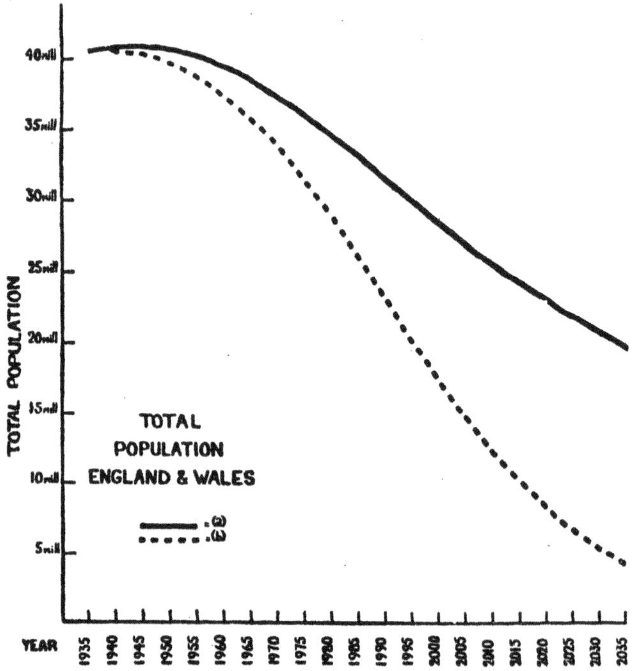

a slight initial rise—and the increase in the first three years has actually been greater than the higher estimate. Estimate (*b*) shows a maximum in 1940, followed by a decline which is slow at first, but soon becomes catastrophic. Estimate (*a*) puts the maximum in 1943, and there is no

effect is to give a slightly low *starting-point*. The age-composition will also be somewhat distorted, particularly if mortality-rates fall; but that is all.

serious decline for twenty years or so, after which it becomes fairly rapid.

The reader should be able to account for the apparent paradox of a rising total with a net reproduction rate of under 0·8. When the population was expanding there was an abnormally large proportion of the population in the younger age-groups ("abnormal," that is, relative to the conditions in a static population). As fertility declined, naturally the effects first became apparent "at the bottom"; there were fewer young children. For a considerable period the number of "potential mothers" (and fathers too, for that matter) not only did not fall, but continued to rise; the large number of children of thirty years ago had "moved up," and so produced an abnormally large proportion of potential parents. For a time the number of births was thus at least partially sustained, despite the fall in fertility; and the death-rate was (and is still) abnormally depressed (again relative to that of a static population), both because the large generations have not yet "worked up" to the top, and because there is a small proportion of infants.

This transition from a high to a low fertility-rate is the main reason why our present age-composition is so wholly abnormal. We can best see how abnormal it is with the aid of a "population pyramid," such as is given on page 36, for the year 1936.

The blocks show the number of males and females of each age, averaged over five-year groups. The dotted line shows the corresponding numbers which would be found in a static population of the same size, and subject to the same mortality-rates. In such a population the figures naturally get steadily smaller as we pass from the younger groups to the older, because each one represents the survivors of the one before.

If we examine the diagram, we find that our actual population shows a deficiency at both ends of the age-scale and a surplus in the middle, which is just what we would expect from the analysis given above. There are other reasons for the divergencies, such as the effects of the war and the fall in mortality-rates—more people who might now be 70 died in their earlier years than would be the case if present rates had prevailed. But the main disturbing element

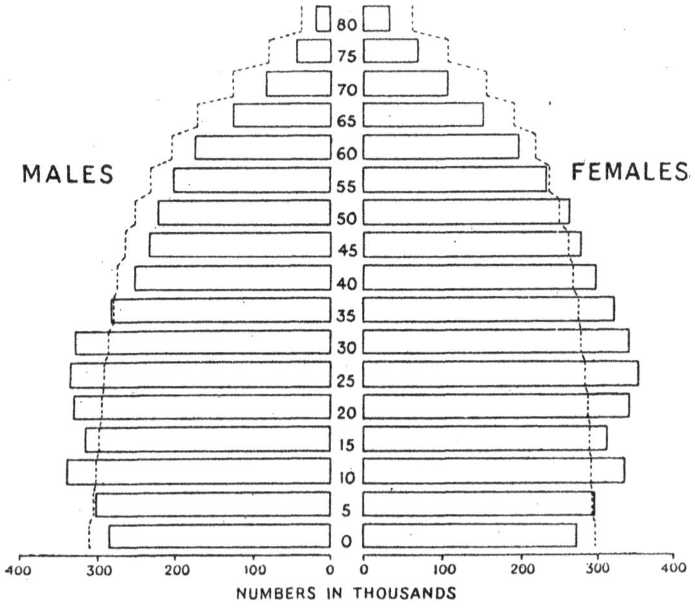

is undoubtedly the progressive decline which we have experienced in fertility.

We may see what is likely to happen in future most easily by setting out Dr. Charles's estimates of future changes in age-composition. The following graphs show for each set of assumptions the proportions aged 0–14, 15–44, 45–64, and 65 and over; these groups are chosen to throw light on the proportions of (*a*) dependent children, (*b*) potential parents, or workers (non-elderly), (*c*) elderly workers, (*d*) pensioners. As a basis for comparison, the reader should note that the percentages in a static population with current mortality-rates would be:—

		Per cent.
0–14	.. ..	22·1
15–44	.. ..	41·9
45–64	.. ..	23·7
65 +	.. ..	12·3

We need not worry with the more extreme results which are obtained by continuing estimate (*b*) for a century. The

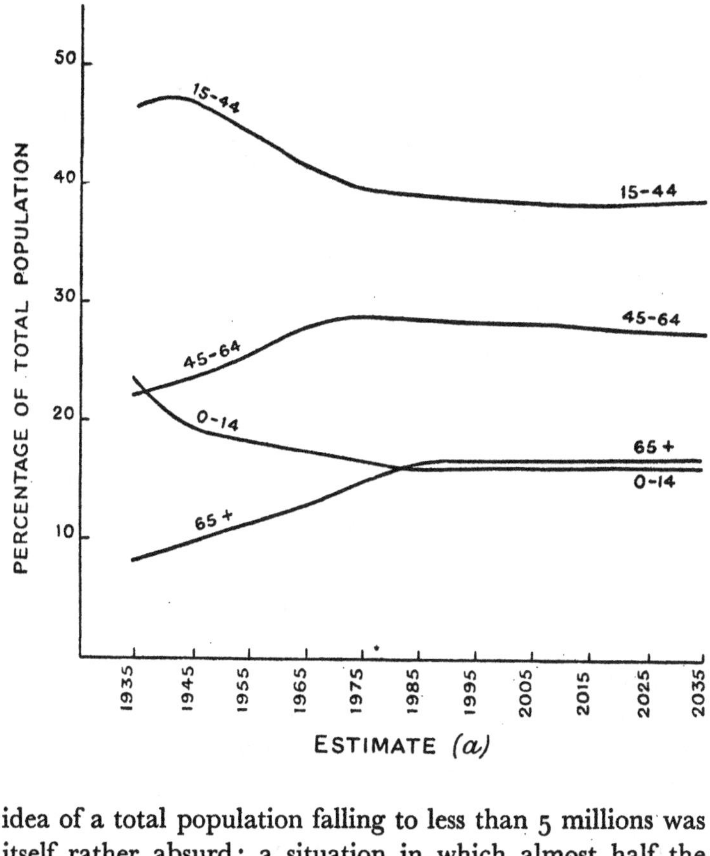

ESTIMATE *(a)*

idea of a total population falling to less than 5 millions was itself rather absurd; a situation in which almost half the nation is over 65 is manifestly impossible. One might as well produce an economic analysis of the end of the world as of such an extreme position.

Even estimate (*a*), however, shows clearly that there will be substantial changes. We see a steady decline in the proportion of dependent children (0–14) and a steady rise in

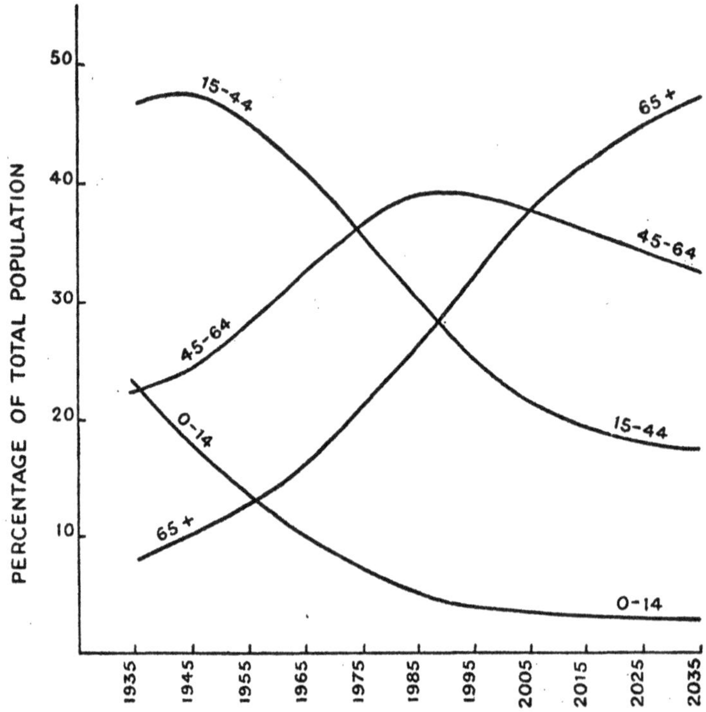

ESTIMATE (*b*)

the proportion of pensioners. The proportion of the other two groups taken together is virtually stable at 70 per cent for more than thirty years, but the elderly workers increase steadily relatively to the others. It is interesting to note the comparative stability of all the proportions after 1970, though the proportion of pensioners continues to rise slowly.

Mr. Colin Clark has made a rather more elaborate

analysis of probable changes in the proportion of the population which will consist of "occupied" males.[1] (The reader is warned that "occupied" is a census term which includes all the unemployed who would like to work, even if over 70.) He assumes that the same proportion of men in each age-group will be "occupied" in future as in 1931, the last census year. His results actually show a rise, which is particularly marked in the case of estimate (*b*), because the proportion of children then falls so rapidly. But it is very doubtful whether this rise is really of much significance, for it is due to the inclusion of men over 65, the number of whom is growing. Even for men over 70, 33 per cent are counted as "occupied," though the chance of their obtaining full-time work is clearly smaller than is the case with younger men. Especially as the average age of retirement is more likely to fall than to rise, it seems better to base our conclusions on the more conservative figures for people between 15 and 65. Even on this basis we can say that, although there will be a rise in the proportion of pensioners to be supported by the active population, yet there will be a corresponding decline in the proportion of children.

A few brief statements may help the reader to appreciate the situation:—

(I) Not even a complete elimination of deaths below the age of 45 would prevent the ultimate decline in numbers, unless fertility rises. We can see this by repeating the calculations made to find the net reproduction rate, but assuming that no females die until they reach 45. The result is known as the "gross reproduction rate," and if it is below unity, then clearly no reduction in mortality-rates can serve to keep up the number of potential mothers. For England and Wales the value corresponding to the 1933 level of fertility was about 0·85, and it has not risen as high as 0·9 even with the aid of the "arrears."

(II) Nor would the decline be averted if all spinsters

[1] *National Income and Outlay*, pp. 20–22.

married, even assuming they bore as many children as the average married woman now does.[1]

(III) With the present figures for mortality-rates, childless marriages and non-marriage, a decline in population is inevitable unless fertile marriages produce an average of nearly three children. This is almost impossible if a family of two continues to be typical.

We may conclude, I think, that an analysis of the effects of a declining population is of very real relevance. Even though the decline in total numbers will not begin immediately and will be small for a considerable number of years, yet it is virtually certain to come (failing a powerful and deliberate "population policy"), and its herald has already arrived in the form of a changing age-composition. Moreover, in the last 150 years we have always had a substantial rise in the total. For many purposes a change from a substantial rise to an almost stationary total is equivalent to a change from a stationary total to a substantial decline. From this point of view an analysis of both phenomena—an ageing population and falling numbers—is already important.

[1] See *Political Arithmetic*, p. 71.

Part II

INTRODUCTION

The statistical facts set out in Part I have become increasingly familiar in recent years. The public has begun to be "population-conscious," though not to the same extent in this country as in others, where the military authorities have regarded the birth-rate as a matter of great importance to them. (As usual, the most effective way of securing attention for a social problem has been to link it up with "national defence.") The only important thing which remains to be done in this respect is to emphasize the magnitude of the issues. Even if the man in the street has accepted the idea that the population is likely to fall "some time soon," he has not been convinced that the next generation will be 20 per cent smaller than the present one. Nor is this attitude difficult to understand, since the annual figures for the total population still show a small increase. The man in the street can hardly be expected to appreciate the subtleties of a net reproductive rate, especially in view of the publicity given to the official figures for the crude birth- and death-rates.

If this book does anything to accelerate the progress of education in the above matter, so much the better. The time factor is highly important in all matters connected with population, because the full effects of a change in the attitude towards child-bearing are so slow in appearing. If we are to adopt a conscious social policy in the matter, the sooner the public and the various authorities appreciate the situation the better.

My main object is not, however, to assist in popularizing the statistical facts—the various writers mentioned in Part I have already done about as much in that direction as the academic fraternity can, and the military publicists will doubtless complete the task as soon as they are really convinced. I want rather to explore the *consequences* of the present trend in population, a task which has been rather surprisingly neglected. It is true that some attempt to take account of population trends has been made by people concerned with such things as school-building and town-planning. But their discussions have naturally been confined mainly to the particular issue involved. Systematic analysis of the more general results has been notable for its absence.

Yet such analysis is clearly of first-rate importance. Without it we cannot really decide whether we should welcome the fall in numbers or not, let alone decide what to do about it. Even if the results of the change are likely on the whole to be beneficial, nevertheless we shall almost certainly have to adapt our social system in various ways to the new situation. If the verdict is unfavourable, then we must not only explore the possible measures which can be taken to mitigate the evil consequences, but also consider whether we should try to raise the birth-rate. Thus our analysis is required as a basis for decisions of great moment.

Some questions cannot be dealt with by an economist. If we are trying to assess the advantages and disadvantages of a declining population, he cannot help if somebody says he regards a reduction of numbers as evil in itself on religious grounds. He might do something to compare the merits of the rival hypotheses about defence—that greater numbers mean greater strength for the armed forces, and that they render Britain more vulnerable to bombardment or blockade. (However, I shall not tackle this question, beyond pointing out that a declining population also means an older one.) But there remain a great many problems where the public can legitimately look to the economist for guidance.

Probably most people's reactions to the news of a coming decline in the population are based partly on rather hazy ideas about its economic consequences. It may be welcomed "because it will reduce unemployment" or dreaded "because it will increase the burden of the national debt." Discussions on this matter show, as is so often the case, a tendency to waver between assertions based solely on a consideration of demand ("A falling population will be disastrous because it will mean a decreased market") and those based solely on a consideration of supply ("Fewer people seeking jobs means fewer out of work"). Alternatively, though this is partly the same thing from another point of view, they waver between ideas based respectively on mankind's difficulty in securing an adequate income from its labours, and on the difficulty of providing an adequate outlet for the available energy. Thus the large number of future pensioners is sometimes regarded as a great burden on the active population ("scarcity of goods," or "inadequacy of incomes") and sometimes as guaranteeing the presence of a large number of consumers who will not compete in the labour market but be "givers" of employment only ("scarcity of jobs"). If economics is to be of any practical use at all, it is surely in tackling problems such as these, by taking account of both sides.

Assumptions.—Any discussion of such a subject must be based on assumptions. The traditional method of economic analysis is to start by assuming "other things equal," so as to isolate the effect of the factor under discussion (in this case the change in the size and composition of the population). Such an analysis can never, of course, be regarded as a satisfactory forecast of what *will* happen, because usually we should expect other factors to change also. Thus we would probably regard it as unlikely that our technical knowledge will remain unchanged; it is clearly more likely that inventions and the discovery of improved methods will continue. Hence we must not use an analysis based on *ceteris paribus* to compare the situation in 1959 with that of to-day; at best we may use it to compare the situation which we expect to prevail in 1959 *in view of the change in population*, with the one which we would expect to prevail then, *if the population factor were eliminated*. Even that is not a strictly legitimate comparison, because a changing population will not have the same effects when it is superimposed on other changes as it would in an otherwise static world.

It is partly because of this last difficulty that I do not propose first to build up an elaborate analysis on the assumption that other things remain stationary, and then to modify it because we know that they will not. I intend to assume from the outset that technical progress will continue at about the same rate as in the past; this is admittedly, and designedly, a rather vague statement, but it is intended to cover a multitude of awkward factors, such as improved education, as well as inventions and improved methods. I shall also assume that the nation will continue to add to its stock of material capital (factories, railways, houses, etc.). This assumption will need further elaboration later on, as will be appreciated by those with a knowledge of trade cycle theory. For the moment, I will do no more than issue a rather vague warning that it is not as simple as it appears. A community may be very willing to do the necessary saving to add to its wealth, but actually fail to do more than an insignificant amount because a slump has severely reduced its income.

I wish to emphasize once more that an analysis of this type is designed to show what sort of problems and changes we are likely to encounter in a period of declining population. It does *not* imply that all the changes, as compared with the present position, are *due* to the declining population. The comparison, if there is to be one, must be in dynamic terms; we must compare the changes which took place in the past when population was increasing (but not, of course, all *due* to the increase), with the changes which the analysis shows to be likely at a time when it is falling.

One more difficulty must be mentioned which also arises out of the time factor. What assumptions are we to make about the general features of our social system? They have shown considerable changes in the past, in the direction of more state control in many spheres; are we to assume that this "trend" will continue? or to follow the Marxian analysis and say that a fundamental change is inevitable? Or are we to invoke our old friend *ceteris paribus*, and assume there will be no change?

This is a very real difficulty, but it seems that the most useful course is provisionally to assume no very great change. We are dealing with a field in which changes can, at least to some extent, be made deliberately. We want to know, therefore, what will happen in the absence of change, so as to deduce what sort of action, if any, will produce favourable results. Of course, some things will be altered for reasons quite apart from our analysis, and it would be better to take account of these. But in this respect I must refuse to play the part of a prophet.

CHAPTER I

UNEMPLOYMENT—PRELIMINARY

The first problem to be tackled is the effect on unemployment. It is an excellent example of the "two views" phenomenon, as any teacher of economics can verify for himself by putting the question to his first-year students. Probably the majority will reply that unemployment will be reduced, because there will be a smaller number of people seeking jobs; most of the rest will say it will be increased, because there will be fewer people to buy; and a great many of both classes will put forward the opposite argument if asked whether they are sure.

Stated crudely as above the two arguments simply cancel out. If we are to make progress we must adopt a less superficial approach. We cannot attempt to say whether unemployment will be higher or lower in different circumstances unless we can produce some analysis of what determines the level of unemployment at *any* given time, such as the present. And the first thing to realize is that unemployment is not a simple phenomenon with one single cause, but a very complex one, with many causes.

These causes overlap with one another, so that it is impossible to make clear-cut divisions. But it is possible, and indeed essential, to make one major distinction, and then further to sub-divide the resulting classes. This procedure has been followed by nearly all writers on unemployment, though they have used a great number of different names.

Our major distinction is between *general* unemployment, alias depression unemployment (alias cyclical unemployment) and *particular* unemployment (alias frictional unemployment, alias Beveridge[1] unemployment). The latter is,

[1] After Sir William Beveridge, whose book *Unemployment: A Problem of Industry*, represents a classic analysis of this problem, and should be consulted by the reader who wants a detailed treatment.

broadly speaking, due to the failure to adapt the supply of particular sorts of labour to the demand with sufficient speed or exactitude. The former is due to the inadequacy of general demand; it is present above all in slumps, but it seems better to give it a name which contains no direct reference to the trade cycle. For in the opinion of many, including myself, it is quite possible to have a considerable amount of "general" unemployment at the top of a cycle; this was almost certainly the case for example in America in 1937. Or the cyclical fluctuations of industry might become far less marked, or even cease, whilst still leaving a substantial volume of general unemployment. It would be particularly dangerous to use a name like "cyclical" if it gave the impression that such unemployment could not be avoided for a time, but would "automatically" disappear as the trade cycle moved along its predestined course. The dominant features of unemployment in a depression are severity and generality—it is to be found in almost all occupations. Hence the name "general," which implies no presumption about a cause or a period of continuance.

We must now proceed with the sub-division of "particular" unemployment. Its general characteristic is that it is due to causes peculiar to a trade, or an occupational class, or some other limited field—causes which are at least partially independent of the general level of trade activity. Our analysis will be brief, but the reader will find a bibliography at the end of the chapter.

We may distinguish the following leading types:—

(*a*) *Seasonal Unemployment.*—Here the name is self-explanatory, and I need say little about it, except that it applies to far more industries than one might expect. Sometimes the conditions of production render fluctuations of employment inevitable (e.g. some sorts of agriculture), sometimes the conditions of demand (e.g. ice-cream selling). But often fluctuations are exaggerated, even if not caused, by nothing more "inevitable" than trade customs, such as the dates of shows, or the perverse habits of customers who *will* all buy their furniture or take their holidays at the same time.

There is one important point to remember. Seasonal fluctuations in the amount of employment in particular occupations are not sufficient by themselves to cause unemployment. We have to find out not only why the ice-cream vendor is no longer pedalling his tricycle in December—that is fairly easy—but why he has not secured another job, say as a purveyor of roast chestnuts. A certain amount of "dovetailing" of jobs is clearly possible. To some extent the peaks of one industry automatically coincide with the low points of others; and even if nature did tend to produce simultaneous declines, man might resist the tendency by encouraging production in slack seasons. Thus winter building might be encouraged by lower wages for that season, or public authorities might deliberately have their work done then; or manufacturers might be induced to make for stock.

We cannot pursue this matter here. It is obvious on a realistic view that seasonal forces are likely to produce *some* unemployment, even if all seasons had an equal number of busy and slack trades. The process of moving from one occupation to another, perhaps requiring quite different qualifications or conducted in a different place, will never work with perfect smoothness. The reader who wants to study the question in detail should read Beveridge's classic work, or *Seasonal Variations in Employment*, by C. Saunders.

(*b*) *Intermittent Unemployment.*—Besides regular seasonal fluctuations, many industries show considerable intermittent variations in activity; one week there may be a rush of business, the next almost none. Sometimes (as with dock labour) the variations are reckoned by even shorter intervals, men being taken on by the day.

Now this does not always lead to unemployment. Banks, for example, experience very considerable variations in the amount of work which has to be done on any one day, but they do not as a rule take on extra men, or dismiss them, according to the volume of work. On slack days the staff may be engaged on various jobs which need not be done at any definite time; or they may simply be working less intensively. At busy periods, such as quarter-days, they work at high pressure and probably stay later in the evenings, often without extra pay; the rough is taken with the smooth.

It is probable that this practice could be used much more widely than it is, given goodwill on both sides. But in some cases it would be impossible, and in a great many others it has not been attempted. So we get, even in periods of prosperity, the phenomenon known as the reserve of labour.

(*c*) *Technological and Structural Unemployment.*—So far we have been dealing with unemployment caused by short-period fluctuations in particular industries' demand for labour—fluctuations which are expected, broadly speaking, to bring us back repeatedly to much the same point. But it frequently happens that their demand for labour, or at least for a particular kind of labour in a particular spot, alters permanently or even disappears. The principal reasons for this are changes in consumers' demand, e.g. supersession of horse transport by motors; changes in the technique of making the original product, e.g. introduction of machinery in place of skilled craftsmen; and changes in the location of industry, e.g. due to discovery of a new coalfield where costs are lower. As usual, we may get two or more of these causes working together.

Now the initial effect of such changes is to throw numbers of people out of their old jobs. The tendency may be resisted somewhat by their accepting a lower wage—if craftsmen's labour becomes less expensive, then the process of mechanization may at least be retarded. But in many cases this will be quite inadequate, and the jobs will be definitely lost. This does *not*, of course, mean that an equivalent number of people will be added to the ranks of the unemployed; as always, it is not enough to show good reason for a man to have lost one job—we must see whether he will find another. But at the very best there is likely to be an interval in which some people are out of work. If the necessary reorganization is on a large scale, as is the case in the depressed coal-mining areas to-day, then the resulting unemployment is generally known as "structural." The term "technological" is generally reserved for unemployment due to changes in technique, but there is really no essential difference between this type and unemployment due to other changes, such as changes in demand for different products. The vital point is that the unemployment arises from delay in readjusting the labour supply to altered circumstances. We shall discuss the factors which influence the extent of this delay in the next chapter.

(*d*) *Unemployment Due to Wage-regulation.*—The question of the relation between unemployment and wages in general must be left until we discuss general unemployment. Here we shall only note briefly one or two special effects of wage-fixation as generally practised under a system of collective bargaining or authoritative regulation.

In the first place unemployment may be caused by prescribing a uniform time-rate for all workers, irrespective of efficiency. This makes it very difficult for the less efficient ever to secure employment. Moreover, it is not even necessary that a man should *be* less efficient, if employers refuse to give him a trial because they *think* he will not be up to standard. This last statement applies above all to elderly workers. Beveridge has shown, both in his book and in recent articles in *Economica*,[1] that old men do not lose jobs any more frequently than young ones; but if once they become unemployed, then they have much greater difficulty in securing a new post.

Unemployment may also be caused if a steep rise in wages is decreed for a given age (generally twenty-one). This means that employers will dismiss a great many workers at that stage, sometimes retaining those who have reached a given standard to occupy more responsible positions, sometimes

[1] Especially the one for February 1937.

not even that. Of course, to repeat the obvious once again, it is not inevitable that all those dismissed will remain unemployed. It may be to their interests that they should be dismissed from jobs such as messenger-boy, and forced to seek "man's work." But, in the absence of a far greater degree of organization than we have at present, any process of readjustment will lead to some loss of labour time. And the fixation of higher wages for those over twenty-one makes some shifting around of the labour force inevitable.

Besides this, we may make a general note that measures which restrict the movements of relative wages in different occupations may make more movement of *people* necessary, and so increase the amount of frictional unemployment. Thus, if demand is tending to shift from coal to oil, the danger of severe unemployment amongst coal-miners will be decreased if their wages are lowered, so that the reduced price of coal can partially offset the attractions of oil. Of course, if any desired number of miners could readily find employment in other occupations, then there would be little point in lowering wages to reduce the need for transfer. But this will seldom be the case, and the number of those who get left, at least temporarily, by the wayside will rise more than in proportion to the number who have to be transferred.

This does not pretend to be a comprehensive account of the causes of frictional unemployment, but it is sufficient for our purpose. We shall say something more in the next chapter about the forces which affect the speed with which adjustments are made, as opposed to the ones which make adjustments necessary. I ought, perhaps, to emphasize that a measure is not necessarily to be condemned because it leads to some frictional unemployment. Thus it is almost a truism to say that trade union restrictions and demarcation rules will make the process of adjustment slower by introducing rigidities, and by sectionalizing the labour market.[1] But they may be very necessary for other reasons, such as the maintenance of professional standards—of craftsmanship, rather than remuneration, though that may also be justifiable. In a dynamic world unlimited competition means insecurity for all, which may be much worse than a certain amount of unemployment.

BIBLIOGRAPHY

SIR WILLIAM BEVERIDGE : *Unemployment: A Problem of Industry*

E. R. WALKER : *Unemployment Policy*

C. SAUNDERS : *Seasonal Variations in Employment*

[1] If they were used to prevent the entry of fresh recruits into the overcrowded casual occupations this would be an advantage, even from the point of view of reducing "particular" unemployment.

CHAPTER II

"PARTICULAR" UNEMPLOYMENT AND A DECLINING POPULATION

WHAT then will be the effects of coming population changes on the problem of "particular" unemployment? At first sight it might appear that we should at least gain in one respect. Each new entrant into industry has to find a job, and there is frequently some delay before he does so. Since a falling population means a reduction in the proportion of new entrants to old members (not merely a reduction in the absolute number), surely this "initial placement" problem will be reduced?

This contention is formally valid. There will be less adaptation to be done both on initial entry and at the age of twenty-one, and consequently less unemployment due to the inevitable friction which prevents any adjustment being made with perfect smoothness. But the former problem, at any rate, has never been a serious one, except in times of acute depression; then it has simply been a part of the phenomenon of general unemployment. And, as we shall see in a moment, there are important disadvantages in reducing the proportion of people who are entering industry for the first time, and are therefore more easily attracted to the right part of it. However, the optimist who sees in a falling population the cure for unemployment can perhaps say that the "twenty-one" problem is a more serious one, and will now be reduced in two ways; firstly, there will be a smaller proportion of people at the dangerous age, and secondly, employers may find greater difficulty in securing juveniles to replace them, because of the still greater reduction in the proportion of new entrants. But it is about the only encouraging feature that he will find in our discussion of particular unemployment.[1]

The effect of a declining population on "particular" unemployment can be analysed in two stages. Will it make more or less adjustments necessary? and will it make the system more or less capable of effecting these adjustments smoothly and without much loss?

The answer to the second question is more or less independent of the particular reason why the adjustments have to be made, so that we can start by reviewing the various causes of disturbance without repeating at each stage that the amount of unemployment caused by them is not necessarily the same merely because the disturbance is the same. To put it another way; we are going to see what the effect of a declining population is, firstly on the number of people who lose jobs, and then on the speed with which they find fresh employment.

The first cause of disturbance is the seasonal factor. It might be possible to produce an elaborate analysis to prove that this will become more (or less) important because the industries which suffer most from seasonal fluctuations are likely to grow (or shrink) relative to those which suffer least. If, for example, we make the apparently plausible assumption that a falling population will mean a much reduced building industry, then the proportion of people who lose their jobs through seasonal fluctuations might be expected

[1] In case the reader still feels that the problem of "finding jobs quickly" is primarily one of placing new entrants into industry, he should compare the total number of engagements made in a year with the number of new entrants. In very round numbers (and that is all that is required to give a sense of proportion) they are as ten millions to half a million. Moreover, a new entrant can much more easily make arrangements in advance, since the date of leaving school is known precisely. This is a matter in which the experience of people who think instinctively in terms of a salaried job with an assured status is hopelessly misleading.

to decline. But such an analysis would require not only a careful investigation of conditions in all sorts of industries, but also very hazardous forecasts ("guesses" would often be a better word) of future changes in demand. It might be of *some* value, particularly if done by an industrial expert, but I doubt whether it would repay the labour involved.

The same is broadly true of intermittent variations in the demand for particular sorts of labour. There is no reason for saying that the requirements of any given industry will become either more or less intermittent. We might proceed to estimate the future importance of industries such as building and dock service, where intermittent fluctuations are greatest; we shall actually have something to say about both of these in later chapters. But beyond that I do not intend to go.

When we examine the effect of changes in demand for particular products, however, we find that a declining population makes a very big difference. In the past it was often the case that a *relative* decline in the demand for one commodity caused little or no disturbance because the general rise in consumption prevented this causing an *absolute* decline in production, or in the industry's labour force. Now it is quite true, and we shall return to this point again and again, that an increasing population is only *one* factor which causes a rising demand. Mere numbers may even be quite unimportant compared with the level of the average man's real income. (Contrast the number of cars sold to China, with a population of over 400 millions with that sold to 1½ million New Zealanders.) But still a rising population *is* a factor which made for greater all-round demand in the past, and which will not do so in future.

Let us see what this means. If the demand for a commodity simply disappeared in a night through the invention of a clearly superior substitute, or through the passage of a law prohibiting its use, then, of course, any rise or fall in the population, or its income, or indeed anything, would be irrelevant. But this is not what usually happens. Take for example the case of transport services. When railways were invented horse transport suffered a relative decline in demand—people no longer spent so large a fraction of their income on it, nor did the horse fill so large a proportion of the demand for transport. But the shift in demand was gradual, and the *total* demand for transport was increasing steadily with increasing population and a rising standard of living; hence there was little need to transfer people out of the industries connected with horse transport—they suffered a *relative* but not an *absolute* decline.

With rather more justification than is usual on such occasions, I shall now assert that the reader can easily think out further examples for himself, and say no more.

The same principle applies almost exactly to the development of new sources of supply. In the past new coalfields have been discovered, new agricultural lands opened up, industries developed in new areas, all of which might seem to threaten established producers with the choice between moving to another occupation or becoming "structurally" unemployed. I do not wish to deny that this problem has been a real one on a considerable number of occasions. Besides the obvious post-war examples I would instance the virtual destruction of the shipbuilding industry on the Thames by the growth of the Northern centres and, to go back still further, the shift of the woollen industry to Yorkshire in the industrial revolution; and I will re-affirm my confidence in the reader's ability to think of further examples. But, as against these, there are numerous cases where dislocation has been avoided, thanks to the steady rise in demand, based partly on increasing population; there has been room for the newcomer without reducing the output of the previous suppliers—indeed this has often continued to expand.[1] Even

[1] Here we might instance the nineteenth-century experience of the British textile, coal, and iron and steel industries, which expanded in the face of growing supplies from other countries; or of the older British coalfields, whose output grew despite the development of new ones.

where the older centre has had to reduce its output, as with British wheat-growing, the growth in total demand has made the transition much less violent.

Indeed, it is quite unnecessary to labour the point. If one industry has to become a less important fraction of the whole this result will be achieved far more easily if it can stand still whilst the others grow than would be the case if it had to suffer an absolute decline. Moreover, the same principle will apply if it is not the industry itself which is to become less important, but only its labour force. If improved methods or the introduction of machinery are reducing the number of workers required to produce a given output of, say, boots, then we shall have far less dislocation if the total number of boots required is steadily rising. This conclusion is not quite as safe as the previous one, because the new methods may call for quite a different type of labour —perhaps even female instead of male. If so, then the expansion of demand will do nothing to ease the position of the threatened workers—the boot and shoe trade is actually a case in point. But this is not always so, perhaps not even usually so.

Another objection might be raised against the contention that a rising population will appreciably mitigate technological unemployment. Will not the introduction of machinery be far too sudden in its effect for such long-period influences to be important? Is it not comparable with the hypothetical case discussed above, where the demand disappeared overnight?

In some cases this objection may well be valid. It is no part of my intention to exaggerate the influence of the change to a declining population, and if the reader likes to console himself with instances where it will make little or no difference, by all means let him do so. (It will of course be a rather poor sort of consolation, for it means that the problem would then be acute even under apparently favourable circumstances.) But changes of industrial technique are generally far less rapid than is allowed for by popular imagination. They are introduced experimentally by one or two firms, perhaps initially on a small scale. If they are resounding successes they may spread rapidly through the whole industry. But some firms will cling to their old methods, and even the pioneers may not completely abandon the old technique until the machinery adapted to it has to be renewed. The disbeliever should study the history of the iron and steel industry, and find how long "obsolete" processes have continued to be employed.

We may conclude, then, that the advent of a stationary or declining population will aggravate the effects of changes in technique, demand, or industrial location in throwing people out of their old jobs. To avoid any overstatement of the case I will repeat that a rising population is only *one* factor which may produce a rising demand for the product in question; it may, however, be a decidedly important one, especially in the case of necessaries or of materials for making them.

Unfortunately, the matter does not end there. Not only will any given shift in demand cause a greater disturbance; but such shifts are likely to be more numerous. The "obvious" reason for asserting this—put crudely, the fact that the altered age-composition will confront us with the problem of changing-over to produce bath-chairs and coffins instead of cradles—is not really the most important. Some re-orientation of industry will certainly be required along these lines, but the transition need only be relatively slow, and the necessity for it can be seen in advance. Moreover, the threatened industries are not particularly specialized or localized, so that producers should not find the problem of transfer insuperable.

The real difficulty arises out of more general considerations. For reasons which we shall explain in Chapter VI, the average person is likely in future to enjoy a rather larger real income. This is, of course, thoroughly desirable, but it has the awkward consequence that he will spend a larger proportion of his income on things other than necessaries. Almost by definition this implies that a larger proportion of his expenditure is liable to be switched from one commodity to another in accordance with the dictates of fashion or passing whims.[1] Hence industry will be confronted with the need for frequent, and possibly rapid, readjustments of a more or less unpredictable kind.

We must now examine the effect of population changes on the ability of the system to carry out adjustments smoothly and with a minimum of loss. Here the main point is as simple as it is unwelcome. It is easier for a young man to change his job than for an old one, so that the adaptability of a community's labour force is greater, the greater the proportion of young workers and the smaller the proportion of elderly; our own development will be in exactly the opposite direction.

The above proposition is often extended by saying that adjustment will be easier, the greater is the proportion of new entrants to established workers, because then it can take the form largely of a direction of the newcomers to the expanding industries. This certainly makes it easier for an industry to *expand*, but the problems of contraction, which are the ones which directly cause unemployment, are unaffected by the supply of new recruits—the crucial question is the proportion of *retirements*. So far as it goes, the fact that more workers will in future be elderly, and, therefore, nearing the age of retirement, actually makes it easier to effect adjustments by allowing the labour force in contracting industries more or less literally to die out.

The force of this argument must not, however, be exaggerated. I have mentioned it more to show that this factor is favourable (and not unfavourable), rather than because it is of great importance. For it is a sad fact that this method

[1] The argument must not be taken as applying to males only.

of painless adjustment features far more largely in economic textbooks than it does in real life—at least so far as major problems are concerned. It is particularly misleading to describe the process of adjustment in this sort of way: "About 2 to 3 per cent of an industry's labour force will die or retire each year; hence it can be reduced by about 15 per cent in six years merely by preventing the inflow of new recruits. Provided, therefore, that changes are only gradual nobody need actually be transferred from the declining to the expanding industries." Formally this contention may be valid, but it takes far too little account of practical difficulties for it to be considered representative of what actually happens.

The first difficulty is that as a rule workers are taken on initially to fill junior posts ("boys' work") at lower wages than an adult would usually accept. It will, therefore, only be possible to reduce the labour force by cutting off the in-flow if employers are prepared to pay some of the adults men's wages for doing boys' work, or if the men who are not promoted accept boys' wages.

The second is that the industry concerned may be the major source of employment in the district. Hence, the boys leaving school will have little alternative but to enter it, despite the poor prospects, or move to another district. If the trade is depressed, perhaps on short time, then the family income will not cover the expense of removal, even if the boy were willing; rather will the prospect of an immediate addition to it force the boy to seize any opening available.

Finally, we may mention the traditions of the family and the district, which are in favour of a son following in his father's footsteps.

These reasons and others combine to reduce the practical importance of the "dying-out" method of making adjustments.[1] It does, of course, help, and for that reason the higher

[1] The Lancashire cotton industry in the post-war period has furnished examples of all the above phenomena—young people entering it despite overcrowding for lack of an alternative; adults earning very low wages

proportion of retirements is of some significance. But it is no compensation for the reduced ability of workers to change their jobs.

This tendency towards reduced adaptability is an inevitable accompaniment of a declining population. It can be resisted somewhat by positive action, as we shall see below; but it cannot be *avoided.* The positive measures would in any case be desirable, and will in future be faced with a more difficult situation. Like the Red Queen, we may find that vigorous running will only just keep us where we are.

Unfortunately, however, this is not the end of the story; the effects are, as usual, cumulative.[1] Where it is necessary to transfer men to a new industry the main question will be to secure an adequate supply of skilled workers. If these are readily forthcoming, then some of the less adaptable men in the declining industry will also find transference relatively easy, because they will take the unskilled posts, either in the new industry itself, or in subsidiary ones. But if the key men are lacking then the new industry will not grow, and five hundred unskilled may remain idle for lack of fifty skilled.

The critical reader may find the above argument unconvincing and demand an illustration. If so, he should consider the present position of those depressed areas from which migration of the more adaptable inhabitants has continued for some time. New industries will not be started there unless there are very considerable advantages to offset the lack of adaptable labour.[2] And the older men who cannot easily

as "little piecers" for lack of better jobs; family firms paying faithful workers men's wages for boys' work; and some reduction of the labour force, painfully and slowly achieved.

[1] Printers of economic textbooks would do well to keep the phrase "vicious circle" permanently in type.

[2] The advantages may take such forms as Government assistance or a feeling of doing good deeds.

move, and would be unlikely to get a job in a strange town even if they did, are left stranded. They could perfectly well do the simple jobs, or they could make a living as retailers, etc., to those employed in a new industry. But they can only fill these relatively passive roles, and there is nobody to play the active part.

This cumulative effect is also inevitable, in the sense discussed above; it can be resisted by human effort, but not avoided. There are other cumulative effects, however, which may be just as important, though they owe their origin to human reactions and are to that extent theoretically avoidable. The ease with which adjustment can be made depends largely on the attitude of the people in the trades which ought to expand. But in a world in which men live by producing for the market it is in the interests of each specialized group of producers to limit their numbers. If we wish to portray this practice in a bad light we describe its object as the securing of monopoly prices; if we wish to be more sympathetic, we say it is to avoid unemployment or losses due to cut-throat competition. (The argument applies equally to a trade union, a professional body, or a cartel.)

Now we have seen that a declining population increases the risks of an industry or its labour force having to undergo an absolute contraction. The danger of allowing newcomers to enter is thus made both greater and more obvious. Each organization will try to be on the safe side, to avoid as far as possible the risk that a subsequent fall in demand will produce a position of over-capacity, human or material. And it must be freely recognized that the trend of public opinion has been increasingly sympathetic towards such practices.

Let us briefly review the methods open to a trade union. The most obvious is a direct restriction on entry, but this is seldom employed "just like that"; the principle of the closed shop, i.e. exclusion of non-unionists, is established, but membership of the union is open to all qualified men. The really important provision is the insistence on a period of training, sometimes formal apprenticeship, and the limitation of the proportion of learners to trained men.

A more subtle method is simply the maintenance of a wage-rate at which the industry cannot expand. This practice is particularly unlikely to be condemned by public opinion as monopolistic or contrary to public policy. An invention in one industry may have made it necessary to transfer workers elsewhere, whilst at the same time reducing somewhat the cost of living. Failing measures of monetary expansion to raise all prices, it may be impossible to reach equilibrium unless the money wage is reduced in the industries to which the workers can most easily be transferred; unless this is done the old employers will not take on more men, nor will new firms be set up. Yet it is clearly asking a great deal of the union concerned to agree to a reduction in the wage (even if the cost of living has fallen somewhat), not because its own members are unemployed, but because there is unemployment in other trades.

Once more I trust that the reader is showing a sufficiently critical spirit to demand an example to support "mere theorizing." The best illustration is afforded by the position in this country in 1925–30. Largely as a result of our return to the gold standard at too high a parity, the competitive position of our manufacturers in both home and world markets was undermined, and unemployment resulted in the staple export trades. Failing an alteration of the parity, equilibrium could only be attained if money wages were reduced. The strain was naturally felt first in the unsheltered trades, and in these, wages were fixed at a relatively low level to meet it. To have reduced them further would not only have made them appear grossly unfair in comparison with wages in sheltered trades, but also might not have had much effect in reducing unemployment. What was required was a transfer of workers to the newer industries, for which demand was expanding, more particularly to those which competed with foreign products. But employers would not expand these sufficiently fast unless wages were reduced there too. And the chance of this happening was remote in industries which were already expanding somewhat, even though a steady fall in the cost of living was raising the real value of a constant wage. Wages do not "go down" (or up) of their own accord. The unions naturally did not suggest a reduction, and the employers had no great reason to do so. The really interested parties—the consumers and the unemployed in other industries—had no power to take the initiative.

The third and most passive method open to a trade union might be termed non-co-operation, though that is rather a harsh word. It may be clear that men from the declining industry will only be successfully transferred if special measures are taken to train them and help them generally. The co-operation of the union in the receiving industry may be necessary to secure instructors, or a change in workshop practice, or simply acceptance of the principle that the new men shall be allowed to work for less than trade union wages until proficient. (For rather different reasons the engineering unions are at the moment of writing being asked to "co-operate" in this sort of way to accelerate rearmament.) By refusing to co-operate except on exacting terms the union may hamstring the whole movement.

This is by no means an exhaustive account of the methods open to a trade union which wishes to pursue an exclusionist policy. The important point is not to give a lengthy description of the various devices; it is to recognize that union leaders would not be human if they did not intensify their efforts to safeguard their members at a time when a falling population was increasing the risks. And these efforts can hardly fail to make the system more rigid and less able to make necessary adjustments.

Moreover, as I have already hinted, exactly the same forces will be working on the side of the employers. For men to be transferred to another industry it will often be necessary for more capital to be invested there in building new factories or extending old ones. But the employers concerned will see in this a danger of over-capacity, especially as demand may always recede, and they will equally want to be on the safe side. With a declining population this fear of over-capacity will be more justified, and the consequence, should it be realized, more disastrous. Employers can frequently do a great deal to hold up an expansion of capacity merely by not undertaking it themselves, for where an industry is made up of a small number of large-scale businesses there may be few people other than the established entrepreneurs who can command the necessary capital, knowledge, and trade connections. And even where this is not the case, trade organizations and restriction schemes are progressively limiting the freedom of outsiders to set up a new business which may threaten the position of existing units.[1]

The conclusion is inescapable that a declining population will both increase the amount of adjustment which is necessary and reduce the ability of the system to effect it smoothly. Besides the factors discussed above the problem of the old men who are thought, rightly or wrongly, to be unable to reach the standard will become more acute because they will be more numerous. It will be more than ever necessary either to reserve special jobs for them where age is no handicap or to let them work for a wage below the trade union rate. But there are difficulties in the way of both courses, and it is at any rate certain that unless a really determined effort is made this factor will add its quota to the swelling total of particular unemployment.

[1] Once more I should like to explain that these practices are not *necessarily* to be condemned merely because they create rigidities. Completely uncontrolled competition may make the producers' position intolerably insecure, just as it might in the labour market; *some* central regulation to secure stability may even be in the interests of consumers, though at present the general community seems to be "more planned against than planning."

So much for the diagnosis; if nothing is done, then "particular" unemployment will become increasingly severe. The next task is clearly to seek a prescription. Is this disaster inevitable, and if not, what measures should be taken?

Paradoxical as it may seem, if you want to combat particular unemployment the most important thing to do is to avoid general unemployment. We shall have to wait until Chapter V to see how this is to be done; but the need for it should be apparent. In the first place it will be difficult to raise much enthusiasm for an attack on particular unemployment if there is a large surplus of labour in all occupations. What, it may be asked, is to be gained by arranging for seasonal jobs to be dovetailed so that the ice-cream vendor can pass easily into winter employment if there is a surplus all round? We may even prefer that one man shall have a job in the winter and another in the summer, so as to reduce the amount of demoralization which comes with prolonged unemployment. And the same objection will be levelled against schemes of de-casualization, training, transfer, and so on.

This lack of enthusiasm is not wholly justified, for such measures would ensure that if revival came, then it could reduce unemployment much further. But it is certain to exist and prevent much progress being made. Moreover, an attack on general unemployment is not only needed to secure enthusiasm, it also contributes directly to the reduction of particular unemployment. For both slumps and the fear of slumps are great breeders of frictions.

The *existence* of a slump means that many workers lose their skill and become demoralized through idleness. The number of apprentices and trainees is also reduced, so that a strong revival generally discloses a shortage of some types of skilled men despite heavy unemployment. Moreover, employers who know they can get good men whenever they need them are under no incentive to even out their requirements of labour, either from day to day, or from season to season; they can often cut down costs by taking men on for very short periods.

The *fear of a future slump* keeps up the amount of particular unemployment even in times of good trade by stimulating exclusionist practices. One great reason why organizations (whether of masters or men) resist the entrance of newcomers is because they are afraid of a subsequent fall in demand. Now demand may fall for a multitude of reasons—change of fashion, development of substitutes, crop failures, and so on; but the most devastating reason of all is a general depression, because it also makes a transfer to some other activity very difficult. Hence the fear of a slump leads craft unions to resist measures such as the relaxing of apprenticeship rules to meet a shortage of skilled labour. The shortage is generally due to the cessation of recruiting in the last slump, and what has happened once may happen again. Similarly, shrewd employers will want to be sure of the permanence of the high level of demand before they go to the trouble and expense of extending their works, and training a lot of men from a depressed industry.

As a converse to the above, a long period of good trade will break down some frictions, *given adequate time.* Men can be trained, extensions built, and so on. Employers may even find that they can not rely on an adequate supply of reliable labour unless they make their demand more stable, or perhaps unless they set up their new factory in a depressed area. Migration from one industry, or one area, to another begins to be worth while if there is a prospect of constant work to be secured at the other end. The genuinely work-shy can be distinguished from the victims of general misfortune, not only by officials but by their neighbours—and that is one of the best checks on loafing. Furthermore, if most businesses are making profits and expanding they will be more likely to look sympathetically on the old and faithful employee, who may be a bit past it but still does his best.

A successful attack on general unemployment is, then, the

first requisite. We must not, however, exaggerate the power of increased business activity to cure all evils, particularly when a declining population is intensifying the problem of "particular" unemployment. Beveridge's analysis should convince everybody that there will still be much to be done, however prosperous trade may be. But I need say little about the supplementary measures which are needed, for his analysis still applies. The leading requirements are:—

(*a*) A really efficient system of employment exchanges to bring the supply and demand for all sorts of labour into direct and immediate contact; here some progress has been made, and if there were a sustained period of good trade, so that employers found difficulty in securing suitable labour without their aid, then the exchanges might well become the main channel. The number of vacancies filled rose to nearly 2·7 millions in 1938, as compared with 1·6 millions in 1929, the last year given in Beveridge's table (page 305). The advantage of having one clearing-house to which both sides would almost automatically apply is considerable at a time of good trade, and to build up their organization the use of the exchanges should therefore be encouraged even when widespread unemployment frees the employer from any risk of delay.

(*b*) De-casualization of dock and similar employment. The proverbial over-crowding of these occupations must be eliminated by giving assured posts to the minimum number required, limiting the number of applicants by means of a register, and making engagements through a central clearing station, so that "multiple reserves" may be eliminated.

(*c*) General discouragement of intermittent hiring of labour on a casual basis. Employers should be encouraged to make their employment as regular as possible, as is done for example by banks. The present regulations for unemployment insurance have the opposite effect, but it would probably be difficult to reverse them. We must rather rely on convincing both employers and the unions of the need to fight this practice. Lower hourly wage rates might be prescribed for men who are guaranteed constant work than for similar men taken on for very short periods. The "permanent" men must adopt a spirit of give and take, being prepared to do other jobs of a non-urgent kind when their own work is slack.

(*d*) Similarly, employers should be encouraged to meet seasonal fluctuations by developing subsidiary activities, reserving non-essential work for the off-season, making for stock, and so on. The "encouragement" need not be wholly moral. In prosperous times they will in any case gain by retaining the services of the best men, who might otherwise go elsewhere. But they can be further encouraged by fixing lower wages for the slack period and by the receipt of Government orders. The device of lower wages in winter applies especially to building, since the products are durable and do not need storage.

(*e*) Labour exchanges, by spreading information, make workers more mobile in space, especially if supplemented by transference schemes. We also require training centres and the like to make them more mobile between occupations. These need not (in fact, should not) be reserved for people who have already lost one job and so need transference. We should try to launch boys into the world equipped with an education that will make them adaptable. And we should try to direct them to industries where they will find permanent work, and away from those which are contracting.

(*f*) We should encourage employers to reserve posts for oldish men where age is no handicap. If need be a law could be passed forbidding the employment of men under forty-five in such occupations without a permit, or at least fixing a maximum percentage of them.

Substantially, these are the same proposals as Beveridge made in 1909, with slight alterations to bring them up to date. We should now add the encouragement of new industries in depressed areas as a major weapon in the attack on structural unemployment. (If the reader is not familiar with the difficulties inherent in this policy and the methods adopted to overcome them, then he should consult the reports of the special commissioners for these areas.) We might add a discussion of the possibility of forbidding, or at least reducing, the exclusionist practices of trade organizations. But it is so difficult to draw the line between practices which are to be considered legitimate (at least on a realistic view of the need for some security in a dynamic world) and those which are to be condemned, that I feel I can do no more than raise the issue, and remind the reader that such practices flourish most in an atmosphere of depression.

This reminder brings us back to our starting-point. I have spared the reader the monotonous task of reading the same warning at the end of each suggestion, so I will now repeat once more that none of these proposals for dealing with particular unemployment will command much enthusiasm unless heavy general unemployment is eliminated. ("What is the use of training coal miners to become hairdressers if there are already plenty of unemployed hairdressers to fill any job that may become vacant?") Our attitude on this subject has changed from the optimistic confidence shown by Beveridge, when he wrote in 1909: "There is, of course, also the possibility that the country may be passing through a general depression of trade. This, however, being a temporary phenomenon, does not affect the argument. Of course, a time of exceptional depression is just the wrong time at which to attempt decasualization."[1] Would anybody now deal with such a topic in a footnote?

[1] Op. cit., page 204, footnote.

CHAPTER III

GENERAL UNEMPLOYMENT
I. ANALYSIS

This chapter is necessarily more difficult than the rest of the book. Those who have little previous knowledge of the subject will find that it requires a great deal of concentrated reading. If they prefer to sacrifice some points of detail and accept various conclusions without fully examining the arguments on which they are based, then they are advised to turn to the summary on pages 89–91 *as soon as they find themselves in difficulties. They should study this carefully, but need not be afraid to go on with the succeeding chapters even if they do not fully understand it. The significance of the various points should become clearer as the general analysis is applied to the particular problems raised by our population trends, and the reader can always refer back to this chapter. By adopting such a procedure he should be able to follow all the more important conclusions.*

THE theory of particular unemployment is not a very controversial subject. But a study of general unemployment involves consideration of highly controversial topics such as monetary policy and the theory of the trade cycle.

At the same time the subject is so important that it cannot possibly be omitted; such a course would (for once) really justify the traditional comparison with a performance of *Hamlet* without the Prince of Denmark. Moreover, we cannot discuss it without putting forward some general explanation of what causes the level of employment to be what it is, and not higher or lower. We cannot sit on the fence and say, for example, that some people consider expansion of credit or public works to be a sovereign remedy for slumps, whilst others say they are disastrous.[1] We must take up some position

[1] Of course, it is still possible to say that the answer will depend on the circumstances of the slump in question.

on the various issues at stake, or an analysis of the effect of a declining population would simply be meaningless.

However, an attempt to do full justice to the subject would call for a whole book, if not two. The discussion of general unemployment which follows will, therefore, be somewhat brief, dogmatic and simplified. The reader who wants to study the question more fully will find a bibliography at the end of the chapter. My main object is to establish certain propositions which would find acceptance amongst a very large number of economists, even though they might differ in their method of approach or treatment of details.

Perhaps we can best start with the old-fashioned and rather simple-minded view which virtually denied the existence of the problem. This rested on the propositions:—

(*a*) That human wants are, for practical purposes, unlimited; at any rate there is as yet no risk of our becoming "unemployed" because we would have no use for all the goods that we would otherwise produce.

(*b*) That the demand for any one commodity consists essentially of the other commodities produced and offered in exchange, money being merely a convenient medium of exchange.

(*c*) Hence that "supply creates its own demand"—whatever the level of output, demand will be equal to it; and

(*d*) Provided that we do not interfere with it, the price system will "automatically" ensure that the level of output will be that corresponding to full employment; or at least it will be always tending towards it.

On a strict interpretation of these propositions, general unemployment could only arise from the insistence by organized labour on a reward in excess of the "competitive," or "equilibrium" level. Failing such a monopolistic policy, unemployment would be limited to such an amount as might be caused by the frictions which are inevitable in a changing world.

It was mainly the pressure of undeniable facts which forced

people to recognize that it was not really "as simple as all that." There were recurrent periods of heavy general unemployment at a time when labour was hardly organized at all and the doctrines of *laissez-faire* and free competition reigned supreme. Such events might perhaps be explicable in terms of frictions, by saying that a rapid change in conditions demanded a reduction in wages so rapid that mere inertia, unsupported by monopolistic organization, had temporarily prevented it. But such an explanation not only involved stretching the meaning of the word "friction" to cover almost everything; it also cried aloud for the obvious retort that the real cause was not the failure of wages to adjust themselves but the mysterious change in conditions which had made the adjustment necessary. An analysis which said nothing about the reasons for this really only begged the question instead of answering it.

The chief defects in the above analysis are the treatment of money as *merely* a medium of exchange, and the great over-simplification involved in regarding the demand for any one commodity as consisting simply of the output of others. We must start by seeing what really does govern the level of demand, and for this purpose it is very convenient to divide production into two broad categories—production of consumption goods, i.e. those goods (and services) which people buy for personal use or enjoyment, such as food, clothing, tram rides, furniture; and production of capital goods, which means broadly those things which would normally be paid for out of capital and counted as capital assets in a balance sheet, such as factories, railways, houses, machinery, and so on. We shall go into the division more closely later on, but it does not really matter very much where we draw the line, e.g. whether or not we believe the advertiser who tells us that his car is an investment. In each category we include all the processes necessary to produce the goods: thus the manufacture of iron to be used for the current output of cutlery is included in the output of consumption.

The demand for consumers' goods in the aggregate consists of the amount of money people spend out of their incomes. Some people may be "living on their capital" by spending it on current consumption, but the nation as a whole nearly always does some net saving. It is in any case certain that the main factor which determines the demand for consumption goods is the level of the community's income. Demand will fall short of this income by an amount which depends on the community's thriftiness. This thriftiness is a complex phenomenon,[1] but we can say with some confidence that a short-period rise (or fall) in the nation's income due to better (or worse) trade will cause expenditure on consumption goods to rise (or fall) also, but by a smaller amount. Over long periods changes in habits have led to a reduction in the proportion of income saved.[2]

So far we have been dealing with the *actual* demand for consumption goods, whereas in reality it is the *anticipated* demand which governs the decisions of entrepreneurs as to how much to produce. We shall return to the distinction later; but for the moment we shall assume that it is not of great importance for a discussion of the entrepreneur's short-range decisions. It is vital if the question is whether or not to build a new factory; but if the question is simply

[1] It is influenced by past movements in the level of incomes and expected future changes, as well as by the ordinary motives that induce people to save. Thus, if incomes have recently fallen from a high level, the desire to maintain customary standards may produce a temporary reduction in thriftiness (particularly if incomes are expected to rise again soon) which would not be maintained if the new level became permanently established. It also depends very largely on the *distribution* of the national income between individuals and classes, and on the policy of company directors in putting profits to reserve.

[2] For a statistical treatment of the relation between income and saving (or expenditure on consumption), see Clark, *National Income and Outlay*, especially Chapter XII.

how intensively to work the existing one, then estimates can be made with reasonable accuracy and are speedily checked.

We have said that the demand for consumption goods depends mainly on the level of the national income. It is clearly also true that the level of the national income depends largely on the decisions of the entrepreneurs in these industries as to how much to produce; for the greater part of the nation is employed in them, and the greater part of the national income derived from them. The scale on which it is profitable to produce any one item in the list of consumers' goods therefore depends mainly on the scale on which other such industries are being conducted. And it might appear that there was no reason why the various industries should not advance (or for that matter, retreat) to any level of output, so long as they kept in step.[1]

To a considerable extent these simultaneous advances and retreats do in fact take place, as any student of the trade cycle knows. But there are two limiting factors. One is the fact noted above that as a community's income rises, so the gap between its income and its expenditure on consumption goods widens; hence an advance by the consumption goods industries will not by itself raise the national income sufficiently to produce its own justification in increased demand. And the second is the tendency of each industry to wait on the others to take the first move; this will at least make progress slow. To secure a really convincing advance we need some outside factor to overcome both obstacles—something which will create extra incomes, and so extra demand, without providing a simultaneous increase in the volume of goods to be bought. Then each consumption industry will feel the impact of the extra demand; stocks will be sold more quickly, orders will flow in freely, and

[1] This condition does *not* mean that they should all increase their output by the same proportion. As a community becomes more prosperous it varies the proportions of its income which it spends on different goods; a smaller proportion, for example, is spent on food. "Keeping in step" means advancing in a way that takes account of this.

higher prices may be offered. Each will be induced to expand, and so will raise demand still further for all the others.

This leads us naturally to consider the key position occupied by the production of capital goods. The people engaged in this work, including the shareholders, etc., as well as the employees, receive incomes in the same way as those engaged in consumption industries. An increased production of capital goods would, therefore, raise the national income, and hence the demand for consumption goods, without, at least for a time, increasing the supply of the latter. Thus it would constitute just that type of outside factor which we have described above as the basis for a general expansion. And correspondingly a reduction in the output of capital goods would tend to produce an all-round contraction.

What then governs the volume of production of these capital goods? There are two main factors: the profits which entrepreneurs expect to make by using them, and the cost at which they can secure the necessary (long-term) finance. A man will put up a factory if he expects that the profits from working it, after deducting all expenses, including depreciation, will exceed the interest he will have to pay on the necessary capital by at least enough to compensate him for the risks involved and any services he may render.[1] If he is using his own capital, then we must substitute the interest he could secure by lending it for the cost of borrowing.

[1] The above criteria apply directly only to capital goods constructed for the sake of the profits they will earn. Besides these there are the works undertaken for the Government (including local authorities) and paid for with loan money. Here the returns are frequently of a non-monetary character, but the same principle is applied as far as it can be—the benefits are compared with the interest charge. It is, however, possible for the Government to count in indirect benefits, and altogether the size and timing of its loan expenditure is to a considerable extent a matter of policy.

Let us examine this statement a little more closely. The first thing to note is the extremely precarious basis upon which the estimates of future profits have to be made. The man in question may be extremely well informed about the present position of the industry. But he cannot possibly know much about the profit he is likely to earn in any but the first few years. Thus the demand for the product may change, the number of his competitors may change, there may be a slump, technical discoveries may render his plant obsolete, or a rise in the running costs (e.g. wages and the price of raw materials) may convert a profit into a loss. A decision under such circumstances must always be largely a gamble, or, to put it more politely, an act of faith. This does not imply that people who take these decisions are necessarily acting stupidly or even illogically. There is a considerable amount of sense in the view that even if the future is uncertain, yet that need not necessarily mean that it is gloomy; the venture may prove unexpectedly successful.

This uncertainty does, however, have important consequences. Where a factory is going to be in use for many decades the probable results in the first year should not, logically, make much difference to the decision. A profit of 20 per cent for a single year does not by itself justify the investment, nor does an initial loss condemn it. But as the more distant future is almost completely unpredictable, the probable initial results almost inevitably *do* acquire an undeserved significance, simply because they are the only ones about which anything can be said with confidence. What is the use, it may well be argued, of building another boot factory if existing ones are working short time? Yet such a slump may actually represent the most favourable time to build; the really important thing is not the *existing* level of demand, but the *prospective* one taken over the whole life of the factory.

This tendency for decisions to be governed by short-period considerations accentuates the fluctuations in the output of capital goods by making it very dependent on the current state of trade. It is reinforced by the fact that the person who takes the decision to build seldom fulfils the whole entrepreneurial function himself. To do so he would have to provide all the capital from his own resources, or be able to borrow it in such a way that the lenders ran a negligible risk. Under such conditions he would assume virtually all the risks himself, and would have to satisfy nobody but himself about the correctness of his judgment. But in practice he will usually have to appeal to the public to do some of the risk-taking by subscribing for shares, the dividends on which will depend on the success of the enterprise. This means that however prepared the initiator might be to take a long view and to ignore the assumedly temporary depression, yet he can do little without his "colleagues." And the public, knowing less about the prospects, will be more insistent on judging by immediate results. If these are likely to be unfavourable, then the would-be initiator will have to postpone his schemes to a period of better trade and greater confidence.

The result is a tendency for the output of capital goods to fluctuate with the state of trade even more than we might expect; and this tendency is yet further accentuated by the existence of a Stock Exchange on which a price is determined for each share every day. These prices should logically reflect the market's estimate of future profits for the whole life of the company. But in fact they are dominated by current conditions, or at best by those expected to prevail in the near future. They will rise in a period of trade activity, and under such conditions it is notoriously easy to float new issues—just as it is notoriously difficult to float them on a falling market.

Summing up then as far as we have gone, the output of capital goods, which has so great an influence on the level of employment, depends on a comparison between the future profits which entrepreneurs expect to make by using new factories, letting new houses, etc., and the cost of securing finance. "An entrepreneur" is by no means always a single individual, but often a combination between an initiator and people whom he persuades to take shares. The estimates of future profits must always be based on very inadequate data, and are in fact dominated by the results of the recent past and the immediate outlook. Unless the other side of the balance (i.e. the cost of securing finance) were to vary in a compensating manner, this must lead to one of the numerous vicious circles found in economics—when trade is good, estimates are favourable, construction is undertaken, and trade becomes better; when trade is bad and existing capacity not fully employed, further construction appears unattractive, and trade becomes worse. The circle is made still more vicious by the existence of a Stock Exchange which encourages flotations in good times, since subscribers expect to see their shares rise, and correspondingly makes them very difficult when share prices are falling.

These considerations are mainly of a short-term nature, showing why the desire to obtain money for capital outlay varies with different states of trade, given the same underlying factors, such as the size of the existing stock of capital, the country's population, and so on. Since in fact the cost of securing finance does not vary sufficiently to offset these changes in the desire to secure it, we have here adequate reason to expect the output of capital goods to fluctuate in the well-known way over a short period, and to cause trade in general to fluctuate also. What we have not discussed is the influence of the underlying factors on the average level of what Mr. Keynes has called "the inducement to invest," about which these fluctuations take place. Why is this average, taken over a trade cycle, higher or lower in one century, or in one country, than in another?

We shall, however, leave this question until the next

chapter. For the moment we must turn to the other side of our balance and see what determines the cost at which our hypothetical entrepreneur can secure his funds. Once again the subject is too large for anything more than an outline treatment, and the reader who wants a fuller one must refer to the bibliography.

It is usual to start by making the simplifying assumption that the amount which entrepreneurs will have to pay for finance can be represented by a single rate of interest. This does not mean that we assume that every borrower pays the same rate; manifestly there will be differences to correspond with each one's "credit status." Rather we assume that there is one "basic" rate, frequently described as the yield on Government bonds, to which all others are more or less closely related; so that if the basic rate rises, then others will rise too.

This basic rate is related to various other phenomena of the economic system in a rather complex manner. One cannot say either that *it* determines *them*, or that *they* determine *it*—all the variables mutually affect one another, just as each of the stars, planets, and other heavenly bodies influences, and is influenced by, all the rest. The most important lines of connection, however, are these:—

1. At any time it is open to anybody who holds an interest-bearing bond to sell it in the market and hold money instead; and vice versa. Hence the price of the bonds must be such as to balance would-be buyers and sellers, i.e. to induce owners of wealth to divide their holdings between money and bonds in the same proportions as these are available.[1]

2. The amount of money (which in England consists mainly of bank deposits) in existence at any time is determined by the policy of the banking system, particularly the Central Bank. (The latter may simply be guided by some

[1] The price of bonds which bear a fixed rate of interest tells us what the "effective" rate is at any time. If $2\frac{1}{2}$ per cent Consols stand at 80, then the effective rate, or yield, is $2{\cdot}5 \times 100 \div 80$, or $3\frac{1}{8}$ per cent.

arbitrary criterion, such as gold movements; but if so, this only means that whoever is in ultimate control has decided to adopt that policy.) The quantity is increased if the banking system grants more loans or buys more securities or other assets; and reduced if it adopts the opposite course.

3. All the money in existence must be held by somebody, but not all of it is really available as a substitute or alternative to holding bonds. A large part of it is needed for the active circulation, i.e. it is required as a medium of exchange to carry on the nation's business.

4. The amount of money required for the active circulation will generally increase as business activity increases. More people are in receipt of incomes, more businesses are in existence, and with a greater turnover larger sums will be temporarily held by firms which have just been paid for the goods they have sold. (As an offset, which is important at the beginning of a revival, some firms which had accumulated idle balances when they had little work in hand will pay them away.)

5. The above tendency is accentuated if greater activity enables business men to raise their prices and trade unions to insist on higher wages.

6. The usual reason why activity increases is, as we have seen, a rise in the output of capital goods. And this tendency is, for a time at least, cumulative.[1]

We may best see how this complicated set of relationships works by taking an example and tracing out a possible

[1] An important reason for this which has not yet been mentioned is the fact that with a higher level of activity business men will want to hold larger stocks. This applies at all stages of manufacture and distribution. Outlay devoted to building up these stocks has just the same effect in increasing demand and activity as outlay on a new factory, since it generates incomes without raising the supply of goods which must be sold before more are ordered. When activity is declining, the desire to reduce stocks, which is equivalent to *negative* outlay, is a serious aggravating factor.

sequence of events. We will assume that activity is more or less stationary at a low level, and the authorities decide to adopt a policy of cheap money. The Central Bank would then buy securities in the market, and so increase the cash reserves of the trading banks in the familiar way described under the heading "open-market operations" in all books on money. The latter would then seek to expand their earning assets in the shape of bills, securities and advances. In doing so they would increase the quantity of money, all of which has to be held by somebody. If they had found borrowers who wished to employ fresh loans in their business, then there would be a direct, and probably a cumulative, stimulus to trade, and the extra money would be largely needed for the active circulation. But at a time of slump this would be unlikely, and the banks would probably have had to rely largely on purchases of securities. The general public would consequently have to hold less securities and more money, and to induce them to do so a rise in the price of securities would probably be necessary. In the first place this would apply mainly to Government securities, since it is these which the banks buy; but the movement would rapidly spread through the market as all concerned tried to make the best use of their funds. It would, therefore, be possible for borrowers to secure funds on more favourable terms, and issues of ordinary shares might also be helped by the fact that some of the people who had parted with securities for cash would be actively seeking an outlet for it.

There is no guarantee that this will suffice to induce new schemes of capital outlay to be undertaken in sufficient volume to produce a significant rise in activity, especially as old ones will be all the time reaching completion.[1] It depends

[1] This last factor illustrates one of the obstinate features of general unemployment. For a satisfactory level of employment to be secured we have to be continually making net additions to the stock of capital. Raising the output of the capital goods trades means increasing the rate at which these additions are made. We may once again find our position

on the state of affairs prevailing amongst the potential users of new capital, with their vague estimates of future profits. But the lower rate of interest and the weight of money seeking employment may suffice, after the inevitable interval whilst schemes are prepared. If so, then the sequence of events is as follows. At first, as we have seen, the banks' purchase of securities and creation of new money leads to a higher price for securities in order that people may be induced to sell them and hold money instead. Then the favourable conditions on which money can be borrowed leads to a greater output of capital goods, and this produces a cumulative rise in activity. This means that more money is needed for the active circulation, and unless there is a further creation of money by the banks, this may well cause interest rates to rise again somewhat. It is unlikely, however, that this will bring the revival to a sudden halt, for the output of capital goods will be sustained for some time by the greater confidence of entrepreneurs and the higher profits being earned.

The reader may feel somewhat surprised to find that this complicated, though really very much over-simplified, account of how the level of employment is determined at any time seems to take almost no notice of the question of wages. With all these complicated interrelationships between employment and the amount of money created by the banks, the forecasts of business men, the thriftiness of the community and so on, is there no room for the apparently common-sense view that wages are the price of labour, and that the amount which is sold, whether of labour or anything else, depends largely on the price?

There are various alternative lines of defence which an author who is only too conscious of the length of this chapter

to be similar to that of the Red Queen—all our ingenuity may be needed to preserve the existing level of employment by getting enough new schemes started to make up for the old ones that are completed.

may adopt. The simplest is to say that, whilst the price of labour is one factor, yet it is a very unimportant one compared with the variations that take place in the conditions of demand in the labour market. After all, this statement is also true of a great many other prices and markets. Anyone who examines the statistics for the sales of steel, for example, will find that far more was consumed in years when the price was high than in years when it was low. Moreover, we can supplement this argument in the case of labour, at least in Great Britain, by saying that in fact, for social reasons, movements in the price of labour are small, so that it is of little more than academic interest to discuss what would happen to employment if they were made larger.

In view of the violent controversy which rages over this question, it is probably best to adopt this line of escape. We may, however, make the following observations:—

1. It is clearly true that if organized labour systematically refused to work unless they received more than the whole value of the product in each industry, then the system of production would simply break down. If employing a man, even under the most favourable circumstances, would only yield, say, 10 bushels of wheat, and he refuses to work for less than 20, then he will be unemployed until some means is found to increase his productivity.

2. Since wages are in fact paid in money, in a modern community this policy means demanding a money wage which would, at present prices, buy more than the product, and raising the sum demanded in accordance with any rise in prices. If this last stipulation is omitted, it is possible to find at least a partial way out of the deadlock by restoring a profit margin through higher prices, provided the banking system creates the extra money required to carry on business under these conditions.[1]

[1] Even if there were a tendency for trade unions to demand "too high" wages and to prevent their claims being dodged by means of higher prices, one need not conclude that the only alternatives are

3. The only case where the wage factor is likely to be important is in causing a disturbance as between one country and the rest of the world. The leading examples are this country between 1925 and 1931 and the "gold bloc" in the period up to 1936. In each case the costs of production in the country concerned were too high to enable industrialists to compete sufficiently effectively in home and export markets. As a result there was a persistent tendency for the balance of payments to become adverse and for gold to flow out of the country. If the authorities concerned had tried to reduce unemployment by measures of expansion—whether by encouraging private outlay of capital through cheap money, or by public works, or by conducting a "spend for employment" campaign, or whatnot—then part of the extra incomes would have been spent on imports, and the position of the exchanges and the balance of payments would have become worse, quite apart from the fact that a greater internal demand might have encouraged trade unions and business men to demand higher prices, and so have made the exporters' position still more unsatisfactory.

Fundamentally such a situation requires that the country concerned shall increase its competitive power by reducing its costs relatively to those of the rest of the world, *as measured in a common currency*. This result might be secured by cutting wages and leaving the exchange rate unaltered—in that sense "too high wages" are an important cause of unemployment. But it is significant that in both the examples quoted the difficulty neither originated on the side of wages, nor was it solved from that side. The trouble arose from the

mass unemployment or wild inflation and soaring prices. The unions will not insist on the fantastic rates which one mentions to make the principle clear, nor do they revise their demands every minute; they do not even, in this and most other countries, make one concerted demand. Especially with technical progress all the time tending to raise real incomes there is no reason why a gentle use of the money pump should not keep production at a high level, despite the tendency of sectional groups to be greedy. Other difficulties are far more serious.

adoption of an unsuitable exchange rate, and competitive power was restored by abandoning that rate. Even for this problem of adjusting the relative positions of different countries the adjustment of wages does not seem to be very important in practice. And it cannot be too often repeated that this type of adjustment, designed to preserve a country's competitive power, only serves to keep countries, so to speak, "in line." It may leave each one suffering from very severe unemployment—it is only designed to make conditions equal, and this may mean equally bad. Expansionist measures are still needed to solve the common problem of all countries.

The only qualification which we have to add to the last statement is that any one country might make its position better than the average at the expense of the others by deliberately seeking a competitive advantage. Theoretically it might solve its whole problem in this way, for an export surplus serves in just the same way as capital outlay to stimulate trade; exporters are receiving incomes without there being any corresponding flow of goods (either as originally produced or secured from abroad) for which a market must be found. Nearly all countries sought relief in this way during the last slump, though most maintained that they were merely offsetting the actions of others. All sorts of devices have been adopted, including tariffs, quotas and exchange controls, all designed to secure an export surplus or eliminate an import surplus. The trouble is, of course, that in a game of beggar-my-neighbour someone must always lose.[1]

[1] For a more detailed treatment, see the chapter on Beggar-my-Neighbour Remedies in J. Robinson's *Essays in Employment*.

SUMMARY OF THE MORE IMPORTANT POINTS

1. It is the rule, rather than the exception, for there to be an appreciable volume of general unemployment.
2. There is considerable controversy as to whether this would be reduced by a general lowering of wage-rates.
3. But this question is not really as important in practice as it seems. The situation has very seldom been reached as a result of labour's insisting on higher rates, and other remedies are both easier to apply than wage-cuts and more certain in their operation.
4. For purposes of analysis we divide production into two categories, production of consumption goods, e.g. food, clothing, and all goods and services which we expect to pay for "out of income," and production of capital goods, e.g. houses, factories, etc. We then find what determines the level of output for each category.
5. The demand for consumption goods as a class consists of the money which people spend out of their incomes; in the case of an individual its size depends mainly on the amount of his income, and similarly for the community as a whole. The most important reason for changes in the demand for this class is, therefore, a change in the size of the national income.
6. Most incomes are derived from the production of consumption goods, so that a rise in the output of one helps to raise the demand for all the others. The consumption goods industries thus tend to "keep in line" so far as output is concerned, advancing and retreating together.
7. Their advance (or retreat) will not, however, be very convincing unless it receives outside help. For as the national income increases (or decreases), so does the gap between income and expenditure on consumption goods; consequently if the output of these goods were raised by £10 millions, the demand for them would rise by less than £10 millions. Moreover, each industry will tend to wait for all the others to take the lead.
8. To secure a really convincing advance we want some factor which will raise the national income (and so demand) without simultaneously adding to the supply of goods to be sold. Then each industry will expand its output and employment in response to the extra demand, and so raise the national income (and demand) still further.

9. The production of capital goods generates incomes without adding to the supply of goods to be bought out of those incomes. Consequently, an increase in their output will provide the desired stimulus, and it is, therefore, extremely important to see what regulates the level of capital outlay.

10. An entrepreneur will undertake capital outlay on building (say) a house, if he expects that the future income, after deduction of all expenses, to be secured from it will exceed the interest on the capital involved by enough to compensate him for his trouble and risk.

11. Capital outlay on private account will increase, therefore, if there is an increase in the number of openings from which a given return is expected by people capable of undertaking the outlay; or if funds can be obtained more easily or at lower rates of interest. (Always providing, of course, that a favourable development in one factor is not off-set by an unfavourable development in the other.)

12. Governmental outlay is, to some extent, influenced by similar considerations, but within limits it can be regulated simply as an act of policy.

13. In the short period, when such underlying factors as the stock of fixed capital and the size of the population may be taken as virtually constant, the main reasons for an increase in the number of openings are:—

An improvement in the state of trade.[1]
Increased confidence about its future state.
Increased confidence about political or social stability.
A greater flow of new inventions.
A reduction in the amount of working capital (particularly stocks) available at all stages of production or distribution.

14. The second alternative will be fulfilled if the monetary authorities increase the supply of money by granting more loans or buying more securities, or if greater confidence makes people want to reduce their holdings of money and buy securities.[2]

[1] Hence the tendency for movements to be cumulative. More capital outlay makes better trade; better trade makes still more capital outlay.

[2] We may get the same effect on interest rates if bad trade is reducing the amount of money which people want to hold for purposes of active circulation. But such a development may have little effect on capital outlay, because at such times borrowers have little faith in their ability

15. When we are confining our attention to one country which has trading relationships with the rest of the world, we have to add a new form of capital outlay—that of supplying foreigners with exports (visible and invisible) to a value in excess of the country's imports. The balance must represent foreign "lending" in one form or another, if we may stretch that term to cover repayment of debt or an import of gold. It has the same expansionary effect within the country concerned as capital outlay on (say) house-building, since exporters are receiving incomes equal to the amount of the excess without there being any corresponding supply of goods to be bought out of those incomes. It has the additional advantage, if gold is imported, that this is likely to encourage the authorities to expand the quantity of money.

BIBLIOGRAPHY

The literature on the subject of general unemployment and the trade cycle is so extensive that it would be impossible to give anything like a complete bibliography. This list has deliberately been restricted to a small number of books which should be helpful to readers who want a more thorough treatment:—

J. ROBINSON: *Introduction to the Theory of Employment*
Essays in the Theory of Employment

J. E. MEADE: *Economic Analysis and Policy* (Part 1)

R. G. HAWTREY: *Trade Depression and the Way Out*

J. M. KEYNES: *General Theory of Employment, Interest and Money*

R. F. HARROD: *The Trade Cycle*

to make profits. The converse case is more important—a period of improving trade increases the amount of money required in the active circulation, and this will produce a rise in interest rates unless the total quantity is increased.

CHAPTER IV

GENERAL UNEMPLOYMENT
II. POPULATION AND CAPITAL OUTLAY

In our analysis of what determines the level of general unemployment at any time we have given the leading role to the amount of capital outlay being undertaken. This is the principal factor which causes consumers to have extra incomes, without also causing producers to have extra goods which they will want to sell before placing further orders or undertaking further production. There are other ways of achieving the result, some of which have already been employed in one or more countries; thus the budget may be deliberately unbalanced, in which case the beneficiaries of the increased expenditure or reduced taxation will have greater incomes available for expenditure. Or we may seek to set the ball rolling by inducing the community to increase its expenditure, and so raise the effective demand for goods and services, without an initial increase in incomes; this might be done by direct propaganda, or by redistributing the national income in favour of those more likely to spend it. But these methods offend a great many people's ideas about correct behaviour; the ideas may not be as well-founded as their holders believe, but they do have very considerable value, if only as a check on irresponsibility. Moreover, so long as they *are* held, measures which offend against them may do as much harm by upsetting confidence as they do good by directly increasing effective demand. We shall have to consider possible alternatives to capital outlay as an expansionary force when discussing a programme of action to combat general unemployment. But, in analysing the effect of a declining population, we must clearly begin with its influence on the normal source of energy, which will in any case be in use, before discussing alternatives which might or might not be introduced.

II. POPULATION AND CAPITAL OUTLAY

The obvious answer[1] seems to be that a falling population will be highly prejudicial to capital outlay. For the most usual object in spending capital on, say, a boot factory is to increase the future output of boots, and this will only be attractive if the market is expected to grow; whereas a falling population seems automatically to imply a declining market. The argument seems particularly obvious when applied to the erection of dwelling-houses, which represents by far the largest single item in the nation's capital outlay.[2] So long as the population was expanding there was a clear need to build additional houses, besides replacing those which fell down or were pulled down, merely to maintain the standard of housing. When there are actually going to be *fewer* people to live in them, surely there will be less incentive to go on adding to the number of houses?

This is the main argument of the pessimists, supplemented of course by the fact which we have already noted, and which will apply whatever happens to population, that capital outlay is incurred to add to a steadily growing stock; as one piece of development is completed, so we have to find some new scheme, merely to maintain outlay at its existing level. Another way in which the argument is sometimes put is to say that the capitalist system will only work in an expanding economy, and that it will be disastrous if one of the main forces of expansion (increase of numbers) is not merely removed but actually reversed.

Let us see what arguments the optimists can muster in in reply. Firstly, we have the undeniable fact (also a previous acquaintance) that an expanding population is only *one* of the possible reasons why a manufacturer may expect his market to grow, and so decide to spend capital in enlarging his works. The level of real incomes enjoyed by the con-

[1] Once again, any teacher of economics can verify this fact by leading his first-year students to this stage, and asking them to continue.

[2] For estimates of the amount of various kinds of capital outlay, see Chapter VIII in Clark: *National Income and Outlay*.

sumers in the market may in some cases be far more important than their number. If this level is expected to rise, so that a far greater proportion of the population, for example, can afford a car, then capital outlay on motor factories will be just as attractive as it would be if numbers were expected to increase, but incomes to remain stationary.

Now if we may anticipate the conclusion of Chapter VI, there is good reason to suppose that the level of real incomes *will* continue to rise, perhaps even faster than in the past, provided we do not become less successful in avoiding slumps. So far as this factor is concerned, therefore, we are in the usual vicious (or virtuous) circle. Every step in the direction of solving the slump problem will help towards ensuring a rising standard of real incomes, and so help to keep up the expectations of an expanding market and the volume of capital outlay.

A rising standard of living means a growing market for most commodities.[1] But to secure an attractive opening for any specific piece of capital outlay we only have to ensure the expectation of an expanding market for the particular product in question. The optimist's second line of defence is, therefore, to say that there will always be particular products of which this is true. New commodities are developed, tastes change, and so on. The population factor itself may contribute to this result; for example, if people have fewer children to support there will be a rising demand for semi-luxuries which they could not previously afford. It may be hard on the manufacturers of cradles, whose plant may even become redundant, but it keeps up the volume of capital outlay on motor factories.

Besides this need for capital outlay to meet changes in demand, the optimist may also refer to the corresponding need for outlay in connection with changes in technique. Inventions and improvements are always being made, and

[1] There are exceptions, of course, where a better article is substituted for a worse one.

there is also the gradual adoption throughout an industry of those already installed by pioneer firms. Once more there may be a certain amount of hardship to individuals where old plant has to be scrapped as obsolete, but we are not for the moment concerned with that.

These three arguments explain why there should be *some* capital outlay in the future, even if the rate of interest does not fall. If capital becomes cheaper, however, then we must also consider a different type of outlay. For capital may be employed not only to increase the future output of (say) boots, but also to secure the same output with a smaller number of men. If the rate of interest falls, or if it becomes easier to secure finance, then it will be profitable to set about adopting methods of manufacture which employ more capital per man. And entrepreneurs can only do this by first embarking on capital outlay.

It has become distinctly unfashionable to say that a dearth of openings for capital outlay of the first type will "automatically" cause the price of capital (i.e. the rate of interest) to fall sufficiently to ensure that an adequate amount of the second type will be undertaken. We have already seen that, within limits, the rate of interest is very much what the authorities choose to make it.[1] However, it is probably true as a long-period tendency that if the demand for new capital at the old rate (averaged, say, over a trade cycle) declines, then this will both make it easier for the authorities to maintain the rate at a lower average level without offending against their traditions, and also encourage them to do so. Since this will stimulate some additional capital outlay of the so-called "cost-saving" type, the system may be said to

[1] They must, of course, accept the consequences of their actions. If they wish to keep the rate up to 10 per cent in a slump, then they must be prepared to see the slump intensified and bankruptcies caused by their progressive contraction of credit. If they keep it down to 1 per cent in a boom by continuous purchase of securities, then there may be a runaway rise in prices. But these are extreme cases—over a considerable range the results of their choice will appear quite sensible.

be (partially) self-adjusting; we should note, however, that the remedy is liable to create a different problem in the shape of technological unemployment as soon as the new labour-saving plant comes into use.

The last argument dealt with the increase in the amount of capital used per man in a single industry. For production as a whole there is a more subtle way in which a cheap and abundant supply of funds can raise the ratio of capital to labour, without involving any change in technique at all. For this ratio varies greatly in different industries, so that if capital becomes cheaper, the cost at which goods requiring a large amount of capital can be marketed will fall relatively to that of goods produced mainly by hand. It will appear profitable, therefore, to expand the output of these industries relatively to those of the others; in this way the average amount of capital employed per man would be raised, even if there were no change in technique in any single industry. In practice, of course, these two factors will both operate together, and both require as a first step that entrepreneurs shall undertake capital outlay. Moreover, in the last case there is no reason to expect any serious amount of technological unemployment when the new plant is ready. The impulse has come from the side of expansion—entrepreneurs in the heavily capitalized industries have found it possible to expand their output, selling it at lower prices. There is no reason why any other industry should suffer severely from this competition, especially as they will be gaining from the increased real incomes of the consumers.

We may illustrate the optimist's five arguments by applying them to the case which at first sight seemed so hopeless—that of outlay on house-building. We must first, however, mention a statistical point which is of great importance in this case. Even the pessimist would agree that, as applied to house-building, his argument must be stated in terms of a decreasing number of *families*. In a stationary or declining population families are naturally smaller than in an expanding one, so that the number of families will continue to rise even after the number of individuals has become virtually stationary, or even started to decline. This is of course only a temporary effect—the number of families will decline when the smaller number of children of one generation leads to a smaller number of adults in the next. But it is particularly necessary to remember the existence of the transition period, because it explains the conditions which have prevailed in recent years and which will continue to prevail for a decade or so. In any estimate of the number of houses required we should go hopelessly astray if we prepared it by "counting individuals" instead of "counting families."[1] With this word of warning we may now proceed to apply the optimist's arguments.

The first is straightforward enough. If people have larger incomes, one of the things which they will very probably want to increase is their "consumption" of house-room. Families who have previously shared a house, say with their grown-up children, will have one to themselves. Lodgers will be informed that their presence is no longer desired, now that their payments have ceased to be essential to the family finances; even mothers-in-law may be encouraged to find a home of their own. Moreover, many of the lodgers who continue to be lodgers will blossom out into the two-room class on the strength of *their* larger incomes. One has only to compare the amount of house-room required by a thousand families in a wealthy country with the corresponding figure for a poor one to appreciate the importance of income-level as a supplement to mere numbers.

The second argument—that openings for capital outlay will arise out of the changing character of demand—also applies to the case of housing. We may regard houses as machines or capital instruments for producing the finished article "living accommodation" or "house-room," which

[1] As we shall see later, however, "families" are very tricky things to count.

is sold to the consumer at a price which we call rent. Now it is clear that house-room is very far from being a standardized product. It is only in a very broad way that one can talk of *the* demand for house-room—there are really a multitude of separate demands for specialized sorts of it, specialized both by the nature of the accommodation wanted and its geographical situation. These demands are interrelated to some extent, for the people on the fringe of each market can be tempted to transfer to another if supplies are abundant there or prices fall; thus all flat-dwellers would not resist the blandishments of a good selection of suburban villas at moderate rents. But they are sufficiently separate for a change in the character of the demand to produce a shortage of special types of accommodation, which can only be remedied by capital outlay on fresh houses of that type, even though there is no shortage of housing in general.

In the past the commonest reason for a change in the character of the demand has been a rise in the level of real incomes. Of course, this is likely to make some outlay on house-building profitable in any case, simply because people are prepared to spend more on house-room. But we can distinguish between the effect of the *increase* in demand and the change in its *nature*. Buying house-room is not like buying butter—if a man wants to increase his consumption, he does not simply order so many extra, standardized sections. He generally alters the nature of his purchase, and the old capital equipment is no longer capable of meeting his requirements, even in part. Hence the need for extra outlay, in addition to that called for by the increased demand.

This distinction is not very important if all classes are enjoying a rise in incomes, particularly if the demand for all types is also being raised by a growth of population; for the changed character of the demand will be met largely by a general "move up," with extra building concentrated at the top end. But it is important in explaining why a rise in the incomes of one section of the community often has an apparently disproportionate effect on the amount of house-building. It is not necessary for the whole community to be able and willing to spend more on housing. If the position of one section is improved, and houses of the right type are not available, then that may call for just as much new building. The houses which they vacate may, in extreme cases, be scrapped, just as industrial equipment is scrapped if the demand for its products ceases; or they may become a drug in the market, let at rentals quite disproportionate to their original cost. But quite frequently they will find a ready market at a somewhat reduced price, and serve to raise the standard of other sections.

So far we have been dealing mainly in general probabilities, without giving any specific reason why there should be changes in demand, apart from those arising out of higher incomes. But clearly the population factor itself may be directly responsible for important changes. Families will be smaller, and the margin of income available for amenities, rather than the minimum of mere shelter, will be larger; this will cause a shift in demand towards comparatively small but well-fitted, up-to-date houses and flats. For certain classes this tendency will be accentuated by the growing difficulty and expense involved in securing maids.[1] The increased proportion of elderly people may also cause a shift in demand. Moreover, even though the absence of population growth removes one reason for house-building, this makes it necessary to do more building in order to meet shifts in demand; we can no longer meet these largely by concentrating the "inevitable" building on the types most desired, and moving people about between existing houses.[2]

[1] See Chapter VII for reasons why female labour is likely to become scarcer.

[2] Besides these factors connected with population changes there will of course be others which will cause shifts in demand—e.g. changes in industrial location. The decentralization made possible by improved transport facilities has probably not yet worked out its full effects, especially as people now have more leisure in which to tend gardens.

The possibility of house-building being remunerative because of changes in the technique of satisfying the consumer's wants should be apparent to anyone who considers the many ways in which modern houses might be improved, if only it could be done more cheaply. It does not follow, of course, that the invention of a cheap method of really keeping all parts of the house at the desired temperature would lead to the scrapping of all existing houses. It might, like electric light or drains, be capable of being installed in an existing house at a cost that was not prohibitive, and the majority of the population would doubtless continue for some time to go without. But the essential point about housing is that the annual output of new houses is such a very small percentage (only about 3–4 per cent even in the recent boom) of the total supply. If quite a small proportion of occupiers decide that they must have a house built according to the new technique, then the effect on the building industry may be enormous, whilst the houses which they vacate may easily be absorbed into the general market.

The optimist's fourth factor is also important in the case of housing. If we revert to our previous analogy, a house is put up in order to add to the supply of living accommodation in the future, just as a boot factory is erected to add to the future output of boots. In each case it will be necessary in the years to come to apply a certain amount of labour and materials to the capital instrument, in order that the output may be forthcoming. In the case of the house the amount may appear to be very small, but this is really an illusion. Quite apart from the obvious painting and repairs, and eventual renewal, there is all the housework, which is liable to be forgotten because it is often done without any direct payment, but which is necessary to a proper supply of "living accommodation." Now the essential point is that the proportions in which capital and labour are combined to produce the finished product can be varied in the case of housing, just as it could in the case of boot-making. We can make houses more durable and incorporate more labour-saving devices in them, provided we are prepared to increase the initial capital outlay. And if plenty of funds are available at lower rates of interest, then it *will* be attractive to invest more capital in each house built, and rely less on the future use of labour, paid or unpaid. To a mild extent this cheapening of the annual cost of various household amenities will also lead to capital outlay on adapting old houses. But its main effect will be to increase the amount of outlay involved per house erected.

The fifth factor is also important. The provision of living accommodation is a highly capitalized industry, and seems even more so than it really is, because consumers are apt to ignore the unpaid work involved in running a house. Hence, if capital becomes cheap and abundant, the cost at which units of living accommodation can be produced by erecting new houses will fall far more than the cost of a great many other things which consumers buy. It is natural that capitalists should expect this fall in price to increase the future consumption of living accommodation—even if a family is prepared to spend no more on rent than before, they will obtain more rooms for their money. And to provide for this expected increase in the "consumption" of living accommodation, capital will be expended on building new houses.

The above discussion of the optimist's five points will probably suffice to convince most readers that it is impossible to deduce at all accurately what the amount of outlay on house-building in any period will be by merely applying arithmetic to the statistics of population and the number of houses in existence. And if this is true in the case of house-building, where the problem might appear relatively easy (once one had appreciated that calculations must be based on the number of families, and not the number of individuals), then it is far more obviously true in the case of most other kinds of outlay.

There may, however, be some readers with sufficient independence of spirit to doubt the proposition, if only on the (very reasonable) grounds that I have given no estimate, let alone proof, of the importance of the other factors compared with the more obvious one of population. One concrete example is generally far more convincing than several pages of theoretical analysis, so the doubters should study the attempt of a highly skilled statistician to perform this feat. In the Housing volume of the 1931 Census Reports the Registrar-General gives an estimate of the number of new houses needed to be built between 1931 and 1941. His final figure, which, as we shall see, was apparently intended to be a maximum, was 1,700,000; this number had been exceeded before six of the ten years had elapsed.

It is interesting and instructive to see how the estimate was made, and why it proved to be so wide of the mark—though our treatment must be brief. The Registrar first calculated the probable size and age composition of the population of 1941, and there can be no question of the failure being due to errors in these estimates, which would in any case have had a negligible effect. He then deduced the number of "families" by a method which had yielded very reasonable results when applied to past censuses; this showed an increase of 917,000 over the decade. However, as he rightly points out, some families share a dwelling, and a deduction of 146,000 was made (again on the basis of past experience) to cover this, leaving 771,000 as the number of additional dwellings needed in 1941 to maintain a position comparable with that prevailing in 1931. To this figure he added 300,000 to allow for slum clearance and 100,000 to allow for houses demolished outside the slums, and so arrived at "about 1,200,000" as the number of new dwellings which must be built to preserve the *status quo*.

The next sentence is sufficiently important to be quoted

in full: "If a further two or three hundred thousand be allowed for existing sharing families, to provide for the overcrowded amongst them and possibly others who might be expected to require separate dwellings were they available, and a still further addition of a similar amount to replenish the reservoir of vacants hitherto associated with a state of housing equilibrium, the minimum of 1,200,000 would be enlarged to a probably more desirable total of 1,700,000 or thereabouts before reaching saturation point."[1]

The reader should note in the first place how much "judgment" is needed to supplement the direct use of statistics. But any doubter who makes so bold as to attribute the failure to the Registrar's poor judgment rather than to the inadequacy of the "statistical" method will find it hard to establish his case. For none of the Registrar's additions had been proved too low by 1937. Only about half his 300,000 slum houses had been replaced, and there is no evidence of much demolition outside the slums; only a negligible number of houses had been built to relieve overcrowding (as defined by the census), which was actually little less serious than in 1931; whilst vacant houses were still scarce by pre-war standards. It is hard to see how one can hope to explain the discrepancy without admitting the inadequacy of the method adopted.

What then *does* account for the startling discrepancy? It is beyond my province to attempt a complete analysis, but a reasonable solution can be found by applying the arguments of the optimist. In particular, an important section of the population (the "salariat") has enjoyed since 1930 a rise in their real income, thanks mainly to the reduced price of food. Many of them wanted to take advantage of this to improve their standard of housing, but suitable houses of the type they wanted were not available. There was, however, an abundant supply of funds, easily accessible through building societies, which could be borrowed at reduced rates

[1] Op. cit., page lxi.

to finance new building. Thus cheap food and cheap money provided a double stimulus to the erection of houses and flats for this class of occupier.

Probably this concentration of demand on a narrow range of types would have been sufficient by itself to cause the Registrar's figures to be exceeded; it is no use counting up the number of dwellings to show the adequacy of the total if they are of the wrong sort. But why has not this new building not led to a trail of "vacants," or even to much "filtering-up" by people of other classes? The explanation of *this* phenomenon is to be found largely in the splitting up of existing "families." The main criticism which may be made of the Registrar's estimate concerns his failure really to examine this possibility. A "family" on the census definition is a somewhat artificial unit, which may include not only adult children but even boarders. It is not enough, therefore, to allow for the possible separation of two "families" who are sharing one house. One must consider also the possible, and sometimes very welcome, division of existing "families."[1] Yet this is what the Registrar, by using his formula to deduce the number of families from the estimated population, had failed to do; he did not even explain what phenomena his assumption was ruling out.

Must we conclude from all this that the pessimist has been trying to scare us with a bogey which has no real substance? It certainly seemed plausible for him to assert that capital outlay will decline both because our stock of capital grows larger with each year that passes, and because we no longer have the prospect of increasing numbers to consume the fruits of that capital; was this apparently simple argument really only simple-minded?

Fortunately for our faith in the powers of common sense, the answer seems to be in the negative. The factors which

[1] Cf. page 97.

the optimist invoked do not constitute a new force which has only now begun to operate.[1] In the past they have all been present, and it has nevertheless been difficult enough to secure a level of outlay which would get us out of slumps, despite the more favourable underlying conditions.

Particularly in the case of house-building, the fact that the Registrar's estimates were exceeded does not dispose of the bogey, but rather the reverse. The current level of activity is so high that, failing special measures, it would in any case be unlikely to be sustained, even if the population were increasing; and the high level of activity in recent years has increased our stock of houses so greatly that the openings for new building are now fewer. It is true that people have been predicting the end of the boom for some time, and repeatedly proved wrong. This need not disturb us, however. Over a short period, as our analysis showed, prediction is very dangerous because building serves mainly to increase the stock of houses, and it therefore only slowly affects the total supply of living accommodation. But for that very reason the probability of a decline in activity is almost certain to increase, unless some quite new factor, such as a vast slum clearance project, makes its appearance.[2]

We may consider the question in a multitude of ways, but perhaps this is the simplest. The optimist's arguments fundamentally amounted to saying that openings for capital

[1] The only possible exception is the argument that as a result of a reduced number of openings for outlay, the authorities will be encouraged to maintain, on the average, a lower rate of interest. But apart from the fact that past slumps have provided abundant "encouragement" to a cheap money policy, this argument assumes the difficulty to exist as a condition for a remedial force to operate.

[2] A striking, if not quite fair, analogy may make this clearer. An heir who is waiting for a wealthy old man to die cannot rely on the statistical argument, based on experience, that he ought to die at age 70. All sorts of factors may upset this prediction, and with the passing of the years he may become exasperated at the repeated failures of his predictions to come true. But he would be very foolish to conclude, because he had been wrong ten times, that he might as well sell his "expectations" for a song.

outlay arise out of the need for more capital to provide a rising standard of consumption for a constant, or even a declining, population, as well as out of the need for more capital to provide the same standard for larger numbers. Previously we have had both factors at work; now our stock of capital is larger, our standard of consumption already higher, and our population no longer expanding. There is no theoretical impossibility about the maintenance of the level of capital outlay, especially if we visualize a great wave of inventions; but the probabilities are all against it, unless conscious measures are taken to secure it.

We must first deal with a plausible but erroneous counter-argument. It is sometimes contended that the smaller number of children will relieve the family budget of many charges, and so automatically create openings for capital outlay by raising the average standard of consumption; this, it is said, will offset the absence of openings due to increasing numbers.

The simplest way of exposing the fallacy in this proposition is to argue in terms of income-earners instead of mere numbers of people. It is quite true that a decline in fertility will have no *immediate* effect on the level of the national income or on the rate of its prospective growth for some fifteen years; the fact that incomes would be spent on rather different things from those bought in the past would actually create additional openings for capital outlay.[1] But there will soon come a time when the number of income-earners will cease to expand, or even begin to contract. There will then be no countervailing "automatic" rise in consumption per head to justify schemes of capital outlay, the level of which will only be maintained if some other factor (e.g. more inventions or low interest rates) becomes operative. The decline in fertility and resultant absence of population increase has a truly depressing effect on capital outlay, even if it be slightly delayed.

If only because this increased danger of slumps is likely

[1] Cf. page 94.

to be easily appreciated, we should also do well to remind ourselves of the vicious circle. Unless we *do* succeed in avoiding catastrophic slumps, and in convincing entrepreneurs that there is a reasonable prospect of demand remaining at a prosperity level, then it will seem very risky to undertake capital outlay which will only be justified if the average person's consumption rises—and not, for example, if real wages are high for those in work, but 25 per cent are unemployed. Economists and others may argue convincingly that if enough capital outlay is undertaken, and goes on being undertaken, then a high level of employment will be secured and the outlay will be justified by results; but a very reasonable caution will suggest to each entrepreneur that he should wait for some solid evidence that others will play their part before venturing.

This brings us to another important point. Catering for a rise in the standard of consumption is almost bound to be a riskier business than extending existing industries to provide for more consumers.[1] Demand is more fickle[2] as between one semi-luxury and another, and if there is a slump, this type of industry will suffer the greatest fall in demand. Moreover, the goods are sold under conditions very different from those assumed to prevail in the "perfect market" of the textbooks, where each seller can dispose of any output he likes at the ruling price, simply by sending them to market or instructing his agent. Semi-luxury goods require an elaborate sales organization and, especially at the start, a costly advertising campaign, which is liable to provoke a rival campaign

[1] For a fuller treatment of this and subsequent points, see my article on "Obstacles to Full Employment in a Wealthy Community," published in the *Economic Journal* for June 1937.

[2] This is *not* the same as saying that demand is more elastic. (Indeed, it may be very inelastic.) The trouble arises out of the risk that consumers may change from one commodity to another because of changes in fashion or the introduction of a more novel novelty. The fact that the producer cannot attract them back by a small price-cut only makes matters worse.

by other producers whose market is threatened. All this makes the undertaking of capital outlay designed to cater for a rising standard of consumption a highly risky proposition. The would-be entrepreneur may be able to calculate his costs of production for any level of output with fair accuracy; but the question of the price, if any, at which he could sell that output, and the expense involved in doing so, is one about which he can know very little. And he will be still more in the dark as to whether he will continue to secure satisfactory results for a long enough time to justify his outlay of capital.

It may be that this riskiness will at times lead to bursts of feverish activity, based on a wave of optimistic ignorance. But he would indeed be an optimist who would assert that such a state of affairs would be likely to continue for very long. Some of the projects are bound to turn out badly, which is liable to cause a general revulsion against further outlay of a similar type. And, in any case, we have the fundamental difficulty that prosperity demands the continual undertaking of new schemes, in order that the level of outlay may be maintained. A sudden burst of construction may produce temporary prosperity only at the expense of a subsequent reaction to a lower level of activity.

There is another factor to be remembered. Many of the possible ways of using extra capital to raise the standard of consumption imply that owners of existing capital suffer. There is indeed nothing very odd about this, for the standard rises largely because capital (and, *a fortiori*, certain sorts of capital) has become more abundant, and it is, therefore, likely to fetch a lower price. Thus the optimist's fifth argument was to the effect that the rate of interest would be lower, and this would encourage the expansion of highly capitalized industries. It would do so because the erector of a new house, to take the example discussed, would be able to let it at a lower rent, and still earn a return in excess of the rate of interest. Clearly such new building is very likely to cause the owners of existing comparable property to suffer a decline in income.

Now in the case of houses there is not, perhaps, very much danger of property-owners securing a restriction of new building in order that their incomes shall not be impaired. But in other cases resort to exclusionist practices is highly probable. The competition between the new plant and the old is more direct, more continuous, and more acutely felt. Particularly if the new plant embodies technical improvements, the return to the owners of the old may not merely fall in accordance with the fall in interest rates, but may completely disappear. The case for "preventing the creation of over-capacity" can be made to sound very plausible.

It is hardly necessary to discuss the various ways in which newcomers may be kept out, and the volume of capital outlay thereby curtailed. The problem is very far from being a new one, though it is likely to increase in intensity when one of the mainsprings of expansion has ceased to operate, and the urge to every group of producers to safeguard their position has thereby been strengthened. But one point is worthy of emphasis. It will very often be the case that the outlay which would appear to be justified, whether by a fall in the rate of interest or a new discovery, will be far more easily undertaken by an existing producer than by a newcomer. The newcomer would have to build up market connections, train personnel, make himself sufficiently well known to investors to raise the necessary capital, and so on, even if there is no actual restriction on his activities, say through a quota scheme. Now if there are a large number of independent producers, one of them may well consider the profit on the new outlay to outweigh any loss to him through the reduced value of his existing plant. But this state of affairs is becoming ever rarer, and the easiest form of common "action" to secure is inaction. Hence, established producers may be able to prevent the new outlay, and so avoid the loss in value of their plant, simply by not undertaking it themselves.[1]

From the point of view of this country we may also add that the prospects of external outlay coming to the rescue are also very poor. Investors have not had a happy experience with their ventures in other lands, and the other lands do not stand in the same need of external capital. Moreover, the power of exporting capital to stimulate trade only becomes effective if it leads to an excess of exports, visible and invisible, over imports—and of this there is no guarantee even if the loans are made, since they may lead rather to the accumulation by foreign banks of funds in London or of gold. On the whole the flow of capital is rather more likely to be the other way, since our best debtors are reducing their indebtedness by means of sinking funds.

The conclusion seems to be that suggested by common sense. Unless special measures are taken to maintain it, the volume of capital outlay undertaken on behalf of private interests is likely to fall. Moreover, it will be of a more precarious nature than in the past, more sensitive to falls in the industrial barometer.

The same conclusion also applies to governmental outlay, although the criterion of what constitutes "special measures" is here less precise. A good deal of this outlay—on roads, telephones, school buildings, harbour facilities and the like—is subject to very much the same considerations as private outlay, and, therefore, likely to decline for the same fundamental reasons. Housing is to some extent a special case, because of the schemes to clear the slums and reduce overcrowding, which have not yet reached the stage of maximum outlay.

Until a year or two ago one might have said that there was still a good chance of expanding the amount of governmental outlay by relaxing our standard as to what expenditure might reasonably be charged to loan account. But

[1] Cf. the history of the Jarrow steelworks.

it is unlikely that our financial scruples will permit the continuous expenditure of an amount greater than the £130 millions a year now being borrowed for rearmament. At any rate, such a change might reasonably be classed as a "special measure."

CHAPTER V

GENERAL UNEMPLOYMENT
III. CONCLUSIONS AND REMEDIES

IN the last chapter we have seen that the amount of capital outlay is likely, failing special measures, to decline. There is, however, one possibility to be explored before we can conclude that general unemployment is, therefore, likely to be greater (again in the absence of special measures).

The reader will remember[1] that the amount of capital outlay was found to be so important for two reasons. In the first place, when there is general unemployment, something is needed to *start* a general expansion movement in all industries; and in the second place, whatever the level of activity, something is needed to make up for the gap between incomes and expenditure on consumption goods. Now the first condition is fulfilled by an *increase* in the amount of capital outlay—no matter what its volume was before, if it increases, then the condition for a general expansion is fulfilled. But the question of what capital outlay will correspond with what level of general activity depends on the community's thriftiness; adequate capital outlay is required as a counterpart to saving. Is it possible that the lower level of capital outlay will be compensated, without any "special measures," by a reduction in thriftiness?

At first sight the answer might appear to be definitely in the negative, for we tend to associate higher incomes with a larger gap between income and expenditure,[2] and we have been accepting in advance the conclusion of Chapter VI that real incomes will continue to rise, at least for those in employment.

[1] If he does not, he should re-read page 77.

[2] It is the *absolute* amount of the gap which is important, not the proportion of income saved.

We must, however, be careful to distinguish between long-period and short-period effects. It is quite true that a nation saves more when a depression gives way to years of prosperity and high national income; but this is largely a short-period effect, associated partly with the fact that in a slump profits, the source of considerable savings, are particularly reduced, and may even be replaced by losses. For our present problem we are interested in comparisons of a long-period nature, from which this cyclical influence has been as far as possible eliminated, e.g. by taking the years of greatest prosperity in two trade cycles. In such a case it will be quite possible for habits or the degree of inequality of incomes to have changed in such a way as to upset our presumption.

The subject has been investigated statistically by a number of writers. There are many difficulties in the way of a reliable comparison, but there can be no question about one thing. Comparing the pre-war and post-war periods there was a big decline in the nation's annual savings, expressed in real values, although real incomes had if anything increased. Moreover, though this is less certain, the proportion of the national income which is saved is still following a downward trend (disturbed, of course, by cyclical fluctuations) which seems more or less to offset the upward trend in the average real income, leaving the absolute amount of saving much the same in comparable years.[1]

It is outside my province to give a detailed analysis of the reasons for these developments, but we do want to know whether the trend is likely to continue. On the whole it seems plausible to argue that the nation will continue to spend an increasing proportion of its income; but this may do little more than prevent the annual amount of saving from rising. In Victorian days the habit of saving was regarded almost with reverence; the more you saved, the

[1] For statistics to illustrate this and subsequent points, see C. Clark: *National Income and Outlay*, Chapters VIII and XII.

better citizen you were in almost every way. The process by which its hall-mark of respectability became progressively fainter has been a continuous one, though it apparently jumped a few stages in the war. It corresponds with a fundamental change in social outlook, which has probably not yet worked out its full effects.

Some of the leading factors which have contributed to produce this result, and most of which are still operative, are:—

The decline in the number of family businesses, to expand which the proud owner sacrificed his own consumption.

The rise in the level of taxes on high incomes, which leaves the recipient less able to save, even if his incentive may be unimpaired.

The rise in the level of death-duties, which not only causes immediate dis-saving on a scale which is likely to rise even if the rates are unchanged,[1] but also causes the national income for future years to be more equally distributed than would otherwise have been the case.

The active desire for a higher standard of consumption, particularly in regard to motor cars, housing, travel, and amusements generally.

To some extent the reduced need to make provision for future emergencies in a "social service state." (But very often the promise of some State provision encourages further private efforts.)

Working in the opposite direction have been the growing habit of life insurance, including pension schemes, the increasing amount of collective saving done by local authorities who repay debt out of sinking funds, and the greater conservatism of company directors in placing sums to reserve.

If we look into the future, we see two factors arising out of population trends which suggest a further reduction in thriftiness. The first is the one mentioned above, that a

[1] See Chapter VIII.

higher death-rate will mean more payment of death-duties "out of capital"; and the second is the corollary to our present saving to provide for old age. At the moment we have only a small proportion of retired people, and the premiums paid and sums set aside by the active population represent almost clear saving (particularly as the habit is a growing one). In future, however, there will be an increasing number of people who are spending their pensions, deferred annuities and so on, and eventually a reduced number of people in the "paying-in" stage; the first factor will remain even if the spread of the insurance habit continues to raise the number of contributors.

Our optimist may, therefore, fall back on the argument that the volume of capital outlay, even if reduced, will still be adequate in view of the reduction in thriftiness. He may support this contention by saying that thriftiness will also be reduced because the lack of openings for new capital will force down the rate of profits, and so lead to a more equal distribution of the national income. But, as we shall see in Chapter VII, there is only a very loose connection between the rate of interest current in any period and the return on old capital; the system cannot be made self-adjusting in this way. Nor can we rely on the alleged tendency for a reduced rate of interest to reduce men's *desire* to save. This is a well-worn theme, and I need only say briefly that much saving is done for reasons which will be little affected—individuals desire the security of a nest-egg or an insurance policy, company directors feel safer with large reserves, a large amount of capital brings prestige and power, very rich people save automatically, etc.; those whose ambition is to secure a given income from their investments will actually have to accumulate more. Altogether the most plausible assumption seems to be that given above—that the absolute amount of saving will not change much unless special measures are taken to make it do so, even though the percentage of income saved may continue to fall.

In judging the force of the optimist's assertion, the reader should also remember that a good deal of the reduced volume of capital outlay will be of the type which does not call for ordinary savings to finance it. Where one form of plant is being superseded by another it is paid for largely out of obsolescence and contingency funds; these are likely to receive larger allocations in future in view of the greater risk of their being needed. Industry proper, as opposed to public utilities and housing, even now makes a relatively small call on the national savings.

Any attempt, however, to prove or disprove the optimist's proposition by means of so-called statistical methods is, in my opinion, pure waste of time. We should remember the fate of the Registrar-General's calculations, of what is one of the easiest items, before venturing on a series of "guestimates." We may obtain much amusement and a fair amount of instruction from writing down figures for the various incalculables, and discussing the matter with fellow seekers after truth. But even after discussion, sensible and unbiassed people may differ so greatly in the numbers they have thought of that the results cannot very well be committed to print.

I shall not, therefore, attempt any proof in support of my own conclusion that the optimist is probably deluding himself. If we consider the distant future and accept Dr. Charles's more pessimistic estimates of population, then I think the reader will probably find this conclusion irresistible. But even in the relatively near future the forces making for a lower level of capital outlay seem to me far too strong to be offset by any likely reduction in thriftiness—always assuming that we do not adopt special measures to deal with the situation, and do not become involved in a major war.

Fortunately (or perhaps one should say unfortunately) it is not necessary to prove this in order to establish the proposition that the risk of slumps is likely to grow greater, and the need to adopt special measures to avoid them correspondingly more pressing. For even if an adequate amount of capital outlay were likely to be undertaken in favourable circumstances, it seems clear that the outlay would be of a type which would be very sensitive to any deterioration in the state of trade or in business confidence, or to other disturbing influences, such as political or social unrest or a setback on the Stock Exchange. Moreover, as we saw in Chapter II, there is certain to be a greater need for adjustments of one sort and another, many of which will be attended by severe losses to particular interests; there will thus be more frequent possibilities of confidence being disturbed, and outlay therefore curtailed. And if once the system starts to slide down the slippery slope, then it is very difficult to reverse the process. For the natural reaction of entrepreneurs is to reduce their orders and meet their sales from stock; there may also be forced sales of bankrupts' goods. This negative outlay greatly intensifies the process of contraction, and makes the undertaking of new schemes appear most unattractive, "at least for the present." So positive outlay is further reduced, and so on, round and round the vicious circle.

Let us review briefly the evidence in favour of our statement that capital outlay will, in future, be of a more sensitive type. Fundamentally, the arguments all derive from the fact that it will be directed towards raising the standard of living, rather than providing for increased numbers, and will therefore be undertaken only if there is a good prospect that the standard will in fact rise in the reasonably near future, and so justify the outlay. But we may make three specific points.

In the first place it will be directed largely to the luxury and semi-luxury industries, and so will be riskier in two senses than outlay directed to the staple ones—the results genuinely are capable of varying over a much wider range, and the potential entrepreneur has very little means of knowing even the limits within which they will lie. His venture is, even more than usual, an act of faith, and will therefore be much affected by the prevailing atmosphere, as we can see by studying the way flotations for such purposes fall off when the trade cycle turns downwards.

In the second place the increased frequency of losses due to the greater need to readjust particular industries is likely to induce a safety-first outlook, with everybody trying to read the signals and making a quick response to signs of deterioration. Much the easiest way to avoid a possible loss is not to undertake the new development at all, or at least to postpone it; and even if industrialists may still be willing, the Stock Exchange may well become apprehensive, and so affect the new issue market.

In the third place even the so-called "cost-saving" outlay is far more sensitive to trade fluctuations than one might expect from its name. Admittedly some outlay of this kind may actually be stimulated by bad trade, for less efficient firms are compelled to overhaul their methods. But many schemes for introducing labour-saving machinery will only be attractive if sales can at least be maintained, if not increased; there may be a minimum scale on which it must be worked to be economical, and the employer may also be deterred by the fact that the new machine would render some of his existing equipment redundant. Moreover, there is the opposition of the trade unions to be considered, quite apart from the reluctance of a humane employer to turn men off at a time of heavy unemployment. Altogether such schemes will be far easier to introduce in times of good trade, so that a greater proportion of this type of outlay will not help to maintain a steady total. The type least affected by trade fluctuations—one which may even expand in a slump if interest rates and construction costs fall—is that "obviously" needed to provide for a growing population; and this is the one which will be missing.

These three factors will increase the danger of slumps, failing the adoption of successful counter-measures. One might perhaps add a fourth point, arising out of the usual vicious circle. If slumps do become more frequent, then the desire to avoid losses caused by undertaking commitments in a time of reasonably active trade will be intensified, and it will be still more difficult to maintain the necessary level of outlay for very long, because people will be expecting a reaction. It cannot be repeated too often that the maintenance of a reasonable level of activity requires that there shall all the time be an adequate number of *new* schemes of capital outlay being inaugurated; this will entail, in the conditions of a declining population, that enough entrepreneurs are expecting the standard of consumption to rise progressively in such a way as to justify increasing the facilities for production, or are finding ways of profitably raising the ratio of capital to labour. The system cannot stand still in respect to its stock of capital without starting a decline in its level of activity.

I do not think that there can really be much doubt about the proposition that the risk of slumps will become greater unless we take special measures. Even if anyone should doubt it, however, this could only lead to a more or less academic battle, and should not affect our policy. For the need to take all possible measures to avert or shorten slumps is in any case obvious, even if their likelihood does not increase; if possible, the problem will, in future, be still more urgent, for we must expect an increase in frictional unemployment, and we cannot hope to cure this unless general unemployment is also tackled.

What measures can we adopt then to fight this evil? Perhaps I can best start by emphasizing that the problem is essentially a "man-made" one, which human ingenuity should be capable of solving. Our difficulty is not to overcome the niggardliness of nature, but so to organize ourselves that we can make use of the (relative) abundance which should be available, but seems likely somehow to elude our grasp.

Let me illustrate the importance of this (fairly obvious) point. I have argued that the decline in population will, in the absence of special measures, increase the risk of capital outlay being inadequate to maintain a satisfactory level of activity. Suppose it were possible, by elaborate action, to raise the birth-rate by an appreciable amount; would this be a sensible thing to do? Failing all else, perhaps it would, and of course there may be plenty of other reasons for wanting to do it. But what a commentary on the ingenuity of *homo sapiens*! That he should be reduced to laboriously increasing the number of children born in order that we may keep up the level of capital outlay, and so avert a slump, by making it attractive to build houses for them to live in! In view of the large gap between what so many of us actually get with our incomes and what we would like to have, surely we can devise (and carry out) some better policy for "maintaining employment" than that?

The literature on the subject of remedies for general unemployment is so vast that I cannot possibly deal with them in detail. A brief review of the more important ones does, however, seem to be necessary, if only so as to put the population factor into better perspective. Moreover, we are bound to lay rather different emphasis on the various factors when we are considering the long-period problem arising out of declining numbers and increasing wealth, instead of the short-period problem of the trade cycle. Some important but rather technical questions about several of them are discussed in Appendix B.

We can divide the proposals into two main categories: those designed in the first place to stimulate outlay, and so start the cumulative effect which we have described so often; and those designed to increase consumption directly, and to raise capital outlay only as a secondary effect, if at all. In assessing the merits of any proposal we must of course remember that it may be beneficial from one point of view, but harmful from the other.

We may start with the first category. Here it is particularly necessary to consider the efficacy of each measure, not only for keeping up the level of outlay in "normal" or good years, but also for giving a special stimulus in bad ones. If we could find enough proposals that would fulfil the first purpose, and could rely on our skill in applying them, then we might neglect the second consideration. But clearly it is as well to be prepared for emergencies.

Amongst the many possible measures we may mention:—

(1) *Public Works.*—We can increase outlay directly by increasing the amount of governmental loan expenditure. There are, however, difficulties in the way of carrying this policy very far, and, as mentioned above, we already have extensive borrowing for rearmament. The Government must either keep within its traditional fields of action, or face the problems inherent in a policy of encroaching on the "preserves" of private enterprise. If it does the former, then it will be very hard to maintain a substantial total, though slum clearance and rearmament offer ample scope for the time being. If the latter, then there will not only be political difficulties about vested interests, but it may also find that it has merely replaced a corresponding amount of private outlay; or, worse still, the fear of further "subsidized competition" may cause a *greater* amount of private outlay to be cancelled.

The whole subject of public works has been discussed so often that there is little more which I need say, except that we should frankly recognize that, if our conclusion about the probable inadequacy of private outlay be correct, then a *continual* stimulus of some kind will probably be needed. This stimulus need not consist wholly, or always, of public works; the best plan may well be to use *this* weapon mainly for meeting exceptional difficulties—we should draw up a programme of abnormal public works to be put in hand as soon as signs of recession appear. But we cannot rely on trade then recovering so much that expenditure can safely be reduced to "normal," let alone "subnormal," again, unless we provide for some other stimulus to take its place.

The optimistic theory that our system is on the whole self-balancing, and that the Government need only use its loan expenditure to even out fluctuations, is even less likely to apply in future than in the past.

(2) *Monetary Policy.*—The obvious way to stimulate capital outlay on private account is by following a monetary and banking policy which will ensure that there is a plentiful supply of funds available at low rates of interest. To some extent we have already assumed this remedy to be in use, when discussing the optimist's argument about raising the ratio of capital to labour[1]; but it is debatable how far it will in fact come into operation "automatically," the debate mainly turning, as is so often the case, on the interpretation of the word "automatically." I need not weary the reader with a review of the controversy which has raged on this subject. The important point is that the monetary authorities can, if they wish, supplement the workings of whatever forces we choose to class as "automatic" by purchasing securities and quoting low rates for advances of all kinds.

There can be no doubt that this remedy should be included in our programme, but it must not be regarded as a panacea. The limits to its effectiveness are discussed in Appendix B, but they may be briefly summarized thus:—

(*a*) Both the central bank and the ordinary banks can only operate directly on the markets for loans (and safe loans at that), whereas more and more of the private capital outlay for which there will be openings will be of the risky type which requires equity capital.

(*b*) It is difficult to lower long-term rates of interest very far, particularly if a subsequent rise is expected.

(*c*) If we are considering the problem of a special stimulus in bad years, the outlook may appear so poor that little private outlay would be undertaken even with very low rates indeed.

[1] See pages 95–96.

The conclusion seems to be that monetary policy can best be used to sustain the amount of private capital outlay in relatively good years and to facilitate the financing of additional public works in bad years.

(3) *Taxing Money.*—The last proposal was concerned with a "cheap money" policy pursued along more or less familiar lines. It has frequently been suggested, however, that an additional force should be used to secure low interest rates. If the holders of bank deposits not only received no interest but actually had to pay a small tax, say ¼d. in the £ per month, then the attractions of holding wealth in "liquid" form would be much reduced. People would be induced to buy securities instead, and so drive down the rate of interest.

This proposal is also discussed in Appendix B. We certainly should not reject it because of its unfamiliarity, or on account of ideas inherited from times when capital was much scarcer. At least in theory it should help to produce a lower average rate of interest, and so to solve our first problem of how to maintain the level of outlay in good years; by raising the tax we might also secure a special stimulus in bad years, though this might not be very large. The problem of administration need not be very serious, especially if we exempt holdings of less than, say, £500; and at the very least we should have found a new source of revenue which ought to encourage enterprise rather than discourage it.

(4) *Technical Improvements in the Capital Market.*—The last two proposals have been concerned with providing a favourable *general* situation in the capital market; to put it another way, they have been concerned with factors affecting that abstraction, "the" rate of interest. Capital outlay can also be stimulated by improving, and cheapening, the technical organization through which potential entrepreneurs are brought into contact with potential suppliers of funds.

Even to-day it might be more helpful to concentrate on

this side of the problem, rather than on trying to reduce the gilt-edged rate. The expense of raising capital of any kind is by no means negligible, and for smaller issues it may be prohibitive. Moreover, in many cases it is equity capital rather than loans which is required, so that a reduction of the rate on Government securities or overdrafts would only ease the situation very indirectly, if at all. To produce results in this field we must organize an outlet for the shares of developing companies.[1]

A declining population will make this question even more important, for it will mean that the openings for capital outlay will be largely in the luxury and semi-luxury industries, with which the investor is not very familiar and which are liable to be risky. Moreover, there is a second reason why a solution will become more urgent. For a declining population increases the need for adjustments of many kinds, and this will lead to increased frictional unemployment unless the newer industries can readily secure capital for expansion.

I do not wish to do much more than draw attention to this question. Various efforts are already being made to deal with it, and the first thing is clearly to push ahead with these. But we also require a greater readiness on the part of capitalists, particularly professional investors such as investment trusts, to buy shares in small or developing companies with a view to holding them for a long time. We need to "de-bunk" the theory that a wise investor should confine himself to freely marketable securities. Admittedly these have the advantage that they can be turned into cash should the holder require it; but few investors need to have the *whole* of their wealth readily available for use. The other supposed merit of marketable securities—that they are "safer," because they can be sold if things start going wrong with the company—is a sheer delusion, unless every holder considers

[1] See A. T. K. Grant: *A Study of the Capital Market in Post-War Britain*, pages 212–23, for a description of recent efforts to do this.

himself to be cleverer than the average at foreseeing the trouble. For every seller there must be a buyer.[1]

(5) *Subsidizing Capital Outlay.*—Another way of increasing the amount of capital outlay on private account is to subsidize it by one means or another. There are obvious difficulties in the way: if the subsidy is general, it will be very expensive, whilst any attempt at discrimination will lead to administrative difficulties and complaints about unfairness. Nevertheless this device has been applied in the past and might give useful results in future.

The most "obvious" sort of discrimination is to confine the assistance to schemes which would not otherwise be undertaken, but these are very hard to define, because the results of capital outlay are usually so uncertain. However, in the case of public utilities and railways it is sometimes possible to decide fairly definitely that a scheme would pay at one rate of interest but not at a higher one. If so, then a convenient way of giving assistance is for the State to guarantee the company's bonds, and so enable it to borrow more cheaply.[2] Such schemes have the advantage of being large and giving little grounds for complaints by rivals.

If the State adopts the device of guaranteeing the borrower's bonds, then it may incur no expense at all, but failures will be costly, as our experience with the Trade Facilities Act has shown. A method which has the advantage of limiting its commitments is to make an annual grant for a number of years. Another of our post-war experiments, the Development (Loans and Grants) Act of 1929, has shown that a modest grant for quite a short period may be surprisingly effective if it covers the interest charges which the company would have to pay during the process of construction. Directors may be very unwilling to reduce dividends

[1] See Keynes, op. cit., Chapter 12, for a further discussion of the "marketability" fallacy.

[2] This procedure was adopted with two recent schemes of railway development, which, it was said, would otherwise have been unprofitable.

so as to pay these charges, and so refrain from undertaking lengthy schemes, even though they might bring in good returns eventually.

Both the above methods involve the making of special arrangements with each entrepreneur. A more comprehensive stimulus may be given by exempting the undertakers of capital outlay from some form of taxation for a period. Thus building might easily be stimulated by exempting all newly built houses from local rates for, say, ten years. This sort of measure could be made particularly effective as a special provision to overcome a slump by limiting the exemption to houses built within a certain period. The effect on the revenues of the local authorities would then be very small; even with the general scheme it would be quite supportable, as the proportion of new houses in a town is seldom large.

This leads logically to the suggestion that the basis for local taxation should be changed, at least in part, to one of site value, so that the undertaking of new construction would not automatically bring a corresponding increase in rates. We must leave this topic, however, and the general problem of revising all taxes so as to make them less deterrent to enterprise, until later in the chapter.

(6) *Promotion of Confidence.*—The importance of "confidence" has been stressed so much in recent years that one almost feels a need to apologize for mentioning this rather elusive factor. There is, however, no doubt that the queer hotch-potch which goes to make up "confidence" plays a vital part in affecting the amount of capital outlay, and we cannot therefore neglect it.

The main element is confidence in the future state of trade, and here we are once more faced with our vicious circle. If we can adopt policies which will avoid slumps for a number of years, or at least prevent them becoming more frequent and more catastrophic, then we shall have gone a long way towards increasing confidence. Once more it is a case of "to him that hath shall be given."

Besides this, however, it is at any rate possible for the Government, and perhaps one should add the labour leaders, not to impair confidence by too aggressive an "anti-business" or "soak the rich" policy. This does not mean that social reform must cease; schemes of income redistribution, as we shall see later, may help to reduce unemployment by stimulating consumption, besides being desirable in themselves. But without denying that there is a conflict of aims here (for there undoubtedly is) it is still possible to adopt a policy of conciliatory gradualism, without making that a polite synonym for standing still.

The above set of proposals are all, in the main, directed to increasing the amount of capital outlay, with special reference to the problem of preventing its falling too far below the average in bad years and ensuring a revival if it does. They do not by any means exhaust the possibilities—thus nothing has been said about the deliberate building up of stocks of commodities by Governments in years of bad trade, a form of outlay which will have still more to commend it in future if the alternative is, as seems likely, the forcible reduction of output under all-round restriction schemes. There is plenty of scope for research in this field, but in a book like this one can only state the general principle and give a few illustrations.

The other main approach to the problem is via consumption. Can we so alter the mechanism of things that a lower level of capital outlay will suffice to give a satisfactory level of employment and trade activity? Here the possibilities are again very numerous, and an exhaustive treatment is therefore impossible; but the following brief list may be helpful:—

(1) *Discouraging Saving.*—The "obvious" method is a direct attack on the saving habit, which causes the gap between income and expenditure on consumption. Up to a point this is undoubtedly desirable; we need to make clear to all

concerned that saving should not be regarded as virtuous in itself, irrespective of circumstances. There is probably a fair amount of saving done, as it were, blindly, without any real object, except to add to the saver's wealth. People who indulge in this habit might well be encouraged to gratify their pride rather by building hospitals and the like, or even, if need be, by ostentatious expenditure on less worthy objects.[1] But from the point of view of most individuals saving is a habit to be fostered rather than frowned upon; the old-fashioned virtues of self-reliance, preparedness, and independence should not be lightly discarded.

Much saving is also done by companies in the form of undistributed profits, and it might seem desirable to discourage this practice. Here again, however, we must tread warily. Whilst there are doubtless cases in which reserves are built up for no very good reason, yet the attainment of a reasonably strong financial position is directly important to the elimination of unemployment. Bankruptcies, with their concomitant of forced sales of stock, i.e. negative capital outlay, can seriously aggravate a slump; and so can the mere absence of credit-worthiness which prevents the raising of new money to finance further development.

It is doubtful, therefore, whether we should place much reliance on a direct attack on saving. It would be very difficult to conduct the necessary propaganda without appearing to assail practices which are desirable on social grounds; and the results would not be wholly beneficial even from the point of view of reducing unemployment.

(2) *Social Services.*—The rather negative conclusion reached about the first proposal does not end the matter. The objections to a direct attack on thrift as such were mainly social in origin, but broadly similar results can be obtained by indirect methods which are socially desirable in themselves.

[1] As a compromise, if they cannot resist the urge to add to their wealth, then they should use their accumulations to start hazardous enterprises in depressed areas.

III. CONCLUSIONS AND REMEDIES

There is no need to labour the point that if high taxes are imposed on the recipients of large incomes and the proceeds distributed in one way or another to the poor, then the gap between the nation's income and its expenditure on consumption will be reduced, because the rich will be less able to save large sums; nor that the process has much to commend it from a social point of view. It does not make much difference, for our present purpose, whether the distribution is in cash, e.g. old-age pensions or unemployment assistance, or in kind, e.g. free education or hospital service. If it is in kind, then there is an absolute guarantee that the money will be spent on consumption ("consumption" expenditure includes payments for services as well as goods); but the same will be almost certainly true of cash allowances. Our choice between the two must depend mainly on social and practical considerations. From the point of view of employment policy the main distinction is that if the distribution is in cash, then there is no direct control over the point to which the extra demand will be directed; in the other case the Government might sometimes be able to assist some specially depressed area or industry.

The advantages of this method of increasing consumption expenditure are not confined to the direct effect. Even if the recipients of high incomes would have spent all the money if it had not been taken in taxes, yet their expenditure would largely have been on luxuries, and probably very variable in its direction. Particularly when demand is in any case likely to be shifting in that direction, on account of larger incomes and smaller families, there is a good deal to be said for reducing the need for industrial readjustment, by redistributing incomes in favour of those who will spend it in ways with which industrialists are familiar.[1]

It requires no great ingenuity to devise new forms of social services to act as channels for distributing the proceeds of

[1] See my article in the *Economic Journal* for June 1937 for a fuller treatment of this and succeeding points.

the taxation, and most of the existing ones could be developed with advantage. There does, however, seem to be a special case for introducing a system of family endowment, whereby allowances would be paid to families with three or more dependent children. The arguments in favour of such a scheme are numerous and powerful, but I need say little about them here, because I have dealt with the subject elsewhere.[1] I will only add that a proposal to relieve parents of part of the expense of bringing up a family should appeal to the nation's sense of what is socially desirable at a time when the population is declining; this factor is of some importance, because it means that the extra taxation will be accepted in a spirit of greater goodwill.

(3) *Taxation.*—The last sentence leads naturally to a consideration of the other side of the medal—the taxation needed to pay for the increased social services. We have seen that this must fall mainly on people with high incomes, but we have not studied the question of how it should be imposed. Yet this is a decidedly important question, and we cannot really decide on the wisdom of expanding the social services until we have examined it. Thus the object of the whole scheme was to reduce the amount which the community would save out of any given level of income, so that we would not need such a large amount of capital outlay to maintain demand and so preserve that level of income. But if we are not careful in our selection of taxes we may offset any good we do in this way by reducing the amount of capital outlay.

This subject is discussed in greater detail in Appendix B, where the merits of various types of tax are examined. Here we may content ourselves with a statement of the general principle that the taxes should fall as far as possible on *wealth*, and not on *enterprise*. We must admit, as we did above, that there is a conflict of aims; but if this principle

[1] In an article in *The Review of Economic Studies*, February 1938. The article is reproduced in Appendix A.

is observed, then we need not despair of doing something *both* to stimulate capital outlay *and* to redistribute incomes through taxation.

(4) *Attacks on Monopoly.*—The last two proposals in conjunction have aimed at securing a more equal distribution of the national income, and so a smaller gap between income and expenditure on consumption, by using the State's taxing power to redistribute incomes after they have been received. It is also possible for the State to try to reach a similar result by influencing the initial distribution of incomes. In particular it can discourage any monopolistic arrangements to "limit competition" where these would benefit rich people, and perhaps encourage them where poor people are combining against rich.

That this factor is important can be seen by anyone who studies the frequency with which efforts are made in one trade or another to maintain profits by some such device. Usually, of course, the practice will be justified on the score that cut-throat competition would prevent even that "fair" return which is all that the scheme seeks to secure. But whether this is true or not, there is no doubt that the object is to obtain higher profits than those which would otherwise prevail. And it is equally certain that profits are the source of large savings, both by the companies themselves and by the receivers of dividends; even if the latter be only at a modest rate, nevertheless they may add greatly to the income (and so the savings) of a millionaire with a large holding.

Unfortunately, however, as the experience of the United States showed, it is extremely difficult to pursue an effective anti-monopoly policy even where popular opinion is in favour of it. Moreover, there can be no doubt that popular opinion now looks far more kindly on these practices than it did in the past, largely because in many cases unrestrained competition would produce a position of great insecurity.[1]

[1] Cf. pages 53–54.

We are not now prepared to be so ruthless in asserting the consumer's right to buy in the cheapest market, whatever the effect on the producers' incomes.

This reaction has almost certainly gone too far, and there is undoubtedly a good theoretical case for a selective attack on the most undesirable practices; this would in many instances stimulate capital outlay as well as consumption, and we have already seen[1] that it would also help to reduce frictional unemployment. But beyond a general plea that the Government and the public should look more suspiciously at the proposals of highly interested parties, I have no concrete suggestion to make. Once again the field is open for valuable research work.

(5) *Budget Deficits.*—If there is a deficit on the budget, this means that some private savings are absorbed in offsetting the negative saving of the State. For any level of employment and national income, therefore, there will be a smaller gap between income and expenditure on consumption, and hence a smaller amount of capital outlay will suffice to maintain that level of activity. It might seem, therefore, that we can always offset an inadequate amount of capital outlay by incurring a sufficiently large deficit.

In a perfectly rational world this solution might be satisfactory. If production were being held up by inadequate expenditure, then the State might behave as if its income were larger and so put to work men and capital equipment which would otherwise be idle. It would not matter much whether it purchased their services directly (e.g. for road work or the giving of free concerts) or distributed money for people to spend. The State would, of course, be careful not to carry the process beyond the stage where it would yield more or less full employment—to be on the safe side it might not carry it as far. But up to that point, for the State to be economical in its consumption might almost be compared with a policy of enforcing economy of water

[1] Pages 66–67.

when the reservoirs were overflowing and flooding the country.

In a perfectly rational world the significance of the process would be realized, and in particular people would appreciate that the Government's borrowing was not "dissipating the national capital," because the higher level of employment was raising the national income, and so the amount of saving. But in our own world one can hardly recommend a policy of deliberate and persistent deficits. Not only is there a risk, perhaps not as great as used to be maintained, that confidence will be undermined and capital outlay curtailed; but the State's credit is likely to suffer. It seems more desirable to reserve budget deficits as an emergency weapon for use in slumps, when for a time we can probably make a virtue of necessity without loss of prestige.[1]

(6) "*Inflation.*"—The word "inflation" has been used, or misused, in so many senses that it should perhaps be avoided. But it serves here as a useful heading to cover a variety of proposals based on this sort of reasoning: "You have said that what is needed to raise the level of activity is an increase of demand unaccompanied by an immediate increase in the supply of goods to be sold. Well, don't worry with your cumbrous methods for causing people to receive extra incomes by stimulating capital outlay, or for making the community increase its expenditure without a previous increase in income. Create the extra income directly by printing it." Sometimes the State is to spend the money on public works, sometimes to use it to remit taxation, sometimes to distribute it to the unemployed, sometimes we are all to receive a national dividend.

The argument of this and the two preceding chapters should have made it clear that these proposals cannot simply be dismissed as "based on a fallacy" with a brief reference to the post-war experience of Germany. The real fallacy—

[1] The above was written in November 1938. The enlarged borrowing programme has already justified it.

and it is one which has cost the world dearly—is the idea that any move towards "inflation" must, under any circumstances, simply lead to wildly soaring prices.

It is extremely important that there should be a proper understanding of these questions, and I might plead this as justification for a rather lengthy digression. Fortunately, however, the matter has been ably discussed by Mr. J. E. Meade in his book, *Consumers' Credits and Unemployment*. I have included at the end of Appendix B a short discussion of the general issues involved; this is intended primarily for those with little previous knowledge of the subject, and does no more than show that *some* scheme of this type, if wisely applied, should make a valuable contribution to our solution. Those who want a more detailed treatment are urged to read Mr. Meade's book.[1]

This completes our list of possible measures to reduce general unemployment. If any excuse is needed for dealing with the subject at what may seem unnecessary length for a book of this kind, I must plead not only its intrinsic importance, but also the need to put the population factor into proper perspective. As with most generalizations, our conclusion about the effect of a declining population on general unemployment had to be qualified by a *ceteris paribus* clause —"unemployment will increase, *unless special measures are taken.*" Without some discussion of the possible "special measures" it is impossible to judge the significance of this

[1] Perhaps I should add the inevitable disclaimer to the effect that this must not be taken as meaning that I agree with all the details of Mr. Meade's proposals. Some of my own criticisms are set out in my brief review of the book in the *Cambridge Review* for May 27, 1938. A longer discussion is to be found in the review by Mr. Keynes in the *Economic Journal* for March 1938, with whose views I am in substantial agreement.

Perhaps I should repeat here the warning that "credits" is really a misnomer for "dividends" or "allowances."

proposition. Moreover, there is a very real risk that the statement will be used without the qualification to support a campaign to raise the birth-rate.

Perhaps we should add the concluding observation that progress can best be made against general unemployment by using more than one of our list of remedies. In particular a wise policy would almost certainly include some measures from each of the two main groups. So long as there is general unemployment the two broad aims—to increase capital outlay and to increase consumption demand—are not rival but complementary, even though some of the particular measures designed to achieve one may be prejudicial to the other.

CHAPTER VI

THE NATIONAL INCOME—I. SIZE

So far we have mainly discussed the question of whether people will or will not secure employment. Now we must investigate the equally important question of how much income will result from their labours. By "income" we shall, throughout, mean "real income," i.e. the amount of actual goods and services, not the amount of money with which people buy them.

We shall make the simplifying, if somewhat vague, assumption that the problem of avoiding general unemployment is solved about as well as in the past. It is not very difficult to adapt the results to see what would happen on any other assumption. Thus if unemployment is, on the whole, higher, then the national income will be reduced, but usually not in proportion to the fall in employment, since the best workers and factories, etc., remain in production; and conversely if it is somewhat lower.[1]

The influence of the change from an increasing to a stationary or declining population is exerted mainly through its effect on the amount of national capital (including land) per head. There are very great difficulties, both theoretical and statistical, in the way of a satisfactory computation of this quantity. But looking at the matter broadly (and that is all that we require) it is easy to see that the amount (per head) of these aids to production has risen in the past because

[1] There is a further difficulty if we want to compare the probable national income of some future period with its level to-day. It is not enough merely to assume that general unemployment will then, on the average, be about the same as it is now. We also want to know what will have happened in the meantime, since this will affect the amount of capital equipment then in existence. But this difficulty does not seriously affect a comparison between the *rates of increase* of the national income in the two periods. The reader might do well to re-read the discussion of "assumptions" on pages 45–47.

accumulation has outweighed growth in numbers, but is likely to rise faster as a result of the change. Therefore, unless people become, on the average, less successful in making use of them, we shall expect the real income per person employed also to rise more rapidly than in the past.

We may approach this problem from two angles—that of income *produced*, and that of income *received*. From the point of view of income produced it is fairly obvious that output per person employed will be higher, the larger the amount of machinery and so on, which each worker has to assist him.

One can see the importance of this factor by comparing the present position of this country with that which prevails in the East, with its teeming millions and shortage of capital. All sorts of operations are there performed by hand because the services of machinery, being scarce, are relatively expensive. As a result a great number of natives are required to do a job which would be done in England by two men, a boy, and a machine. Even when due allowance is made for the men employed in producing the necessary fuel and keeping up the stock of machines, it is clear that the output per person employed will be much higher in England. There may of course be certain occupations where little help can be secured from the use of capital, and in these the output per head will only be higher if the Englishman works more effectively. But these are sufficiently rare for the average, taken over all industries, to be far higher in England.

It may be helpful to examine the mechanism of the process. We have already seen[1] that a rise in the average amount of capital per worker may take two more or less distinct forms. The obvious one is the adoption of labour-saving machinery in one or more industries; and the more subtle one is the expansion of the heavily capitalized industries relatively to those where the ratio of capital to labour is low. Both movements are stimulated by the abundance and

[1] Pages 95–96, 100–101.

cheapness of capital, and we shall expect to find both more strongly at work in future, helping to make the average output per person employed rise more rapidly than in the past.

Another way of arriving at the same result is to consider the use which will be made of our additional capital. In the past a great deal of this was needed merely to provide for the increase in population. In future there will be little or no need to use our savings merely to duplicate existing equipment in this way, and there will be correspondingly more available each year to raise the level of output per head. It is true that some of the new capital will be needed to enlarge those industries, the demand for whose products will have grown owing to the higher standard of living. But this will not affect the rise in the average amount of capital per workman, unless other capital is rendered useless. For these trades will simply be absorbing men who might otherwise have been employed in the industries which have installed labour-saving machinery. The absence of population increase must mean a more rapid rise in capital per head.

Strictly speaking, the above conclusion should have been stated subject to a proviso, which I hope the reader will now insert for himself, if he has not already done so. However, for the benefit of those who could not get it beyond the tip of their tongue, here it is in all its simplicity. The annual supply of additional capital must not fall too much. In the past the supply has been sufficient both to take care of the increasing population, and to provide a surplus with which to raise the average amount of capital per worker. The whole supply might fall to the level of this surplus, in which case the rise in productivity due to extra capital would merely continue at the same rate as before.

There are two reasons why the supply of new capital might fall off. The nation might, on the average, have a higher level of general unemployment, causing the national income (and so savings) to be reduced; we have assumed that this will not be the case. Or the nation might become less thrifty, so that it saved a smaller amount despite the maintenance of the old level of employment. We have seen[1] that there has been some tendency in this direction, and one class of measures for combating general unemployment would reinforce it. Clearly, therefore, we cannot be dogmatic on the subject, but thriftiness would have to fall considerably in order to off-set the population factor. Our conclusion is probably sound, though any reduction in thrift naturally reduces its importance.

We may now see how the thing works out from the point of view of income *received*. The average amount of capital owned by each person will be higher in future than in the past for the following reasons:—

(1) The average person will be older, and will, therefore, have had more time to build up savings himself.

(2) His father will, on the average, have had more capital to leave, because the amount of capital per head has grown with each generation.

(3) His father will have divided his fortune amongst a smaller number of heirs. (As an interesting illustration of this we may consider the division of the paternal land in peasant countries, where the effect on productivity is also particularly obvious.)

Of these factors, the second simply represents the continuance of the previous rate of growth. The first and third, however, reflect the accelerating effect of a change to a stationary or declining population. It is easy to see how the possible off-sets work—number one may be counterbalanced by reduced thriftiness of the spontaneous sort, and our special measures might include higher death-duties.

Now, if the average rate of return on capital has remained the same, it is clear that the increase in the average amount

[1] Pages 113 ff.

held will mean a corresponding increase in the average person's unearned income. If, as is more likely, the rate falls there will still be *some* increase in this income unless the fall is more than proportionate to the increase in his holding of capital. And there will certainly be some gain in the real value of the average earned income; for capital will still be yielding its physical product, so that either wages will rise or prices will fall.[1]

From either point of view then we see that the increase in the amount of capital per head makes for a rise in the average income per person employed, and that probably this quantity will rise more rapidly in future than in the past. (It is, when all is said and done, not a very startling conclusion.) But this is very far from being the end of the problem; we have only shown that *this* factor will be working in the right direction, without examining the possibility that others may be counteracting or re-inforcing it. Strictly speaking, the words *ceteris paribus* ought to have appeared repeatedly throughout the last few pages—the reader may like to go back and put them in.[2]

One other factor may be dismissed very briefly. We assumed at the very beginning that technical progress will continue at about the same rate as in the past.[3] So far, therefore, as better knowledge of how to make use of our resources is concerned, incomes should rise at about the same speed as in the past. Of course, we have not proved this—if somebody else likes to make some other assumption, only the march of time can show who was right; and even after the event the inevitable vagueness of the concept and the difficulties in the way of collecting and interpreting the statistics might prevent agreement as to the verdict. But it is as well to make some assumption about this factor, if only to prevent

[1] We return to this subject in the next chapter.

[2] The really observant reader will have noted the all-embracing proviso on page 137: "unless people become, on the average, less successful in making use of them."

[3] Page 46.

its being forgotten; for it is very important, and we can at least say, with considerable confidence, that it will be operating to raise incomes, even if its influence be not so strong as heretofore.[1]

Both our knowledge and the supply of capital are therefore likely to be working strongly in the right direction. What can we say about the human element, which has to make use both of the knowledge and the capital? We have included the effects of improved education and so on under technical progress, but what about the changing age-composition?

We must be careful to distinguish between three distinct problems which we may wish to solve. In each case we are trying to estimate the future national income "per head," but there are three different senses in which we may interpret "per head." We may include in the divisor:—

(*a*) Only those people actually taking part in production—this would be most natural if we were wanting to judge the system's efficiency in turning out goods and services with a minimum of labour.

(*b*) Everyone who is either at work or seeking a job—i.e. the "occupied" population on the census definition. Since the unemployed do not set much value on their enforced leisure, this is perhaps more important than (*a*) as a test of efficiency from the social point of view.

(*c*) The whole population. Since everyone—breadwinner and dependant alike—must be a consumer, the importance of this concept is obvious.

[1] If anyone should think that technical progress has lost any of its previous virility, let him study the figures for output per head in Special Memorandum No. 75 of the Royal Economic Society. Some of the rise is doubtless due to the use of more capital per man, but a great part may be fairly attributed to the factors we have grouped under the heading "technical progress." If anything, it seems more reasonable, in view of the greater energy now devoted to research, to assume a higher rate of progress. But we must not forget that little advance is possible in some branches of economic activity, notably many kinds of services, which are becoming progressively more important.

There are other possible interpretations, and not a few difficulties in connection with those given—such as the treatment of people who live on their means, but do a little work occasionally if it is available. However, the broad concepts are clear enough for our purpose.

Before trying to find out any of the answers, let us examine the relations between them. We saw on page 38 that there is not likely, in the next thirty years, to be any very significant change in the proportion of the population which will be of working age. We ought perhaps to qualify this by saying that ideas may change as to what should be regarded as the limits of a man's working life; thus people may well stay longer at school and retire earlier, especially as a richer community can more easily afford such practices.[1] But even if the average working life were reduced by two years this would only make a difference of about 4 per cent, and it seems reasonable to offset the probable movement in this direction against the slight rise in the percentage of people who would fall within the present age limits. We may therefore conclude that, for the next thirty years, the answers to problems (*b*) and (*c*) will be substantially the same; the increased proportion of pensioners will balance the decreased proportion of dependent children, so that, for example, a 10 per cent rise in the national income "per occupied person" will also mean a 10 per cent rise in income "per head of population."

The relation between (*a*) and (*b*) depends simply on the percentage of the occupied population which is unemployed; so long as this remains constant the two will move together. Now we have assumed for the purposes of this chapter that *general* unemployment will remain about the same. But it would hardly be plausible, in view of the analysis of Chapter II, to make the same assumption about "particular" unemployment. The forces making for a rise—the reduced

[1] If the problem of general unemployment becomes more acute, then there is likely to be an agitation for making such a change compulsory.

adaptability of the labour force and the greater need for adjustments—are too strong. We must therefore expect that the rise in income per person employed will be larger than the rise per head of the occupied population.

We must not, however, exaggerate the importance of this difference. If the measures described in Chapter II are adopted, the rise in particular unemployment need not be very large; even if they are not, it would hardly reduce the number of people at work by as much as 5 per cent. Particular unemployment is a disease which may have a devastating effect on individuals, or on special trades or areas; but so long as it is not aggravated by the simultaneous existence of severe general unemployment, its effect on the national income is not very great. If our assumption about the latter holds good, then we need only make a comparatively small deduction from the rise in the first average to find the rise in the second.

We are left, then, to solve the question of whether the changed age-composition of the people actually employed will make for a rise or a fall in the national income. At first sight it might appear that the increased proportion of elderly workers will have an unfavourable influence. Although this view is widely held, there seems to be very little evidence with which it can be supported. Old men undoubtedly find greater difficulty in securing a new post if they become unemployed—that was one of the reasons why we anticipated a rise in particular unemployment. But they are no more liable to *become* unemployed than young men, which suggests that those who remain in work are quite capable of doing their particular job. We are dealing with the efficiency of those who are actually at work, and must judge this by the man's skill in his own trade, not his adaptability at turning to something quite different.

If the reader remains sceptical, let him consider the number of posts where experience counts for more than muscular strength, or where age is no handicap to one brought up in the trade. Or let him consider whether the despised elderly man would be likely to be paid more, on the average, than their juniors if they were really so inefficient. (Admittedly the extra payments may in some cases be simply the result of semi-automatic promotion to positions which a young man could fill just as well if given the chance; but this is not always so.) If we consider the whole field of economic activity, the changed age-composition of the *employed* population may on balance be favourable, even if some of the elderly are not really up to standard; for there will be a smaller proportion of boys and learners to pull down the average.[1]

In short, the most important thing to be said about the effect of the changing age-composition on the productivity of those at work is probably that it has had little effect one way or the other in the past, and is not likely to do so in the relatively near future. (It would of course be a different matter if Dr. Charles's pessimistic nightmare about the population of A.D. 2035 came true.) It is likely to cause some increase in particular unemployment, and this factor will exert a small depressing influence both on the average income per person "occupied" and also, since this group represents a more or less constant proportion of the whole, on the average income per head of population.

So much then for capital, knowledge, and the quality of the people; the outlook continues to be cheerful, so long as the vital assumption about general unemployment holds good. There are, however, a number of other factors which are, or may appear to be, relevant, and which must therefore be discussed. In the first place, will the absence of population growth (and still more the existence of a decline) have a

[1] Not only are boys less efficient than men, but the fact that they are relatively cheap encourages the use of methods which are wasteful of labour. Employers will be stimulated into mechanizing much "blind-alley" work when they no longer have an adequate supply of boys who are willing to work for low wages because these will bring an immediate relief to the family budget.

seriously adverse effect by depriving us of the advantages of large-scale production?

This is a question to which I cannot hope to give a really satisfactory answer. I can only set out some of the relevant considerations, state my own opinion, and leave the reader to form his. We may start with an old friend—the fact that the size of the population is by no means the only factor in determining the size of a market; particularly in the case of luxuries and semi-luxuries, the rising standard of consumption may produce at least as rapid a rise in demand as we have experienced in the past. Then we must remember that it is comparatively seldom that the whole output of a commodity has to be produced by one company for the economies of mass production to be realized; provided we can prevent monopolistic exploitation, we may meet the situation by reducing the number of companies rather than by reducing their size. Furthermore, there will in some cases be off-sets where a larger output involves rising rather than falling costs, e.g. if there is a limited supply of suitable sites or of raw materials.

Provided we confine ourselves to a period of stationary population, there is, of course, no possibility of an actual loss of efficiency due to this factor; the worst that can happen is that we shall no longer secure a rise in incomes through producing for a larger market. But even in a period of modest decline, the expanding market for luxuries may well offset the effect of any contraction in that for necessaries; there is more to be gained by raising the scale of output to the stage where mass production first becomes possible, if only for one factory, than by expanding output still further or by having a number of large factories.

For the period with which I am most closely concerned (the next thirty years or so) I conclude that any scare about the population factor leading to smaller-scale, and therefore less efficient, production is quite out of place. There is likely to be some actual gain through the larger market for luxuries, but this will not prevent the dynamic comparison with previous periods from being unfavourable; the expansion of markets will be making for a rise in incomes, but not as strongly as in the past. If we were to go on and consider a period of headlong descent to a population of four or five million greybeards, then of course there would be serious loss of productivity due to smaller markets. But I have already likened an analysis of such a period to one of the economics of the end of the world. The really determined believer in "pessimism in our time" should rather hold forth on the danger of uneconomically small markets due to economic nationalism.

This brings us to another point. The rise in the average level of incomes has in the past owed a good deal to the development of international trade—not so much because larger markets enabled England to make her particular products more efficiently, though that doubtless helped in some cases, as because we were able to concentrate on these products and obtain in exchange things which we could only produce with difficulty, if at all. Even apart from the effects of economic nationalism, it seems unlikely that this increasing specialization can henceforward hope to play such an active part in raising incomes; the movement seems rather to have gone into reverse.

We shall return to this subject in the chapter on international trade. Here it is perhaps sufficient to say that the disappearance of a factor which previously caused incomes to rise will of course tend to make the future rise less rapid, and there is a real danger that attempts to deal with general unemployment by restricting imports may turn this into an actual depressing influence. But in any comparison with the experience of the recent past, as opposed to one with pre-war times, we must remember that this depressing factor has already made its appearance. Moreover, it has been quite insufficient to prevent a rise in the national income per person employed, as we can see by comparing the figures for 1937 with those of 1929—both peak years in the trade cycle, with similar amounts of unemployment. The average real wage has undoubtedly risen—using the Ministry of Labour's indices of weekly wages and the cost-of-living, we find a rise of slightly over 10 per cent. And Mr. Clark's more comprehensive, if more speculative, calculations of the actual quantity we are discussing, i.e. the real national income per person employed, show if anything a greater rise.[1]

Finally, we may deal with an issue which seems to be causing many people some concern. It is argued that when the population is declining we shall be left with "a burden of redundant capacity" in many directions—railways, houses, factories, public buildings, sometimes even roads. It is then argued that this will have an adverse effect on the national income, the specific reason being sometimes given that property values will fall and property incomes disappear.

Now there are many things which might be said about this mixture of ideas. In the first place, of course, the arguments can have very little application for some time, i.e. until the population actually begins to decline at a significant rate; even their most ardent supporters would hardly maintain that we should be better off if a growing population caused the supply of these things to be inadequate, and so led to a rise in their value.[2] At most they might make some reference to capital developments, e.g. water supply schemes, undertaken on the assumption that population would grow.

There is, however, no need to evade the issue in this way. Even when the population is declining the nation will very seldom suffer from the resultant rise in the amount of house-

[1] See *National Income and Outlay*, page 208. The table only goes as far as 1936, but may be supplemented with figures from his article in the *Economic Journal* for September 1938.

[2] The reader should distinguish between such a false proposition and the true one that a growing population, by making it attractive to incur capital outlay, may help us to avoid a slump. We are dealing with the (real) national income per person employed.

room, or other capital, available per head. The *owners* of that particular sort of capital, even perhaps of most sorts of capital, may suffer a loss of income; for they will have to sell the services of their property more cheaply. But the community as a whole, even including the owners, will generally find no reason to regret such a state of affairs. The fall in rents, for example, will lead them to increase their consumption of living accommodation, to the benefit of their real income. If there really is so much house-room per head that nobody has a use for part of it—or, more strictly, that nobody is prepared to pay a rent for it sufficient to cover the costs of maintenance—then some of the houses can simply be allowed to decay. It is contrary to common sense to say that the community as a whole can be worse off because it is "burdened" with so many houses that it cannot make use of them all.

Put like this I do not think anyone can fail to appreciate the truth of the proposition. It is useful, however, to see what has led so many people to be scared by such a fallacy. Members of left-wing parties may say that it is simply the capitalists who are frightened at the possibility of their incomes suffering, and who cannot see that true wealth derives from plenty, not scarcity. Such a view would undoubtedly represent a part of the truth, but there are two, or perhaps three, other elements which should be distinguished.

In the first place, a great reduction in the income earned from some form of capital, say houses, will generally mean that our descendants would have preferred us to have devoted our energies to a different *type* of construction—perhaps bath-chair factories, perhaps merely a different type of housing. The existence of an abundant supply of houses cannot be a "burden" to them, unless they actually get in the way and so necessitate expensive demolition schemes. But even if no house is actually left unused, our descendants may still feel that the money spent on them could have been used to greater advantage; they may say that families would have been happier with one well-built house equipped with labour-saving appliances, although the existence of two "desirable villa residences" enabled the old folk to have a separate establishment. In other words, the people who bewail this hypothetical glut of houses are not without some justification. Our descendants will not be worse off than we as a result of it, but a violent fall in house rents would truly show that things were not as much improved as they might have been.

The above point is valid, so long as there are other forms of capital which would have yielded a larger return. (Indeed, we are likely to experience this phenomenon on a minor scale even before the population starts to decline, because the changing age-composition will change the direction of demand and make us wish we had a different type of equipment.) There may be cases, however, where the damage is not limited to the partial loss of an advantage which falling numbers would have brought, if people had shown more forethought. For it may be that the smaller numbers will reduce the demand for some product below the minimum level which justifies working a single large-scale plant, even if the owner is prepared to forgo the whole of his profit. In the case of houses, we could say cheerfully that if the demand falls away so much that the owners can get no return, then any surplus can simply be scrapped; the capital devoted to housing has been used to build a large number of separate units, and the abandonment of a part does not interfere with the use of the remainder. But if, for example, we considered a town which had previously supported one cinema, the fall in population might so reduce the demand that the proprietor could not even cover his working expenses, whatever price, high or low, he charged. The whole capital would become valueless and be abandoned, and the consumers would be deprived of a desirable facility for making one type of purchase. Clearly then the "redundancy" of capital would here correspond with a real loss to the community—and the same would be true if the service were maintained, but at higher prices[1] or on an inferior basis. But we must emphasize that there will in general only be a real loss if it is impossible to abandon a part of the capital used for a certain purpose without thereby affecting the efficiency of the rest, and if the complete elimination of profits will not maintain the volume of sales. In effect we are simply faced with a special case of the phenomenon discussed above, where a reduced market leads to the loss of economies of large-scale production.

A third reason why people class this phenomenon as a disaster of redundancy instead of a blessing of abundance applies particularly to the case of public buildings and the like which have been financed by means of loans. If a municipality, for example, has constructed a car park and the reduced population leads to a reduced demand, then the profits may no longer suffice to cover the interest on the loan; and this is regarded as being a disaster, since it will involve a charge on the rates. It seems clear, however, from a physical point of view that the community is better off if there is no longer so great a pressure on the limited supply of parking space—perhaps the charge will be lowered so as to keep the park full. How then can we reconcile these two ways of looking at the problem?

The answer is not difficult. So long as the owners of the bonds issued to finance the construction are included within the community, the community as a whole must gain; it has better, or cheaper, parking facilities, and the levying of rates to pay interest is merely a transfer between its own members.[2] It may, of course, nevertheless be true—very

[1] This will apply mainly in cases where the owners were not previously trying to make the maximum profit—otherwise they would have raised prices earlier. An excellent example would be the case of a little-used country road. The reduced amount of traffic would not reduce the cost of maintenance proportionately, and there would be no gain through reduced congestion; hence the effective price to the ratepayers per unit of service would rise.

[2] It may, however, involve difficulties, as we shall see in the chapter on Public Finance.

probably it will—that the community would have been still better off if its ancestors had used the capital devoted to building the car park to making a smaller car park and something else as well. But that is the extent of the "burden" so long as the financing is internal. If the money has been borrowed from outside, then truly the members of our community will have to pay the penalty, as ratepayers, of being partners in an unsuccessful enterprise, and cheap parking facilities will only be a partial consolation.

Perhaps we may summarize the main results of this chapter in a table. The first column shows the factor considered, the second its absolute effect on income per person employed, i.e. whether it makes for a rise or a fall, and the third its relative effect, i.e. whether it will be making for a more or less rapid rise than in the past.[1] The table is based on the assumption that the problem of avoiding general unemployment is solved about as well as in the past, and—a rather belated addition—that we shall not be involved in a major war, which would clearly swamp all other considerations, at least temporarily. It applies mainly to conditions of comparatively small change, such as we can expect in the next thirty years or so; considerable alterations would be needed for a period of violent decline.

Everyone is free to make his own assessment of the quantitative importance of the various factors. It is clear, however, that the total effect is going to be a rise, and very probably a more rapid rise than we have experienced in the past. Furthermore, if we are interested in consumption, rather than in income, we can add another favourable factor—the probable decline in thrift, which we noted when discussing the supply of capital.

To obtain the results for income per head of population

[1] Alternatively the comparisons may be regarded as "static" and "dynamic" respectively.

we have to make a small deduction to allow for the increase in particular unemployment. The picture is still a fairly rosy one—not entirely on account of the population factor, though that was clearly helpful on balance, particularly in its effect on the supply of capital per head. I ought, however,

FACTORS INFLUENCING THE REAL NATIONAL INCOME PER PERSON EMPLOYED

Factor	Absolute Effect	Relative Effect
Capital Supply	Very Favourable	Favourable
Technical Progress, etc.	Favourable	Nil
Age-composition	Perhaps slightly favourable	Unimportant
Scale of Production	Unimportant	Unfavourable, but not very important
International Trade	May be unfavourable, but probably not very important	Unfavourable

once more to display the skeleton in the cupboard—the increased risk of slumps. Again the population factor is not wholly responsible—to some extent this danger is the inevitable consequence of increased wealth. But, to put it crudely, whilst this and other developments are increasing the potential plenty, they are also increasing the risk of a large part of it remaining only potential.

CHAPTER VII

THE NATIONAL INCOME
II. DISTRIBUTION

We have now discussed the questions of how many people will secure employment, and how much income will be created. The next problem to tackle is that of the distribution of this income, both as between property and labour, and as between individuals.

We saw that one of the main effects of the change-over from a rising to a stationary or declining population was to raise the ratio of capital to labour, and we shall start by discussing the effect of this development. The problem has been analysed by various economists with the aid of simplifying assumptions, and by making these drastic enough it is possible to present a fairly simple treatment.[1] In broad outline the analysis would run something like this:—

It is assumed that capital can be treated as a homogeneous factor of production—not, of course, because all machines and so on are of one type, but because money is assumed to have been spent on each kind in such a way that the return per £100 is the same in each case.

Similarly, it is assumed that labour can be treated as a homogeneous factor, on the ground, presumably, that men will move from one occupation to another so as to equalize "net advantages."[2]

It is further assumed that perfect competition prevails, so that each unit of capital, or labour, receives the same reward; that the rewards are so adjusted that the whole

[1] See, for example, A. C. Pigou: *Economics of Welfare*, pages 658 ff. J. R. Hicks: *Theory of Wages*, Chapter VI. (But the reader is most particularly warned that he must examine their assumptions with extreme care, especially those about equilibrium and perfect competition.)

[2] I.e. wages, with allowance for any other features, such as pleasantness of work, which may attract or repel.

supply of each is hired; and that there are no other factors except these two.

Now suppose that the amount of capital is increased, all other things (knowledge, consumers' tastes, etc.) remaining unchanged. In order that this additional supply may secure employment, the charge for hiring capital will have to be reduced. This will, as we have seen before, stimulate the use of capital in place of labour for jobs where this is technically possible, and will also cause those industries to expand in which capital plays an unusually large part; and the process is assumed to continue until equilibrium is once more established, with full employment of both factors.

On this analysis it is clear that the return per unit of capital must fall, for that is the force which causes the extra capital to be employed. Three considerations will affect the extent of the fall; it will tend to be small on the following conditions:—

(*a*) If there were previously a large number of jobs, or parts of jobs, which could be done almost as cheaply by using extra capital in place of some of the labour.

(*b*) If a small reduction in the price of goods produced by highly capitalized industries relative to other prices would lead to a large increase in sales.

(*c*) If the change in the size and distribution of the national income caused by the introduction of the extra capital leads the community to change the direction of its demand in favour of goods produced mainly by capital.[1]

If every unit of capital, old and new, receives a lower rate of return, then the rate of wages is virtually certain to rise. The least favourable case, apart from the theoretical curiosity mentioned in the footnote, would be one where the extra

[1] In an extreme case such a change might cause the initial fall in the return per unit of capital to be subsequently replaced by a rise.

capital was all used on jobs previously performed by labour. To illustrate this we may visualize a limiting position, suggested by Professor Pigou, in which there would actually be no rise in wages, and no fall in the return per unit of capital. This would be so if capital could only take the form of mechanical men which performed the same functions as their human rivals. Clearly the two types would then receive equal "wages," both before and after the increase in the number of robots; and, in the absence of other factors of production, the whole product would be absorbed in making such payments. Since there is no reason to suppose the productivity of a "man" would be changed with greater numbers, wages would be unaffected.

At the other extreme is the case where it is impossible to substitute capital for labour anywhere, so that all the extra capital has to be absorbed by expanding the capitalistic industries.[1] Real wages will then rise strongly, particularly if these industries are faced with an inelastic demand. The rise may take the form of higher money wages—for the owners of the new capital will have to attract workers to operate it—or of lower prices, due to the reduced charge for hiring capital, or both.

Another way of expressing this result is to say that the rise in wages and the fall in the rate of return on capital will be greater the smaller the degree of rivalry between the two factors, and the greater the degree of co-operation.

The analysis may be extended to give formal answers to such questions as "Under what conditions will the total earnings of capital rise or fall?" or "Under what conditions will wages represent a larger proportion of the national income?" But I am too sceptical of the value of such work, except as an exercise in pure theory, to reproduce it here—any reader who is interested can consult the passage in Hicks

[1] If the demand for the products of these is sufficiently inelastic or if all industries use about the same proportions of capital and labour then the price of capital might sink to zero before it was all absorbed.

referred to above. It seems more useful here to discuss briefly some of the practical limitations in the way of such a treatment, and to indicate what part of the results may nevertheless be reasonably assumed to hold good.

In the first place, can we really draw this antithesis between the remuneration of capital on the one hand and of labour on the other, as if there were a single rate paid to a unit of each? It is clear that neither factor is homogeneous in the ordinary sense of the word; neither is composed of units sufficiently identical to be interchangeable for productive purposes, and one might plausibly argue that there is a greater justification for classing steam-shovels with navvies, and clerks with adding machines, rather than for talking of "labour" and "capital." The connection between the demands for the services of men and machines which fulfil similar functions seems closer than that between clerks and navvies, and the forces affecting their rate of remuneration more similar.

To this type of objection the orthodox answer would be somewhat on these lines. "What you say is largely true in the short period when the supply of different specialized types of capital and labour is more or less fixed; a sudden rise in the demand for trenches would initially tend to raise the remuneration of mechanical and human diggers alike. But with the passage of a little time each rate will return to a level in conformity with the rates payable to capital and labour in general. The new capital which becomes available each year will be pressed into lines where the return to capital is higher than the average, and as machines become worn out they will not be renewed in lines where profits are low. Similarly, new workers will enter well-paid occupations and retiring workers will not be replaced in ill-paid ones, so that adjustment will be made in time even if the mobility of established ones were nil. Thus the returns to different types of capital will at least tend to equality, being governed by the supply and demand for capital as a whole; and similarly with labour. But capital and labour are distinct things, and must be treated separately."

I do not propose to criticize this contention at length. As a statement of a broad tendency, it clearly has considerable force, though one might legitimately say, for example, that human beings should be split into a number of separate factors[1] because social considerations so greatly reduce mobility between classes. But one question is vital, and must be carefully considered.

A key-point in the analysis given above was the effect of the extra supply of capital on the return to the old capital. On the assumptions made (homogeneity of capital, perfect competition, and equilibrium) it clearly followed that the return to each unit of capital, new or old, would have to be the same. Since the new capital could only secure employment by accepting a lower return, the old would have to accept one also. This was the great reason for saying that real wages would rise. Whilst it would generally be helpful to secure the services of the new capital at cut rates, yet the really important thing was the revision of the bargain with all the old capital.[2] The question is, then, whether the facts will be sufficiently close to the assumptions for this conclusion broadly to hold good.

To answer this we must consider how the extra capital comes into existence. Each year there are savings available which entrepreneurs may secure and use for any project which they think will yield a return sufficiently in excess of the rate of interest to justify the risk involved. If the demand for the product of the chosen industry were expanding, then this might not affect the selling price or the return to any old capital at all. But under the conditions postulated—an increase in the amount of capital with a constant labour force—the dearth of such openings would

[1] Cf. Cairnes's famous "non-competing groups." An increased supply of capital may affect these groups very differently.

[2] Cf. Hicks, op. cit., page 115; Pigou, op. cit., page 660.

require a fall in the rate of interest. Hence some at least of the new capital would enter industries in which demand was not expanding, the extra output being only saleable if prices are reduced. The newcomer is prepared to sell at this reduced price, because he has obtained his capital more cheaply, and his competition also forces down the return on old capital invested in that industry.

So far, so good. But whatever the rate of interest may be, the return on old capital in other industries will not be affected (except possibly indirectly) unless some of the savings are directed into them too; the profits of the railways, for example, will not be reduced because lower interest rates have encouraged an increase in the capital invested in houses. The general fall in the rate of return to capital will only take place in the all-embracing manner postulated by the theoretical analysis if the new capital is suitably distributed between all possible uses.

On a realistic view it seems clear that this condition will not be fulfilled, at any rate in its entirety. The reasons for this are numerous, though they overlap somewhat. In the first place there is the general uncertainty which plays such a large role in all matters of capital outlay. In deciding whether or not to add to the stock of one type of capital the potential entrepreneur is faced with a most formidable problem. He should not simply be guided by the current level of profits earned by producers in that industry. Even if these are known to be high he may fear a change in conditions within the lifetime of his fixed plant—the long-run adjustments which are supposed to result from a process of trial and error can only be relied upon if conditions remain static. When our knowledge about the present is often inadequate and our knowledge about the future almost non-existent we clearly cannot expect delicate adjustments in the amount of capital applied to different uses, such as would be necessary for the assumption of homogeneity.

Then there are more specific considerations, directly

related to our present problem. Competition is very far from perfect, and the newcomer is at a great disadvantage, particularly in industries where goodwill plays an important role. It may, therefore, be quite possible for the rate of interest to fall a long way and yet for the old companies in such an industry to continue to make the same good profits, without attracting outside competition.[1]

The same result will be achieved if the established producers have an advantage of some other kind—trade secrets, or a superior site, or an excellent management or organization. They may be passing on the benefits of all these to the consumer in the form of low prices, in which case the newcomer should see clearly how hopeless his task is, despite the fact that he is now able to secure capital more cheaply than they did. But even if they are using their advantage to secure very high profits he may still hesitate before giving battle.

Another reason why the return on some types of old capital will not fall is that in many cases it is already considerably below the level which would induce the building of the existing plant, were the owners free to decide again. Either the conditions have altered since the time of the original outlay, or the industrialists simply miscalculated. Whatever the reason there will be no further outlay on capital of that type, even if the supply is greatly increased and the rate of interest greatly reduced; hence the argument about the revision of old bargains will not apply here.[2]

[1] Cf. the discussion of forces affecting capital outlay on pages 107–110.

[2] It may be objected that these low profits are only a temporary phenomenon, that capital would in time leave the industry through absence of renewals, and that the rate of interest will then again affect the total supply and so the earnings of that type of capital. But the process is extremely slow, as our depressed industries have shown, and the level of profits which will retain existing capital is, even in the theoretical long period, far below that which would attract new. For different items of equipment do not wear out simultaneously, so that failure to make renewals involves scrapping sound plant; and some capital expenditure, such as preliminary expenses, losses during development, expenditure on surveys, etc., never needs to be repeated.

For these and other reasons, such as the existence of legal monopolies, we must not expect the theoretical argument for a rise in earned incomes to apply in full force. It does not, of course, lose all its validity; the presence of additional capital seeking employment will to some extent make the terms of other bargains, beside those in which it actually takes part, more favourable to the working community, either in their capacity of earners or of consumers. This is particularly likely to occur in the case of goods produced mainly by capital, whose prices will be reduced—especially as these are frequently sold in a fairly stable market, which permits of more exact calculations. House rents, for example, are likely to fall as the result of lower interest rates, and, although the market is a very imperfect one, this will apply to some extent to the rents of existing houses as well as of those newly erected. The discussion given above was not intended to minimize the importance of such results, which may, in particular cases, be very great, and the total effect of which on real incomes will undoubtedly be significant. But in assessing its influence we must remember that the connection between the rate of interest and the earnings of old capital is extremely loose, and sometimes non-existent. The fact that new capital can be obtained more cheaply is as likely to mean reduced earnings for special groups of workers as for special kinds of property.

This conclusion seems to me inescapable, and is my main reason for omitting any elaborate attempts at exact analysis based on the assumption of a uniform return to each unit of capital. I may add that we shall be even less able in future to rely on the profits of all sorts of capital being adjusted "in accordance with the changed conditions of the capital market." For the importance of goodwill, trade connections and the like are becoming ever greater as the demand for non-standardized luxuries and comforts grows relatively to the demand for those staple goods which are sold in a more or less perfect market. Moreover, the effect of this is accentuated by the growing tendency for established producers to combine in the employment of monopolistic devices to protect their position. We should not, however, place all the emphasis on goodwill and the imperfection of the market. In many spheres the possession of that other intangible asset—an efficient staff and organization—may give the existing firms so great an advantage over anybody starting from scratch that their position may be unassailable. Their profits will be unaffected, however cheaply funds can be secured for the construction of physical assets.

There is also the question of changes in knowledge. It has been suggested[1] that a general fall in the rate of profit would stimulate research and inventions designed to find fresh ways of using capital in place of the labour whose price was steadily rising. The unknown extent to which this may happen makes exact analysis even less useful. Altogether, the broad fact that an increased amount of capital per man will make for higher wages, as described above, is best left as it stands.

The historically-minded reader, remembering the rise in wages after the Black Death, may feel that I have put the case for some rise in real earnings too mildly; he may even say that the reason is that I have argued too much in terms of capital increasing rather than of population falling. To the latter contention I have, of course, the obvious defence that this is very much what will, in fact, happen for a considerable period. But this escape is not necessary. There is really no great difference between the two cases, *so long as the change is gradual.* The Black Death, with its resultant sudden shortage of labour, is of little use as a guide to what we should expect in anything but a period of violent decline. Even for that case it will exaggerate the probable rise in wages, for in the Middle Ages production was so largely concentrated on agriculture that the human and material factors could more reasonably be treated as homogeneous.

[1] See Hicks, op. cit., pages 124 ff.

There is little which can usefully be said about the influence of other factors on the division of the national income between labour and property. At a time when labour is becoming relatively expensive research may, as we noted above, have a slight bias in the direction of finding ways of replacing labour by capital; if so, this would reduce the effect of the increased capital supply. Probably, however, the main consequence of technical progress will be, as in the past, to raise the real value of all incomes, whatever their source; to put it another way, the benefits of increased knowledge will simply accrue to consumers as such. This will apply particularly to the type of progress which involves little change in technique, but simply consists in the discovery of an improved method whereby the same amount of capital and labour is made to yield a larger product. The reader should be able to think of examples for himself—agricultural research has produced a good many in the form of better breeds of live-stock, better varieties of wheat, and so on; in industry it may be a question of improved organization or the elimination of breakages and faulty products.

More interesting than the broad division between earned and unearned incomes, is the effect on particular groups within the category "labour." Thus it is clear that boy labour is going to become relatively scarce, so that juvenile wages will approach more closely to those of adults. Three factors will limit the rise. Firstly, as the wage increases, so the goods (or services) produced mainly by boy labour will become expensive, relatively, to others, and the amount bought will therefore fall away—in some cases perhaps to nothing. Secondly, there will be some jobs for which it will soon pay to employ men instead of boys, because their greater efficiency will no longer be offset by the (reduced) difference in wages. And thirdly, and similarly, with the rise in boys' wages it will pay to substitute machinery where the difference in cost was previously not great.

The reader will, I hope, have detected the resemblance

between these three factors and those which we met so frequently in discussing the changed ratio of capital to labour. We ought perhaps to sub-divide the third into two parts; firstly, the application of mechanical methods which were already known, but would not pay before the rise in wages; and secondly, the stimulation of the search for new ones.

I do not feel competent to make any detailed estimate of how large the rise in wages will have to be before the combined effect of these factors reduces the demand to correspond with the fall in the supply. That it is likely to be substantial, even on a relatively optimistic view about fertility, we can easily see from a study of the changing age-composition. If we take the age-group 15–19 as representative of the supply of juvenile labour, we find that on Dr. Charles's first estimate this falls from 8·63 per cent of the population in 1940 to 7·30 per cent in 1945 and 6·74 per cent in 1950.[1] These figures are almost bound to be very near the truth, because they refer to people already living at the time the estimate was made. They show beyond all question that juvenile labour will become markedly scarcer in the near future. Moreover, this tendency will be very strongly reinforced if there is any effective raising of the school-leaving age; even if we extend the scope of juvenile labour so as to cover all workers under twenty-one, nevertheless an extra year at school would reduce the supply by about a sixth, in addition to the reduction due to changing age-composition. We certainly do not need to embark on speculative long-range forecasts to prove that our point is an important one.

Actually the proportion of juveniles will not fall very much further after 1950, unless fertility declines—the percentage given by the first estimate becomes virtually stabilized at about six after 1980. Naturally the second estimate continues to show a relentless fall, which brings the figure down to

[1] See Table VI on page 85 of *Political Arithmetic*, or Table XII on page 14 of Special Memorandum No. 40.

1·53 in 2035. I hope it is unnecessary for me to explain why it would be a waste of time to use this figure for any careful estimate of the probable rise in juvenile wages on the alternative assumptions that the school-leaving age is, and is not, raised.

Similarly, although to a lesser extent than in the case of juveniles, the supply of adult female labour is likely to contract relatively to that of male. We cannot be so certain of this, because it depends on the continuance of existing practices with regard to the period for which women seek paid employment. But unless there is a very material change in this respect the conclusion will hold good, at least on a modified scale. For women mostly retire from the labour market at a far earlier age than men, so that the number seeking paid employment depends largely on the size of the age-group 21–30, rather than on the total number of adults; and this will be a diminishing proportion of the whole.

If, as is sometimes maintained, juveniles and women represent alternative sources of cheap labour for various simple jobs of a routine or automatic nature, then the fact that *both* will become scarce simultaneously will reinforce the tendency for each wage to rise. The argument may be extended, though with less certainty, to cover the case of unskilled wages in general. If some unskilled men find openings in jobs previously done by women and juveniles, then the premium on skill, which depends on its scarcity, will be reduced. Such arguments simply represent particular applications of the general rule that a contraction in the supply of any one factor will improve the position of those which are predominantly rival to it, relatively to that of factors which mainly co-operate with it.[1] But the reader is warned that the different bargaining strengths of different groups

[1] Cf. page 155.

is liable to distort the results, especially in conditions far removed from full employment.

A study of the distribution of the national income should not stop short with its division between factors of production. Such an analysis might suffice if we only wanted to look at the question from the point of view of income *produced*, as part of a study of the productive process. But we are also very much interested in the question from the point of view of income *received*, i.e. in the distribution between individuals. It is not enough, for example, to find out how much income is paid "to capital" or "to land"—the social consequences will be unintelligible unless we trace the progress of such income from its source to the individuals who receive the benefit, and explain why so many of these channels lead to the same destination. Similarly, if we divide "labour" into a number of different factors, as we must for a realistic treatment, we must find out what determines the numbers in the different groups, why particular individuals are in one rather than in another, and so on. And we should then examine what might be called a third stage, namely, the *re*distribution of incomes effected by the Government (including local authorities) by collecting money in taxation and social insurance contributions and paying it out for debt interest or social services.

However, whilst I should like to emphasize the importance of this subject, and urge the reader to study it carefully,[1] yet it would be out of place for me to say much about it here, because the same influences will continue to be at work in much the same way as at present. Thus the question of whether or not a man gets a good start in his career will continue to depend mainly on his opportunities in the way of education, upbringing and social connections—natural

[1] *Inter alia* he should consult—Dalton: *Inequality of Incomes*; Wedgwood: *The Economics of Inheritance.*

ability is undoubtedly important *within* any one social class, but the inequality of opportunity between the children of rich and poor parents is, and will probably remain, the factor which dominates the scene. From then onwards his industry and the vagaries of fortune will largely determine a man's progress, but the starting-point is the most important influence on the incomes earned by the majority of men. Indeed, unless positive measures are taken to prevent it, inequality of opportunity is likely to exert an even greater influence in future; in a world which has, in some respects, ceased to expand it will be even more difficult to force an opening for one's talents, even if they are above the average, unless one knows the right people and is of the right social class.

Similarly, with incomes from property, it will continue to be largely a case of "to him that hath shall be given." If a man receives a large inheritance it not only means that he automatically secures a substantial unearned income, but he will also be far better able to increase it by saving and so adding to his capital. Moreover, it will very often be the same person who receives both a good opportunity and a large inheritance, so that he will also have a large salary, and the cumulative effect will be still stronger.

It is tempting to say that the inheritance factor will in future exert a greater influence in the direction of inequality because fathers will have fewer children amongst whom to divide their fortune, and, on the average, larger fortunes to divide. There are, however, several complicating factors which prevent any dogmatic assertion to this effect. In the first place the proposition is decidedly ambiguous. Are we to take account only of income *directly* derived from inherited wealth—comparing it presumably with income from other sources—or are we to include the indirect or cumulative effects? The latter will be extremely difficult to estimate, even broadly—for one thing it will be important to know at what age people receive their inheritances. (Presumably this will tend to rise, since the average age at death is rising with the advance of medicine; but it may not do so if children are born when their parents are older.) And how exactly are we to measure inequality? This is not an academic question, for Daniels and Campion[1] have shown that the number of people who have some capital to leave is increasing; are we to say that the disequalizing effect of inheritance is thereby increased (because more people are given an inheritance, and so an advantage over the great majority), or that it is reduced, because this privilege is no longer confined to so small and exclusive a minority?

However, even if we waive these difficulties we are still faced with another problem. We have seen that the increase in the amount of capital per head will tend to raise the average earned income, and to lower the average return to a unit of capital. We have, however, left unanswered the questions of how large these movements will be, and of whether the absolute or proportionate share of the national income accruing to capital will rise or fall. Without an answer to the last question we cannot even say whether the influence of property incomes as a whole will increase, let alone separate out the effect of incomes derived from inheritances. As a guide to practical policy we must be content with a warning that the division of fortunes amongst fewer heirs may accentuate the influence of inherited wealth, and therefore make it more desirable to prepare counter-measures.

If counter-measures are needed, then the obvious one is an increase in death-duties. The principle of these might at the same time be changed somewhat by increasing the importance of legacy duty (payable by each heir separately at a rate now dependent only on his relationship to the testator) and making the rate dependent on the heir's financial circumstances. A more effective stimulus might also be given to legacies to charitable institutions and other good causes. It seems obvious to suggest that the increased revenue from higher death duties should be used to reduce inequality

[1] In *The Distribution of National Capital*, especially Section IV.

by expanding the social services. For other reasons besides a desire for poetic justice, we may recommend that it be devoted especially to improving education and other services of a constructive type which promote greater equality of opportunity.

CHAPTER VIII

PUBLIC FINANCE—I

No treatment of the economic consequences of our population trends would be complete without some discussion of their effects on the public finances. Certain issues immediately suggest themselves, at least to the minds of those who appreciate that these imply a changed age-composition as well as an eventual decline in numbers. Will the charge for pensions make a satisfactory budget impossible? Or will this increase be offset by a reduced charge for education? And how about that more or less fixed item, the interest on the national debt? Will that become a crushing burden when there are fewer people to pay taxes?

I shall endeavour to answer all these questions, and others which are almost as "obviously" relevant to a discussion of public finance. But I want to start by emphasizing the overwhelming importance of an issue which may not so naturally suggest itself, but which, as always, dominates the scene. This is the problem of avoiding general unemployment—a problem which, as we have seen, is made more difficult of solution by the falling trend of population, but which should nevertheless not be beyond the wit of man.

Once it has been mentioned, the importance of this issue is obvious, and little need be said about it. The experience of all countries in the last slump has shown the close connection between the state of trade and the state of the budget. The connection becomes more and more intimate as a nation becomes richer and the role of the State grows in importance. In an "advanced" country unemployment is likely to be more severe (it can hardly be heavy in a poor country where 75 per cent of the population are engaged in primitive agriculture), and public opinion will insist on much more generous provision for the unemployed from State funds.

Moreover, the yield of high and progressive income taxes will fluctuate greatly with the level of prosperity and profits. A slump will, therefore, confront the Government with an irresistible demand for more expenditure at a time of rapidly falling revenue. It may well be that no amount of vigilant economizing or drastic raising of tax-rates will cope with such a situation. And, indeed, we have seen that such a policy is undesirable; for by reducing effective demand it will very probably intensify the depression and so defeat its own ends by cutting down the yield of all taxes.[1]

Our first conclusion then is simple. A falling population increases the risks of prolonged depressions, "unless something is done about it." We have seen that this prospect should not be regarded in a spirit of helpless fatalism—the problem is in a real sense a man-made one, or at least one that man should be able to solve. But if it is not solved, then the outlook for the budget is gloomy indeed.

We may now turn to the more specific questions affecting public finance. First of all, what about this pension bogey? Is it really as frightening as it might seem?

As usual we cannot give a single answer to such a vague question. We must sub-divide it, and we can best start by emphasizing the difference between the "social" and the "budgetary" problems. The "social" problem can best be appreciated by imagining that the national income were all pooled and distributed amongst the members of the community as a father might distribute a family income. The fact that a much larger proportion of the population had retired from work would clearly impose a certain burden on the others; this is what we mean by the "social" problem. Its magnitude naturally depends on how much the proportion of pensioners is assumed to rise. If we take Dr. Charles's more pessimistic assumption about fertility, and consider the

[1] This effect may not be apparent until the *next* year, particularly in the case of income-tax, which is assessed on the previous year's income.

position a hundred years hence, then the problem would indeed be frightening; for half the population would be over 65. But if we take either a shorter period, or a less gloomy view of the birth-rate, then the social problem is appreciable but not overwhelming. Quite apart from any compensation to be derived from a smaller percentage of children there is the increase in productivity to be remembered. Even if the conclusion of Chapter VI (that, slumps apart, the average income per head might well rise faster than in the past) were too optimistic, yet *some* increase is almost certain, despite the increased proportion of pensioners. Our imaginary paterfamilias would merely find that he could not raise the dividend as much as he otherwise might have done.

There still remains, however, the budgetary problem. The national income is not placed freely at the disposal of a central authority, to distribute as he may think fit. Measures have to be devised for making the first recipients surrender to the Treasury a portion of the incomes which they regard as "theirs." Even though the payment of old age pensions out of receipts from, say, income-tax is "merely a transfer, not a destruction of income," yet the process involves serious problems. Not the least of these is to evolve a system of taxation which will both be considered just and will not prevent income from being created, e.g. by penalizing enterprise.

Granted that the production of the country should be adequate to afford a reasonable income to those who have retired without making the active go short, there are various ways in which it may be arranged that the desired amount shall actually reach them and not somebody else. In some cases there will be no need for State action. The old men may themselves own property, or they may be supported by their children; they may have worked for a firm which has a pension scheme for its employees, or they may themselves have arranged for a pension from an insurance company or a trade union. But these private arrangements will seldom cover more than a part of the field and will nearly always have to be supplemented by some State scheme; indeed it might now be more reasonable to describe the private arrangements as supplements to the State scheme, rather than vice versa.

In England State action takes two main forms, the contributory and non-contributory pensions. Between them these secure a very modest income for nearly all people over 70 who are not otherwise provided for (in recent years some 75–80 per cent of the people over 70 have been receiving a State pension) and for about half of the people aged 65–70.

We need not say very much about the non-contributory pensions. Broadly the position is that 10s. a week is paid to anybody who can satisfy a test as to means, nationality, and residence. A reduced pension may be granted where the applicant's means are not very far above the limit, but this provision has been unimportant in practice. The whole cost is borne directly by the Exchequer out of ordinary revenue. The scheme has been in operation, with various modifications, since 1908, but its importance has been declining since the introduction of the contributory scheme.

The latter is part of a wider system of social insurance inaugurated by the Widows', Orphans' and Old Age Contributory Pensions Act of 1925. Under this and subsequent Acts it is laid down, broadly, that membership is compulsory for all people insured under the Health Insurance scheme, i.e. virtually all employed people except non-manual workers earning more than £250 per annum, and there are minor provisions for voluntary subscribers.[1] The rate of weekly contribution was fixed initially at 9d. for a male employee and 4½d. for a female, of which the employer had to pay 4½d. and 2d. respectively. The male rate was to rise

[1] Under the Widows', Orphans' and Old Age Pensions (Voluntary Contributors) Act, 1937, it has been made possible for many people (primarily blackcoated workers) to insure for pensions only on rather different terms.

"unless Parliament should otherwise determine," to 11d. in 1936, 1s. 1d. in 1946, and 1s. 3d. in 1956, the female rate being always half the male; the first increase has been duly enforced. These payments entitle the contributor, as of right, to various benefits, of which the most important are:—

Widow's Pension: 10s. a week, plus 5s. for the first dependent child and 3s. for each subsequent one.

Orphan's Pension: 7s. 6d. a week until age 14 (or 16, if still at school).

Old Age Pension: 10s. a week from 65 onwards, plus 10s. for the man's wife when she reaches 65.

The finance of the scheme is somewhat complicated, and we can only deal with it very briefly. A special account, known as the Treasury Pensions Account, was set up, into which the contributions are paid. The first important point to note is that both widows' and old age pensions are only paid out of this account until the beneficiaries reach the age of 70. After that they are, in effect, automatically granted an old age pension of the non-contributory type, but without any of the tests as to means, nationality, or residence. It makes little difference whether we call these pensions contributory or non-contributory—whatever the name, the important thing is that the whole cost is met by the Exchequer out of ordinary revenue, although the pensions are granted "by virtue of" the beneficiaries' contributions.

Despite this relief the scheme is now, as it has always been (and, one may safely add, as it always will be), hopelessly insolvent from the actuarial point of view. The explanation is not far to seek. The contributions were, broadly speaking, fixed so that they would cover the costs of the benefits in the case of people who enter at age 16.[1] But at the outset

[1] The calculation of the necessary amount with such a complicated set of benefits and conditions is a very difficult task, both because it involves a great deal of technical work and because this has to be based

of the scheme the vast majority of contributors were older than 16, so that they would pay premia for a much shorter period before receiving benefits. Moreover, some of the then existing widows and orphans were given pensions, to be paid for out of the fund, although naturally not a single contribution had been paid on their behalf. The scheme, therefore, started with an actuarial deficit (still ignoring the pensions after 70) which the Government actuary estimated at £620 millions.[1]

This sort of "back-service liability" is a common feature which is encountered whenever a company, for example, sets up a pension scheme for its employees to which the older ones are admitted on equal terms with the young. It is normally met either by a capital grant from the firm, or by an arrangement for gradual liquidation over a period of years. The important point to note is that unless the fund receives an income corresponding to the interest which would be produced by this amount of investments, then the actuarial deficit will not merely remain, but will grow progressively larger; for in calculating the contributions needed to pay for the benefits, allowance is made for the interest which they would earn in the intervening years. There may for some time be no lack of ready cash to make all the payments actually due, but future liabilities will be accumulating without a corresponding growth of assets.

on some rather hazardous assumptions—e.g. about future mortality-rates, the probable age of a deceased contributor's widow and/or children, the probability of the widow's remarrying, the future level of unemployment (since contributions are not payable during unemployment) and so on. But we may say broadly that those who entered at 16 in 1926 were paying premia which, if accumulated with compound interest, would almost exactly have covered the eventual cost of their benefits (except for pensions after 70); whilst later entrants, who paid the higher contributions from the outset, would do more than this. See the Government Actuary's Report on the 1925 Bill (Cmd. 2406) and his first decennial review of the scheme's working (H.C. 82 of 1935), especially pages 19–20 of the latter.

[1] Cmd. 2406, page 17.

In the case of the national scheme the State accepted in principle the liability to make good any deficit which might emerge, whether on account of the initial position or through subsequent developments, such as the continued entry of many people at ages well above 16. However, it adopted neither of the methods described above to "clean up the balance sheet"; it made a small annual grant from the outset, but its procedure was really not very different from that known as "pay as you go." In other words it decided to do little more than see to it that the fund always had sufficient cash to make all the necessary disbursements, without really worrying about the balance sheet position at all.

The history of the scheme is set out in the Government Actuary's decennial report, referred to above. The actuarial deficit has, naturally, grown considerably, both because the Government grant has been far less than the interest on the initial deficit, and because the Act of 1929 granted pensions to another batch of pre-1926 widows, in respect of whom no contributions had been paid. In the early years, however, the fund accumulated a cash balance which reached £46·4 millions on March 31, 1931, mainly because the number of people who have qualified for benefits is always small at the outset of such a scheme.

Even this relatively insignificant balance is fast disappearing. The Act of 1929 provided for the annual grant from the Exchequer to rise from £9 millions in 1930–31 by annual increments of £1 million until it reached £21 millions in 1942–43, at which figure it was to remain stable for four years. It was reckoned (and the Actuary confirms this in his review) that this procedure would lead to an excess of cash outgoings over receipts in each year up to 1946, and that these would absorb virtually the whole of the accumulated balance. The position would then be reviewed afresh, the intention clearly being to make the future grant just sufficient to meet the difference between receipts and outgoings.

With this brief description to help us, what is the extent of the budgetary problem which the future has in store for us? Is there to be a dreadful day of reckoning as a result of this rather improvident finance?

I shall assume that the existing arrangements are maintained, merely noting the fact that 10s. a week is not a very large sum, even as a basis to be supplemented from private savings, children's help, etc. I shall also make no attempt to disentangle the part of the Bill which is attributable to old age pensions from the total grant needed for the whole contributory scheme.

First, then, the cost of pensions to people over 70, the whole of which is borne by the Exchequer. The amount paid in 1936–37 was, to the nearest million, £46 millions.[1] In his report on the 1925 Bill the Government Actuary published an estimate of the cost for a number of future years,[2] of which we may select the following:—

1945–46	..	£52·6 millions
1955–56	..	£61·6 millions
1965–66	..	£64·4 millions

Unfortunately, these estimates are almost certainly too low, mainly because mortality-rates have already fallen below those used by the Actuary.[3] For 1935–36 his figure of £40·6 millions was 5·8 per cent below the actual cost, and the discrepancy is, from the nature of the case, likely to grow

[1] This and subsequent figures for 1936–37 are taken from the *Statistical Abstract*, published in 1938. They refer to Great Britain and N. Ireland.

[2] Op. cit., page 16.

[3] These were based on the experience of 1920 and 1921. The reason for choosing these years is given in a footnote on page 6, and is a rather striking illustration of actuarial reluctance to "invent" figures, even in cases where a reasonable "guestimate" would almost certainly be better than blind faith in the repetition of past experience.

"The death-rates of these years were below the present level and their employment gives such effect as is practicable, *without the introduction of hypothetical methods*, to the probability that the general tendency of the death-rate in future will be to diminish." (My italics.)

greater, especially as he also assumed there would be a substantial amount of emigration. In the absence of revised official figures we must, therefore, attempt an independent estimate.

In his decennial review the Actuary states (page 22) that the proportion of the over-70's drawing a pension is likely to be about 80 per cent. If we apply this ratio to the number of such people given by Dr. Charles's two estimates, making a small allowance to cover Northern Ireland, for which there are no figures, we arrive at the following sums (to the nearest million pounds):—

(£ millions)

	Estimate (*a*)	Estimate (*b*)	Mean
1936–37 (Actual)	46	46	46
1945–46	56	57	56
1955–56	63	71	67
1965–66	70	82	76
1975–76	78	97	88

The reader will note what a difference the assumption of falling mortality makes. Estimate (*b*) may perhaps claim to be slightly the more probable, or at least to have the more logical basis; but those who, like the author, feel that a certain caution is desirable in the assumption that past trends will continue to hold good over a long period, may prefer to "play safe" and work with the simple average. In any case it is clear that the cost of pensions to the over-70's is going to increase very considerably. It is not merely a case of "the burden becoming more formidable because there will be fewer young people to bear it," as one might perhaps imagine from some current discussions of population decline. The burden will be heavier in absolute terms, simply because the present number of old people does not reflect the great increase in the average expectation of life.

We must now consider the contributory scheme, to which the Exchequer contribution in 1937–38 was £16 millions. The Actuary prepared a careful analysis of the probable working of the scheme for each year up to 1965–66.[1] According to this the annual grant needed to cover the difference between receipts and outgoings after 1946 would not show much increase over the £21 millions which it will reach under the existing arrangements. Thus we have the following figures:—

1945–46	..	£21 millions
1955–56	..	£22·7 millions
1965–66	..	£25·1 millions

If these figures could be used as an adequate measure of the seriousness of the problem, then clearly there is nothing to cause undue alarm, especially as, for reasons which I hope the reader can work out for himself, the years quoted are ones which present the matter in its least favourable light. But such a procedure is hardly legitimate, even if we accept the actuary's forecast as perfectly accurate.[2]

The reason is, of course (and by inserting those words I am showing my faith in the reader's power to answer the conundrum posed above) that the smallness of the increase in the Exchequer grant is largely due to the provision for raising the rates of contribution in 1946 and 1956. On each occasion this produces an increase in the annual income from contributions of some £5 millions—and a corresponding

[1] See pages 28–29 of his decennial review.

[2] Because the scheme has so many aspects there is a very good chance that any factor which fails to behave according to the assumptions will produce compensating errors. Thus a fall in mortality reduces the number of widows and orphans who qualify for pensions, but increases the number of people who reach 65.

fall in the grant needed to equalize receipts and expenditure; the latter then slowly rises during the next decade.

Now it may be true that such an increase in contributions, even though it brings no promise of extra benefits, can be enforced without provoking so much "squealing" as would be the case with an equivalent amount of extra taxation. Nevertheless, the direct effects are very similar to those produced by imposing higher rates of taxation—with the corollary that the taxes chosen are extremely vicious ones. Thus the employee's share is a flat-rate levy on wage-earners, which, *inter alia*, leaves them less able to pay ordinary taxes; whilst that of the employer is a direct addition to his costs, exactly equivalent to an all-round rise in wages, and very similar to an all-round excise duty. He will naturally seek to pass it on to the consumer in the form of higher prices, and as his (British) rivals are all in the same position, he will probably succeed. Industries subject to foreign competition will find their competitive power reduced.

We are likely, therefore, to get a more accurate impression of the increased burden if we either add on to the figures given above an amount corresponding to the extra receipts due to higher contributions, or simply work with the total cost of benefits, however met. The two methods would give very similar results, but I propose to use the latter. In effect this amounts to amalgamating the insurance fund with the ordinary budget, and in view of the adoption of the pay-as-you-go principle there is a good deal to be said for such a procedure.

The table on page 180 therefore sets out, to the nearest million pounds, the total cost of pensions paid under the scheme—widows', orphans', and old age—in 1936–37, and as estimated by the Government Actuary for three subsequent years.

Before we proceed to combine the two sets of charges we ought, I think, to take account of a more favourable development in the pension world. I refer, as the reader may have guessed, to the progressive reduction in the charge for war pensions, which may very reasonably be considered here, especially as we have included the rising figures for widows and orphans. This relief is not, of course, *due* to the changing size and age-composition of the population, and anyone who wants to isolate that factor may like to rearrange the figures, or work with the column giving old age pensions only; but if we are interested in the question of the state of future budgets, then it seems more helpful to put all pensions together.

No official estimate of the charge for war pensions has

(£ millions)

	Widows and Orphans	Old Age (65–70)	Total
1936–37	24	20	44
1945–46	28	24	52
1955–56	31	25	56
1965–66	33	28	61

been published since that given by the Government Actuary in his report on the Pensions Bill in 1925.[1] But the estimates for the intervening years have proved reasonably accurate, so that this set of figures should suffice for our purpose.

The table on page 181, then, sets out the estimated charges for pensions under various heads (to the nearest million pounds).

The inclusion of war pensions enables us to present a far less gloomy picture than at one time seemed probable. The growth in the absolute total is not really alarming; it could be made more so if we had taken estimate (*c*) for the cost of pensions to people aged 70+, and this item showed a further rapid increase between 1965 and 1975. A really determined pessimist would also lay much stress on the eventual decline

[1] Cmd. 2406, page 26.

in the number of active citizens who have to foot the bill, whether by means of "contributions" or straightforward taxes. This phenomenon, however, is not likely to be important in the period covered by our table, in which the worst danger is another war.

The increase in the bill for pensions has its origin in the coming rise in the number of elderly people. It seems logical,

(£ millions)

	Old Age			Widows and Orphans	War	Total
	65–70	70 +	Total			
1936–37 (Actual)	20	46	66	24	40	130
1945–46	24	56	80	28	32	140
1955–56	25	67	92	31	21	144
1965–66	28	76	104	33	10	147

therefore, to look next for any favourable consequences of this phenomenon, and the obvious item to consider is the yield of death-duties. We have seen that the crude death-rate is virtually certain to rise, even if mortality-rates are further reduced. Does this mean that the revenue will benefit because a larger amount of the nation's capital will pass under the axe each year?

In general the answer must be "Yes." All the capital of the nation must be owned by somebody, and unless steps are deliberately taken to alter its distribution in favour of those who are unlikely to die, then the higher the death-rate, the higher the yield of death-duties. Moreover, the influence of smaller families will sooner or later make itself felt; the father's estate is divided amongst fewer heirs, so that the average inheritance is larger, and with progressive duties considerably more will be taken in taxation when *they* die. And, of course, if the nation's capital continues to increase, then this development alone would make for a higher yield in future, quite apart from the population factors. Altogether the outlook seems fairly rosy.

The reader may feel somewhat puzzled (as the author did at first) about this conclusion. The argument seems (and indeed is) incontrovertible; but it also seems very plausible to argue that the frequency with which property will pass under the axe simply depends on the interval between generations. Thus if a father bequeathes it to his son, who is thirty years younger than himself, then on the average it should be taxed again after an interval of thirty years; if this were the typical case, surely one thirtieth of the nation's capital would be taxed each year, and the fraction would only change if there were a tendency towards earlier child-bearing?

There are two fallacies in this argument. In the first place it deals only with inherited wealth, ignoring the man's own accumulations. At present we have an abnormally large proportion of people in age-groups where much saving and few deaths are to be expected, and an abnormally small proportion of old men about to die and surrender a part of their accumulations to the Treasury; in future this position will be reversed. But even if we consider only property which has already passed at least once by inheritance, there is still the difficulty that the amount of such property which is taxed in any given year will be affected by the number of property-owners who died about thirty years ago. Now we have seen that in the past, since the population was expanding, there has always been an abnormally small proportion of old men, and so an abnormally small number of deaths. ("Abnormal," that is, relatively to the position in a static population; with a declining population the position will eventually become "abnormal" in the other direction.)

Hence the amount even of this kind of property which now passes under the axe each year is depressed by the abnormality of the age-composition thirty years ago. Moreover, this is not the only reason. In a period when mortality-rates are falling progressively the number of deaths is temporarily depressed below what one would expect with a steady rate (even at the new figure), because many of the people who "ought" to have died this year survive for another one. To look at it another way, the fact that the son lives longer than the father makes the interval between deaths more than thirty years.

In brief, our present age-composition is quite abnormal, on account of the change from high fertility- and mortality-rates in the past to much lower ones in the present. Several factors have, as it were, conspired to produce a period in which deaths are few and the Chancellor of the Exchequer must contain his soul in patience. Thus the generations which formed our present supply of elderly people were smaller than those which followed; they were abnormally depleted (by present standards) in the early stages by being subject to relatively high mortality-rates in infancy, and indeed throughout most of their lives; and now the survivors are managing to prolong their lives and so keep the Chancellor waiting.

The worst years, however, are almost over, and the postponed harvest will soon begin to be reaped. The conclusion that, *ceteris paribus*, more deaths will mean more death-duties cannot be upset by any arguments based on the simple one-thirtieth rule, which can apply only with a population which is stable both in numbers and age-composition.[1]

There are, however, two qualifications which have to be remembered in considering the extent of the rise. In the first place death-duties can at present be quite simply and legally evaded by gifts *inter vivos*; so long as he does not wait

[1] Even then, of course, it would be subject to corrections for such things as the leaving of sums to people other than children.

too long before doing so, the father can give his whole fortune to his children without the Inland Revenue taking a penny. This practice clearly might become more widespread than it now is, and might be difficult to check, even if the attempt were made. And in the second place there is the alleged tendency of high and progressive death-duties to eliminate large fortunes, and so reduce the yield in subsequent years.

About the latter I will only say that whilst these duties naturally have some tendency in that direction, other forces are at work to restore the fortunes or create new ones. After all, the millionaire's heir will still have a large unearned income, despite the death-duties, quite apart from anything he may earn. Even if taxes on that income make it difficult, or unattractive, for him to save sufficiently to build the fortune up again, these hardly affect the other method by which money breeds money, i.e. a successful investment policy. Particularly with the general rise in security values due to lower interest rates, "capital appreciation" has done much to keep up the number of large fortunes; whilst each generation produces a number of business leaders who succeed in amassing large sums even though they started with comparatively little.[1]

It seems fairly safe, therefore, to predict a rise in the average yield of death-duties—we must take an average over a few years because the yield in any one can be seriously affected by the number of millionaires who happen to die in that year, and also by the level of security prices. To attempt to forecast accurately how large the rise will be would,

[1] The reader who, quite rightly, suspects arguments based only on theoretical analysis should consult *The Distribution of the National Capital*, by Daniels and Campion. Their statistical investigations lend no support to the thesis of the disappearing plutocrat. Comparisons between pre-war and post-war years are dangerous, because of the great inflation of private fortunes caused by higher prices and the vast increase in the national debt. But Tables I and V in particular show that any slight tendency towards reduced inequality within the post-war period is due to the increased number of people who own small and middle-sized fortunes; the number of large ones shows, if anything, an increase.

however, involve both a great deal of work and a great number of rather hazardous assumptions. Thus it is not sufficient merely to calculate the probable number of deaths in any one year, for the average size of a person's estate depends largely on his age; and we know that the average age, both of the living and of the dying, is going to increase. (In particular, even if fertility-rates are constant, the number of births will probably decline, and so the proportion of infants among the deaths will fall.) And there is always the increase in the national capital to take into account.

We do, however, want some idea of the order of magnitude

Period	Death-Rate (Total per 1,000)	Yield (£ millions)
1935–39	12·9	80
1940–44	13·7	85
1945–49	14·5	90
1950–54	15·3	95
1955–59	16·1	100
1960–64	16·9	105

of the sums involved—whether they are likely to be reckoned in millions of pounds, or tens of millions, or even perhaps hundreds of millions. As all the other factors, except a possible increase in gifts *inter vivos*, are likely to make for a higher yield, it seems reasonable to assume that for the next thirty years or so the rise will be very roughly proportionate to the rise in the crude death-rate for England and Wales as given by Dr. Charles's first estimate, i.e. the one which does not allow for a further fall in mortality-rates. If we take £80 millions as our starting-point for the period 1935–39 we arrive at the above figures, to the nearest million pounds.

The coincidence that the results are all multiples of five may help to impress on the reader that the table does not pretend to do more than give him an indication of whether this factor is likely to be about as important as, say, the increased charge for pensions, or to be negligible in comparison with it, or to dominate it. We find that, if war pensions are included, the two factors more or less offset one another, with death-duties if anything having the advantage.[1] It would be easy to apply minor "corrections" so as to make the calculation seem more plausible; but they would really do little more than obscure the issue and give a false air of exactness. The death-rate is actually likely to be somewhat lower than that shown, but the rise in the size of the average estate should if anything outweigh both this and the fact that the population will be somewhat smaller in the later years.

Before leaving the subject of estate duties we should emphasize that the yield *per head of population* is likely to go on increasing after 1965, and that the greater the fall in fertility, the more it will rise. Indeed, our table does little more than carry the process up to the stage where the present abnormally low yield (due to the temporary deficiency of eligible coffin-fodder) has been more or less corrected. With present mortality-rates a stationary population would have a death-rate of between 16 and 17 per 1,000; it is only after 1960, therefore, that the yield per head becomes "abnormally high," in the sense that the surviving population gain because there are so few of them to share in the taxes on the old men's estates. If we like to strain our imaginations so as to visualize the great fall in fertility assumed by Dr. Charles's second estimate taking place "whilst other things remain equal," then the death-rate of 47 per 1,000 in 2035 should cause estate duties to yield sums which would be very large indeed in relation to the small number of survivors. Even without any fall in

[1] Perhaps a more logical course would be to compare the probable rises in the yield of death-duties and in the cost of pensions to those over 70. The latter, on the above calculations, is likely to be rather larger.

fertility below the level of 1933 the death-rate will continue to rise until it becomes stabilized at about 21 per 1,000 after 1990, unless mortality declines.

The next item to consider is the cost of education. To many people this might have seemed the obvious counterpart to the pensions issue, on the grounds that "a smaller proportion of children" and "an increased proportion of old people" were twin consequences of "a declining population." We have seen, however, that it is the increased *number* of old people which made the pension issue a lively one, and the *number* of these people is bound to increase for reasons which have nothing to do with a declining population—indeed, one important reason, the fall in mortality-rates, is a factor which is helping to postpone the decline. Even if we are interested in proportions, rather than absolute numbers, there would have to be a phenomenal rise in fertility to prevent the proportion of old people from increasing.

Nevertheless, whether the two phenomena are really due to a common cause or not, it seems somehow "natural" to examine the influence of a decline in the younger age-groups after dealing with the increase in the older ones. And it seems very plausible to argue that the reduced number of children will mean a substantial "saving" on the £100 millions or so which our governments (central and local) now spend on education. But the question is not quite as simple as might appear.

That there will be a substantial and progressive reduction in the number of children is almost beyond question—indeed the decline has already begun. There are, however, very serious difficulties in the way of making any careful estimate of the effect on the cost of education. In the first place the size of the relevant age-groups cannot be estimated for more than a very short period without making some assumption about the future level of fertility—and this, as we have seen, is the most uncertain of the various quantities used by the statistician. The importance of this point should be apparent from the fact that the assumption of declining fertility causes Dr. Charles's second estimate to show a figure for the age-groups 4–14 in 1950 which is only about $\frac{5}{6}$ of that given by the first—and the divergence naturally grows ever greater with the passage of time.

Even if we could prepare reliable estimates of the number of children, however, we would still be faced with the problem of how to allow for changes in the proportions who would attend the various sorts of schools and in the cost per pupil. To some extent a falling-off in numbers will cause the latter to rise without there being any corresponding gain in the quality of the education; this will be particularly the case in small or scattered communities where the number of pupils of any age will become inconveniently small, and where the existing schools will still have to be maintained, though no longer of the appropriate size. But more important is the probability that the chance will be seized of giving each child a more expensive education, as soon as that is possible without an increase in the total bill. This might be done in two main ways—we might increase the average time that each child spends at school, whether by raising the leaving age or by enabling more children to attend nursery schools; or we might provide a more intensive education by such measures as installing better equipment or reducing the size of classes, many of which are now far too large. The last possibility is particularly likely to be adopted, if only as an automatic consequence of doing nothing.

Now most of these developments would be highly desirable under any circumstances, and it is one of the undoubted advantages of a downward trend in population that they should become available so painlessly. At the same time this downward trend also makes some of them more necessary, and to that extent the advantage of the new situation might be said to be somewhat illusory. Thus we have seen that the increased danger of frictional unemployment will call, *inter alia*, for a more thorough education, probably of a rather different, and more expensive, kind, *merely to prevent the situation getting worse*. Perhaps one might add that the various measures similarly required to prevent an increase in general unemployment mostly require an understanding public if they are to be really effective—though the greatest need here is for better instruction of people holding positions seldom filled by men who have attended State schools. It would be a difficult problem in social values to say how large the net advantage is when the downward trend of population makes the education both more necessary and less costly.

Fortunately, however, this is a problem which for our present purpose we do not need to answer. The immediately important point is simply this. In our capacity of citizens we need not deplore this tendency to seek a higher standard of education as numbers fall. Yet from the narrow budgetary point of view it does, I think, mean that we should be unwise to look for any substantial relief within the next thirty years or so. We must content ourselves with the reflection that improved services are likely to be secured without any additional burden.

From the nature of the case I cannot attempt any elaborate "proof" of the soundness of the above conclusion. It has been tacitly based on the assumption that Dr. Charles's first (i.e. higher) estimate will prove to be fairly near the truth. For England and Wales this shows a fall of roughly one-fifth in the size of the age-groups 4–14 between 1938 and 1965. Such a fall seems hardly sufficient to counterbalance the probable extension of the average period at school and the rising cost per pupil. We must remember in this connection that the number both of teachers and class-rooms in a school is frequently determined rather by the number of different ages than by the total number of pupils; and that the reorganization of schools so as to obtain a better distribution of pupils is generally costly, and often hampered by the need for schools to be near children's homes.[1] A slight fall in fertility below the 1933 level seems to be the condition most likely to stabilize the cost of education.

Some such assumption seems to me about as reasonable as any that one can make. The reader may, however, be interested to see what would happen if fertility continues to decline in the way assumed by Dr. Charles for her second estimate. In this case the age-group 4–14 would be reduced to less than half its present size by 1965, and we should clearly expect some fall in the cost of education. It would, however be extremely difficult to estimate even the order of magnitude of the fall, for with such a revolutionary change in numbers the whole educational system would have to be revised; any elaborate calculations could be regarded only as statistical exercises.

If we glance at the position after 1965 we find that the second estimate shows such a decline in the proportion of children that the cost of education, even reckoned per head of population, would presumably become very small. This fact is, however, mentioned only for the sake of completeness, since the position visualized by this estimate for the later years is so unstable that it could hardly exist, and could not be analysed in terms of concepts appropriate to present conditions even if it did. The first estimate shows only a slight further fall in the *proportion* of children—the absolute number continues to decline as the population grows steadily smaller, but constant fertility- and mortality-rates soon establish a virtually constant age-composition. In view of the difficulty of adapting the educational system to the decline, we should then expect the cost per head of population to

[1] Various aspects of the relationship between population and the cost of education are discussed in articles by N. Wilson in *Public Administration*, January 1935, and D. V. Glass, in the *Review of the Headmasters' Association*, April 1938.

rise somewhat, quite apart from any improvements in the quality of the service.

The last paragraph should help the reader to appreciate an important point. It is the change-over from an increasing or constant population to a declining one which eases the burden of providing education of any given standard by reducing the proportion of children; once the transition period is over the burden will actually begin to increase again unless fertility falls further so as to accelerate the decline in numbers and further reduce the proportion of children.

We may perhaps conclude this section by reverting to the distinction made earlier in the chapter between the "social" and "budgetary" problems which arise out of our changing age-composition. For some time to come we are likely to have a more or less constant proportion of dependants in the population, owing to the coincidence that the rising proportion of old people will roughly balance the falling proportion of children. From this we might roughly conclude that no "social" problem would arise—the national income should continue to be about as adequate (or inadequate) for the needs of the new type of population as it was for those of the old.

A similar argument could not, however, be applied to the budgetary problem. The requirements of children are mostly paid for by their parents, and consequently involve no strain on the public finances comparable with the charge for pensions (often supplemented by out-relief). From the budgetary point of view we cannot, therefore, regard the smaller number of children as an adequate off-set to the increased number of old people—more especially as the relief which "ought" to accrue to the budget as a result of fewer pupils is likely to be intercepted. There may well be minor savings on such things as dependants' allowances paid in respect of children of the unemployed, and income-tax payers will not be able to claim so much in "reliefs."

But these cannot alter the fact that it makes a big difference to the public finances whether people are dependent because they are too young to work or because they are too old.

The other topic which usually occurs to people when discussing the effect of population trends is the burden of the national debt. This is a large subject, however, which must be held over until the next chapter. I want now to clear the decks by dealing briefly with a point which might easily be overlooked, though it is really important.

We have seen in Chapter II that the population factor will make for a higher level of frictional unemployment. This tendency may be counteracted by the adoption of various measures, including the improved educational system mentioned above, so that no additional unemployment actually results; such a course might well be the best way of dealing with the situation, even if we judge solely by the effect on the public finances (using that term, as is really most convenient, to cover the semi-autonomous social insurance funds as well as the budgets of central and local governments). But in any case there is certain to be increased outlay, either for these constructive schemes or for extra unemployment assistance, insurance benefit, or poor relief.

It is extraordinarily difficult to make any estimate of the possible cost of this item, but there is no question that unemployment is an expensive luxury for the State to enjoy. The following very round figures may help to impress this fact on the reader, and perhaps to give him *some* idea of the sums involved.

For a considerable period the number of "occupied" people in the United Kingdom will not vary greatly, and may be put roughly at twenty millions. If an extra 1 per cent of these became frictionally unemployed, and the average amount paid to each from public funds of one kind or another were £1, then the extra cost would be rather over £10 millions a year. Or to put it another way, if the money were raised by flat rate contributions from those in work, then the levy would have to be about 2½d. a week.

There is, of course, no particular virtue in the figure of 1 per cent. It might, I think, quite easily be exceeded, so that the sums involved are capable of being very substantial, though they are not comparable with the financial effects of a slump. We must repeat that unemployment, even in the comparatively mild form of "frictional" or "particular" unemployment, is an expensive disease, even in the narrow budgetary sense. Respect for vested interests or cherished axioms of orthodoxy must not be allowed to make it worse.

CHAPTER IX

PUBLIC FINANCE—II

THE main subject to be dealt with in this chapter is the national debt. In the past, particularly after the Napoleonic wars, the burden of this, i.e. the severity of the taxation needed to raise the interest, has been much reduced by the growth of population. If, it is therefore argued, the population is to decline, will not this relief be replaced by an intensification? And as the debt service is a large item in the budget (roughly speaking, between one-fifth and one-fourth) will this not be a matter of great importance?

We may start by rejecting the argument, sometimes advanced in reply, that there is really no difficulty because the debt is an internal one. It is, of course, true that the problem is only one of "transference"; if there will be fewer people to pay the interest, yet there will be correspondingly fewer to receive it. But the reader should by now be well aware that this fact does not prevent the budgetary problem from being a very real one. As we seek to increase the proportion of the national income which the Government is to extract by taxation, so the difficulty of doing so equitably and smoothly increases, even if the money is to be returned "unused" as debt interest or pensions. Hence the greater the fraction of the available revenue which we have to use to fulfil contractual obligations, the less there is for such desirable transfers as family allowances and social services generally. Moreover, if we are to include public works, budget deficits and State guarantees in our campaign against slumps, then the State must be in a position to borrow cheaply and on a large scale; its credit must not be undermined by danger of default.

In considering this question we must, however, retain a sense of proportion. In the first place the actual decline in the population will be negligible for about twenty-five to thirty years—this will be true of the active population (which is what really matters) even if fertility continues to fall. During this period the problem will, therefore, not become worse than it now is; it is merely not going to become easier as a result of rapidly increasing numbers. We have managed to bear the burden so far with reasonable success, and should, therefore, continue to find it tolerable for some time to come. Admittedly, this only affords a breathing space, but it is a fairly long one.

The proper use to make of a breathing space is for a discussion of possible remedies. Before embarking on this, however, we must try to get the population factor in perspective. It is quite true that the increase in numbers during the nineteenth century made the national debt far more manageable than it otherwise would have been; but it is equally true that this was by no means the only factor at work. The great rise in productivity and in trade was at least as important. After all, the burden of a debt is reduced far more if the national income is doubled owing to greater productivity than it would be by a mere doubling of numbers. With the evolution of our progressive system of taxation this distinction should be even more important to-day than it was in the last century.

Now we have seen that the average real income per head should continue to rise at least as rapidly as in the past, provided that we do not allow the potential benefits of better knowledge and a more ample supply of capital to run to waste in prolonged periods of heavy general unemployment. The new trend of population is not, of course, wholly responsible for this favourable conclusion, though on balance it makes a substantial contribution to the potential gain. But whatever the reason, the attainment of anything like the cumulative rise of about 1 per cent per annum experienced in the last century would rob the debt problem of its terrors for a very long time. The yields of nearly all important taxes would rise automatically without any increase in rates—this would be particularly true of income-tax, surtax and all taxes on luxuries[1]—and new burdens could be borne much more easily.

It would be very convenient if we could translate this general statement about the rising yield of taxation into quantitative estimates, and at first sight it might seem possible to do this by observing the relation between national income and tax-yields as the former varies during a trade cycle. But such a course would be quite inadmissible. The yield of any set of taxes depends very much on the distribution, as well as on the size, of the national income. Thus the great rise in revenue from income-tax during the last few years has been due primarily to the revival of profits from their slump levels, rather than to the growth in total income. A secular improvement in productivity would clearly have a quite different effect on the revenue from that exerted by a trade revival.

This question of distribution is indeed the rock on which all attempts to make an exact estimate must founder. It would be difficult enough to estimate how much the revenue would gain from a small rise in the national income, even if we knew that all incomes would rise by the same percentage; the difficulty would increase greatly as we went on to consider the later years, in which the rise would be greater and national habits might be quite different. But the problem is insoluble unless we have some guidance as to whether the extra income will accrue mainly to a few rich people or be spread thinly over the great mass of wage-earners. However much the Chancellor of the Exchequer might prefer the

[1] In this connection we may mention briefly some special effects associated with the population trend:—

I. The reduced claims for income-tax allowances, mentioned above.
II. The increased consumption of dutiable luxuries when fewer people are directly dependent on each breadwinner's income.
III. The increased consumption of tobacco and beer arising out of the substitution of elderly people for children in the dependent class.

latter on humane grounds, in his professional capacity he will be all for the former.[1]

We have explained in Chapter VII the obstacles which prevent any very definite statement being made on the question of distribution in future years. A rise in real incomes may be expected for a number of different reasons, and in no case is the effect on distribution really clear-cut. To take an example, we might reasonably assume that the income paid in the year under discussion to the owners of the new capital created during the intervening period would go mainly to rich people, and that the Chancellor would, therefore, receive in direct and indirect taxes decidedly more than 5s. 6d. in the £. But even in this case we left unsettled the question of how much of their profits the competition of this new capital would compel the owners of existing capital to surrender to their workpeople or to consumers. Since the newly created capital is by no means the most difficult factor to handle we had better rest content with the generalization that a 1 per cent rise in the average income should raise the yield of existing taxes (per head of population) at least in proportion. Even this apparently safe statement would not hold good if the inequality of incomes were substantially reduced.

If the rise were strictly proportionate, it might appear that an annual rise of 1 per cent in average incomes would just prevent the burden of the debt from increasing if population were declining by 1 per cent per annum (which is about the rate of the eventual decline with our present mortality- and fertility-rates). Actually the question is far more complicated than that, depending largely on what exactly we mean by the "burden" of the debt. If debt interest were the only fixed item in the national expenditure, all others moving in proportion to population, then the burden would progressively fall under such conditions, in the important sense that

[1] At the same time, if equality of incomes is reduced "naturally," there will be less need to raise money for purposes of redistribution.

tax-rates could be reduced. For the opposing movements in average incomes and in population numbers would maintain the yield of existing taxes, whereas items covering more than three-quarters of the expenditure would be showing a reduction. However, we must not press these calculations too far, for "overhead" expenditure on such things as armaments will not fall in this automatic way, and a rising standard of real incomes will inevitably bring demands for a higher standard of social services (e.g. bigger pensions).

Despite its lack of precise calculations, which would only be misleading, the above discussion should have helped to put the influence of a declining population on the debt burden into a better and more comforting perspective. It should also have served to re-emphasize the importance of avoiding general unemployment, which not only lowers the national income for the year in question, but also reduces the amount of capital equipment (and so productivity) in subsequent years. We are thus dependent on maintaining the level of activity for relief to the debt problem, both immediately and in its long-term aspect.[1]

The first of those "remedies" which we promised to discuss (and the desirability of reducing the burden of the debt is obvious enough, even if we are sufficiently optimistic to assume it will not grow heavier) is, therefore, our old friend, "Avoid general unemployment." To this we may add with equal brevity, "Avoid wars," for these are the creators of all major debts. Indeed, a major war would simply make our whole discussion of public finance (if not the whole of this book) virtually irrelevant. If only for this reason, perhaps I may be permitted a very brief digression

[1] This is not, however, the case where activity is maintained purely by stimulating consumption, and may be the reverse of the truth if the only stimulants are budget deficits or valueless public works. We shall return to this possible clash of objectives later.

on the subject of war finance. It may well be, of course, that financial niceties would be completely ignored; but we may lay down the axioms that it should be financed as far as possible by taxation, be followed (if administratively practicable) by a levy on war wealth, and that under no circumstances should the burden of the inevitable debt be subsequently increased by encouraging a general reduction in prices and money incomes after the war.[1]

Apart from this we have two methods open to us to alleviate the burden of a given total of debt. We can reduce the rate of interest which has to be paid on it by conversion schemes; or we can reduce the real equivalent of the money paid as interest by securing a general rise in all prices (including the price of labour and other services).

As regards the first there is, unfortunately, little scope in the near future for saving very much by means of voluntary conversions, even if we could establish a level of interest rates that would seem really low as judged by past experience. It is doubtless easy to be wise after the event, but the Treasury's handling of the national debt in the dozen years or so after the war could hardly have been more ill-suited to take advantage of the fall in interest rates which has subsequently taken place. Very large loans had then to be raised (mainly for refunding old ones) at a time of high interest rates. The ideal policy would, therefore, have been to place no obstacle in the way of these being repaid or converted as soon as interest rates fell. But the Treasury not only failed to reserve to themselves the right to redeem the loans, such as Victory Bonds, 4 per cent Funding, 3½ per cent Conversion, 4 per cent Consols, until very long periods had elapsed; they also chose to issue bonds with a comparatively low nominal rate of interest at a large discount, rather than ones with a higher rate at par. For example, 4 per cent Consols were issued in 1927 at 85, to give a flat yield of just under 4¾ per cent;

[1] See J. M. Keynes, *Treatise on Money*, Volume II, Chapter 30, Section 3.

the Treasury retained no right to repay them until 1957, and then, of course, only at par. Thus, although the interest paid on every £100 actually received in cash was to be £4 14s. 2d., no saving by conversion was possible unless the rate fell below 4 per cent. If the original loan had been issued at par with a nominal rate of 4¾ per cent, then the full benefit of any fall in interest rates could have been secured. The 3½ per cent conversion loan was actually issued at prices varying round 77, to yield rather over 4½ per cent; it is not "callable" until 1961, and even then a saving will only be possible if and in so far as money can be borrowed at less than 3½ per cent. The issue of a loan on such terms could only have been justifiable on the assumption that a material fall in the rate below 4½ per cent was most improbable.

The consequence of this policy, and of the fact that large conversions have already been effected, is that there are only two loans which will be convertible in the reasonably near future so as to give a material saving. In 1940 some £375 millions of 4½ per cent Conversion Loan may be called, and in 1944 some £323 millions of 5 per cent Conversion Loan. If these were replaced by 3 per cent stocks, the saving would be appreciable (about £12 millions gross), but still very small in comparison with the annual interest charge of about £225 millions. After that there will be no loans outstanding with a nominal rate of more than 4 per cent; substantial savings would depend on securing a material reduction in the 3½ per cent now paid on nearly £2,000 millions of War Loan.

For what it is worth, however, we should certainly adopt the measures suggested in Chapter V to secure cheap money. The longer we have cheap money, the easier it is to secure a further reduction in rates in the later years when something may yet be done in the way of converting, for people will become accustomed to the lower rates and not refrain from buying bonds "because there is sure to be a reaction sooner or later." Moreover, there would otherwise be a danger of the interest burden actually growing. Besides the floating debt which has to be renewed every three months (and which now costs little more than ½ per cent per annum) there are various short-term loans which now bear low rates of interest and will have to be renewed. Whatever its other merits, cheap money is certainly wanted to ease the interest charge on the budget, more especially if new loans are to be floated for rearmament or public works.

We must now consider the second possibility—that of reducing the value of the money in which the debt service is paid. This is necessarily a somewhat delicate subject. There are nice questions of equity involved: for the State to borrow, and then deliberately to reduce the real amount of its liability by monetary manipulation, smacks rather of sharp practice, if not of fraud. Moreover, even if our consciences can be stifled and our hearts hardened against the inevitable pleas made on behalf of widows and orphans, yet it will be hardly expedient to blazen it abroad that such a policy is to be adopted. Lenders may then insist either on a higher rate of interest or on some sort of "commodity clause," whereby the amount to be paid each year will depend on an index of prices. Equities will be preferred to bonds, and non-governmental seekers of capital will be better able to compete for funds by meeting this demand; or they may offer bonds bearing higher rates of interest in the confident expectation that the rise in prices will prevent the service being burdensome.

Once again, however, a sense of perspective is essential. The proposal is not to raise prices at a rate comparable with that of the German inflation period; it is not even necessary to raise them by 5 per cent every year. A great deal can be accomplished merely by seeing to it that the gradual drift towards higher prices which has persisted throughout many centuries shall continue. An average rise of 1 per cent per annum, probably composed of larger ones in some years and declines in others, would do a great deal to reduce the burden and would have very little effect on the behaviour of investors, who are mostly concerned with more immediate considerations.

The crucial factor is the general level of money wage-rates, both because this is a very sticky element, and because, *for industry as a whole*, it represents such a large element in costs, since the level of wages also influences material and transport costs, etc. To secure a slow secular rise in these rates is not really very difficult, provided we do not allow a state of depression to become more or less permanent. In periods of good trade they can be relied on to rise more or less of their own accord. This does not mean, of course, that the process will be independent of human volition or conduct, like the rise of a barometer, but simply that no general action need be taken by any central authority; the trade unions in the various industries will be pressing for higher wages, and the employers will concede a part of their demands. The process will be spasmodic and piecemeal and hardly sensational—in the recent period of improving trade, despite the fact that there were "cuts" to restore, the Ministry of Labour's index of weekly wage-rates rose from 94 in 1933 to 102 in 1937. But this sort of pace is amply fast enough for our purpose of slowly reducing the real burden of the national debt. Indeed, if it continued without interruption for a decade or two, the results might well be undesirably large.

The real problem is to prevent these gains being subsequently lost in a period of depression. There are two possibilities here, though they overlap somewhat. We may discourage attempts to cut wages if a depression does come. As we saw in Chapter III, a large (and growing) body of opinion holds that wage-cuts bring no benefit which could not be better secured by other means, or which does not simply represent the snatching of a competitive advantage over another country. Or we may seek, by all means in our power, to avert, or at least mitigate and shorten, the depression. It is as part of our programme for achieving the latter objective that "monetary manipulation" comes into the picture, though that is perhaps rather a grandiose name for a not very startling policy.

This subject is really covered by the analysis in Chapter III,[1] but we may set it out briefly thus. An improving level of trade activity will call for a larger amount of money in the active circulation, quite apart from any rise in wages or prices. The rise in wages (and in other prices too, for they are interconnected, each reinforcing the other) will, however, increase the requirements still further. There is usually a fair amount of "slack" in the financial system which will enable the two processes to continue for some time without producing any stringency; but this will be exhausted sooner or later, and unless the authorities act in time the whole movement will be brought to a halt (if not put into reverse) by a shortage of money and rise in interest rates.

This does not imply that a willingness to expand credit is sufficient to ensure the continuance of prosperity. Whatever the policy of the banks—and of the unions too, for that matter—there are plenty of other causes which may bring an advance to a halt. But it does mean that an increase in the money supply is a *necessary* condition for the continuation of the rise, whether it be in activity or wage-rates.[2] And if we do slip into a depression, then monetary expansion and low interest rates will at least help to make a speedy recovery possible, even if they will not be really effective unless coupled with other measures.

In short, then, a slow reduction in the real value of the debt service seems hardly to call for any new policy at all. If we apply the measures which have already been found desirable for maintaining a high level of activity (and

[1] See in particular pages 82–85.

[2] Cf. page 86, especially the footnote.

incidentally a buoyant revenue), then we can rely on more or less "natural" forces to do the rest. Moreover, as far as the money supply is concerned we do not even have to diverge in any way from traditional rules. The great rise in the price of gold since 1931 has raised the value of the then existing stocks to a level which would permit of a great increase in the quantity of money without any departure from the old traditions; and it has so stimulated the annual output (besides automatically raising its value) that the authorities may be forced into expansion whether they consider it desirable or not.

There is, however, a certain amount of disharmony concealed under the apparent coincidence of policies designed to secure different ends. Included in the list of possible measures for maintaining activity (and so for promoting a secular rise in prices) were such things as public works and budget deficits. These involve an addition to the total amount of governmental debt, and hence to the interest bill in subsequent years. The public works may, of course, produce a direct return which will cover this interest, and it is important that we should choose schemes which will yield some return, or at least be of real value to the community, instead of simply seeking to "give employment." But in general there will be some net addition to the Exchequer's payments.

It follows, therefore, that there is some clash of objectives. Borrowing for public works may lead to a rise in prices which will reduce the real value of the interest on the existing debt, or raise the level of activity and so the revenue from taxation, or both; but it will also increase the amount of money to be paid as interest in future years.

Similarly we must not exaggerate the extent to which the same policy is desirable both to secure the conversion of the debt to a lower interest basis and to reduce the real burden of the interest by raising prices. Both policies may be classed under the heading "cheap money"; but "cheap" is a relative term, and the implied standards are not the same. For the limited objective of furthering conversion schemes cheap money is an end in itself—we want rates simply to be reduced as far as possible, and to secure this we may usefully resort to such measures as a ban on new issues; indeed, one of the most powerful weapons at the authorities' disposal is to allow a really thoroughgoing depression to develop[1] before proceeding with monetary expansion. Obviously, however, this is not the type of cheap money policy which we want for our second objective or for a campaign against slumps. These require that money shall be cheap in order that it shall be used, not that obstacles shall be put in the way of its use to make it cheap. The standard of cheapness is now the level of rates which will ensure an adequate amount of capital outlay. We do not much mind what the actual figure is; if, for example, a burst of inventions increases the demand for funds so much that rates have to be raised to prevent a wild boom, then this simply means that our task is all the easier.

Honesty and clear thinking demand that we should point out these disharmonies, but we must be careful not to over-stress their importance. Many of the measures designed to keep up activity, and so to encourage an upward trend in prices, involve no increase in the deadweight debt; the latter is in any case so large that a 1 per cent rise in prices would offset an addition of about £80 millions. All the types of "cheap money" include a liberal monetary and credit policy as a leading item in their requirements, and it is clear which objective is the most important. If we could believe that this or any other policy would succeed in preventing depressions without establishing really low interest rates, then we would cheerfully renounce the prospect of converting the national debt. I fear, however, that there is little "risk" of this happening.

[1] In case this sounds too callous, perhaps we should add that they may be unable to prevent it, and simply seize a golden opportunity.

Perhaps we may conclude our discussion thus. The gravity of the "population and debt" problem is very frequently exaggerated. For a considerable period the decline in the size of the active population will be negligible, so that the problem, as usually stated, simply will not arise; in fact the burden of the debt should be reduced by the rise in productivity, and so in the average (real) income. Even in the later years, when population really is declining, reasonably skilful management should make it quite tractable, particularly if we begin *now* the process of lightening the burden by encouraging a slow rise in prices and money incomes. Admittedly it would become serious, and probably unmanageable, if the population declined rapidly for a century or so in the manner illustrated by Dr. Charles's second calculation; but such a state of affairs would raise so many far more important problems in other directions that we need hardly discuss it.

The idea underlying this scare—that a constant or even increasing outlay would have to be met by a falling number of taxpayers—is really far more disturbing when applied to other "overhead" items in the budget, notably the cost of defence services. In these cases there is little to be gained by raising prices and money incomes, since this will increase revenue and expenditure alike; at best there may be a time-lag. We cannot even derive much comfort from the thought of increasing productivity, for at least one item in this (technical progress) is also likely to mean "improved" and costlier engines of war.

The main problems which are really likely to make the task of budget balancing a difficult one in future are[1]:—

[1] On the other hand, quite apart from the automatic rise in the revenue per head from existing taxes (already discussed), we must not forget that with the passage of time taxpayers can be induced to accept new taxes, or increased rates on old ones, even though the tax-burden had previously been described as being already "at, if not beyond," the limit of what is tolerable. We have seen in Chapter V that some developments in this direction are in any case desirable as part of a policy of combating unemployment, quite apart from the social gain through reduced inequality.

(*a*) The difficulty of avoiding slumps and wars.

(*b*) The cost of the defence services, expressed as a fraction of the national income—and one need hardly add that the national income is not the only variable here, let alone its constituent factor, the size of the population.

(*c*) The increasing burden of maintaining the social services at their existing standard.

(*d*) The inevitable (and in many ways highly desirable) pressure for improved standards in these services.

All four of these factors are, to a greater or lesser extent, already troubling us. At the moment the second is dominating all other considerations: a cynic might say that if expenditure on defence rises by hundreds of millions in a few years, then it is no use worrying about the influence of population trends or anything else. The last two will exert an increasing influence before the "population and debt" factor can come into operation at all, though it is only fair to mention that the changing age-composition which is largely responsible in this period for (*c*) brings substantial offsets through the higher yield of death-duties and other taxes.

The final item is worthy of closer attention. Our cynic might say that extra outlay under this head was an automatic consequence of our political system, irrespective of any rise in real incomes, or of the effect on employment, or of population trends, or indeed anything. Be that as it may, if we are to enter "rising revenues as a result of a higher average income" amongst our budgetary assets, then we must expect irresistible pressure for bigger pensions, etc., and make an appropriate entry amongst the liabilities. And, still more obviously, if we are to rely on measures such as these to maintain effective demand, and, therefore, estimate the probable revenue on the assumption that the slump risk will be *pro tanto* reduced, then we must not forget the other side of the account. Moreover, this is another case where monetary manipulation can do little to help us. The State may not be under any contractual obligation to raise pensions if prices rise, and could very probably get away with a rather smaller real payment under such conditions, at least for a time. But quite apart from the social undesirability of such a procedure, it might prove to be bad tactics even from the narrow budgetary point of view; the rise in prices, by compelling some consideration of the matter, might well precipitate a revision of standards which would raise the pension bill more than in proportion to the rise in prices.

CHAPTER X

INTERNATIONAL TRADE

THAT population trends have a bearing on international trade is a fact which has been fairly widely realized. Thus the author not infrequently came across arguments of this type in Australia: "Now that Britain's population is about to become stationary or even to decline, we cannot expect any great increase in the absorptive capacity of the British market; Australia should concentrate on developing outlets for her products in the expanding markets of the East." The discussion seems, however, always to stop at this or some similar point; we are provided with some interesting fragments, but a comprehensive analysis is not attempted.

There are perhaps special reasons for this neglect in the case of international trade, quite apart from the general failure to examine the effects of population trends. International trade has recently been influenced so largely by political considerations that any discussion of its future by an academic economist might be regarded as a waste of time. It seems to me, however, that there are issues of sufficient importance to justify at least a brief discussion in a book which seeks to look further ahead than the next international crisis. There are plenty of other factors which influence the volume and character of international trade besides the actions of governments, as we can see from the fact that the world total was about the same in 1937 as in 1929 (the previous "all-time high," if we may import an American phrase), despite all the multitudinous restrictions imposed in the meantime. We can usefully say something about the probable development of some of these, and also about the reactions which governments are likely to make to various economic changes which we must expect.

Let us begin at the beginning by seeing what it is that

makes it advantageous for the peoples of different countries to trade with one another. In some cases the answer is obvious: many highly desirable commodities would cease to be available at all in England if it were not for international trade, because they simply could not be produced there. But this is only an extreme case of a more general rule. We import many commodities which it would be physically possible to produce here, perhaps even in such a way as to yield more of the product per person employed than is secured in the exporting country.

The fundamental condition for trade to be advantageous may be grasped in this way. Suppose that a careful comparison were made between our facilities for satisfying our requirements of various commodities and the corresponding position in the rest of the world. Different countries are supplied with specialized factors of production[1] (human and material) in very different proportions, and their demands for different commodities also vary greatly. Such a comparison would, therefore, show that our position with regard to some commodities was far less satisfactory than with regard to others. If international trade were impossible, this would cause the former to be relatively expensive, the latter to be relatively cheap; it is to the advantage of all countries that we should import the former and export the latter until the price difference no more than covers transport costs. This may mean that we do not produce some goods in the former category at all, because our supplies of the necessary factors of production are either non-existent or else better employed in other uses; but frequently we shall continue to supply a *part* of our requirements because we have good facilities for doing so, e.g. in the case of meat and many other agricultural products.

[1] It is important to note that the number of these is very great. The traditional division into land, labour, capital, and enterprise is obviously quite inadequate, because each category covers a multitude of types which are not interchangeable.

The essential point to note in the above analysis is that the advantage of international trade arises out of our being better placed, in comparison with the rest of the world, in regard to some commodities than in regard to others. Another country might appear more (or less) efficient in some physical sense at producing every single commodity, and yet international trade would be advantageous if the degree of superiority varied as between different commodities. The industries where it was greatest would offer high prices to attract the factors of production, the country's income would be large, and so the other industries would be faced with a large demand and a small supply of human and material resources.

It follows that population trends, or anything else, will reduce the fundamental advantageousness of trade between Britain and other countries if they cause our facilities for satisfying our requirements of the various commodities to be more similar to those prevailing in the rest of the world. They will make little or no difference if they affect our position with regard to all commodities equally, conditions elsewhere remaining stationary; or if they increase the ease with which all countries could produce any one commodity.

Now an exhaustive analysis of the ways in which population trends would influence the position in respect to all the different commodities would be a Herculean task. We have also decided to assume that capital will continue to be accumulated and technical progress to be secured; these factors would complicate the matter still further—particularly the latter, since progress would take different forms in different countries. But one or two conclusions seem to be both safe and important.

Thus the very fact that technical progress will probably take different forms enables us to make a fairly safe prediction about the composition of our trade. It is almost certain that the more backward countries will improve their efficiency in producing the simpler kinds of manufactures—e.g. above all, textiles of a simple kind—perhaps up to the point where they are as (physically) efficient at producing them as we are. Progress with us, on the other hand, is more likely to be in the newer and more complex industries, and it is in these that we shall have a comparative advantage. In other words the trend will continue, whereby our exports progressively shift from standard goods to specialities or new commodities, yesterday's novelty being to-day's standard line. Only by continually leading in this way can we expect to maintain our incomes at a level so much higher than that of the backward countries.

The pressure in this direction is likely to be accentuated by the different trends of population, since those of the backward countries are mostly still growing. This is important in another respect. A second great reason why it is beneficial to all concerned that we should trade with these countries is the very different ratios of capital to labour in the two areas. This makes it advantageous for us to export goods produced by highly capitalized industries, e.g. machinery, and import those which require little besides cheap labour, e.g. peasant handiwork. The basis for this trade is likely to be strengthened in future by a further increase in the ratio of capital to labour in England. British labour will be so expensive relatively to, say, Indian that only those industries will be able to compete in which it can be combined with a large amount of capital.[1]

Another case in which population trends are likely to be important is that of our trade with the Dominions and other primary producing countries, such as the Argentine, whose population is still expanding. Here it is the existence of

[1] The use of broad categories such as "capital" and "labour" is sometimes dangerous, since it is the abundance or otherwise of particular sorts of each that is important. The absence of an adequate supply of textile factories in India in the past may be better ascribed to lack of trained labour to operate them than to lack of capital in general. Frequently the factors reinforce one another—an industry requires both a lot of capital and a labour force skilful enough to use it.

different ratios between the supply of labour and that of land[1] which furnishes the basis for much of the trade. Clearly this discrepancy is about to be reduced, and with it the advantage to be gained from such trade.

Let us examine this case in rather greater detail and see what the implications of these developments are. We must distinguish between two types of comparison, both of which are useful and interesting for certain problems, but confusion between which is a fertile source of muddles.

The first contrasts the position which we expect to prevail (in the absence of further political interference with trade) in future with that which would prevail if population continued to expand in the way which was considered normal in the nineteenth century; whereas the second contrasts it simply with the present situation. The first is designed roughly to isolate the influence of the population factor, the second to show what is likely to happen.

Let us begin with the first comparison. If our population continued to expand, we should require larger imports of food and so on merely to maintain our present standard of living. We have good facilities for producing a part of our requirements ourselves, and do in fact do so; but it is probably safe to say that most, if not all, of the extra supplies could be better obtained from abroad, because the obstacles in the way of agricultural expansion are much smaller there, whilst there is no great reason to suppose industrial expansion to be easier in one place or the other. It follows, therefore, that it would be advantageous for our food imports to increase *more* than in proportion to the increase in population, even if standards remained unchanged; failing Government action, this is what would happen. The effects of any rise in standards would be in addition to this.[2]

[1] In this case the use of broad categories seems to suffice.

[2] The reader should remember that with a few commodities, e.g. wheat, a rise in real incomes causes a *fall* in consumption. The total effect, however, is clearly an increase.

With a stationary population, however, our food imports will only increase as a result of a rising level of consumption per head. This might be due to a rise in the real national income, or a change in its distribution in favour of those who would spend more on food, or both. Since the proportion of a person's income which is spent on food decreases as his income increases, the second condition means a redistribution in favour of families whose income per head is low. A rise in wages relative to salaries and profits would do something, but the importance of the family element shows that an equivalent amount transferred as child endowment would do far more.

Now we have seen that the average real income is likely to rise in future, and that distribution may become less unequal even without any further political action—the smaller size of families in itself reduces one sort of inequality which is very significant in this connection; we have also recommended various schemes for furthering this process. Even ignoring the latter, we may reasonably expect, therefore, a considerable rise in our consumption of food, which will mean, in the absence of Government action, a corresponding rise in imports. But this is a point which is primarily relevant to the *second* type of comparison, with which we shall be dealing in a moment. For our present purpose we are only concerned with the *additional* rise (if any) in the average consumption, which is due to the absence of population increase; this is the only element which we have to balance against the loss of potential consumers.

There can be little doubt about the answer. Admittedly, the new trend in population is likely to make some contribution to the expected rise in the average income, and it will probably also help to reduce inequality somewhat. But an annual rise of 1 per cent in the number of consumers, which would be quite moderate by nineteenth-century standards, would outweigh the total effect of all the factors making for a higher average consumption, let alone a part of them. The only plausible counter-argument would be to say that the falling trend of population might induce the Government to institute a scheme of family allowances or an effective nutrition campaign, which would not otherwise have been introduced. This might in one year have more effect than rising numbers or incomes could have in several; but there is no guarantee that this will happen, and it would clearly be a special case.

The Australian primary producer is quite right, therefore, in saying that the falling trend in Britain's population is a bad thing for him. But this is not the same thing as saying that it will lead to an actual contraction in Britain's imports of food. To answer that question we must make a comparison of the second type, and it should be clear from what we have already said how it is to be done. For some time to come there will be no significant change in the number of consumers, and the important question is, therefore, the level of the average income and the degree of inequality. The general trend should be slightly upwards, with the usual disturbances due to depressions.

The total demand for food imports is really a less interesting subject than the varying fortunes of individual commodities. Clearly the wheat-grower cannot expect a higher average standard to provide any compensation for the failure of numbers to increase, for bread consumption falls as people can afford more expensive foods. On the other hand, producers of fruit, eggs, butter, and other of the semi-luxury foods may even regard rising standards as more important than rising numbers (though naturally preferring to have both). These will benefit particularly if the average amount spent on food rises mainly as a result of improvement at the bottom, such as would be secured by child endowment. It is worth noting, however, that at least one of the commodities which should benefit (fresh milk) is not at present imported;

rising standards may turn demand more in the direction of foods which can best be produced at home rather than imported.

This last point illustrates a question which is of considerable importance to a discussion of the future of international trade, and which has been the subject of some controversy. Does an increase in the average real income of a nation make it advantageous for it to have more or less international trade?

Briefly, the main arguments on either side may be put thus:—

(I) As real incomes rise, so the variety of goods bought increases greatly. Not only are people able to satisfy other wants besides the bare necessities of life, but these other wants are spread over a vast range of different goods, partly because different people have different tastes, partly because we often only spend a little on each thing. Moreover, this increasing diversity is not confined to the market for finished products—all sorts of raw materials and special machinery are also required. No single country can hope to be efficient at producing all this multitude of articles, so that international specialization is essential if the full benefit is to be derived from man's improved command over his environment. Hence the view that "it is the rich country which cannot afford the luxury of a self-sufficiency policy."

As evidence in support of this argument its supporters point to such phenomena as the simultaneous importation and exportation of goods all classed as "steel," which is a feature of the trade of most advanced countries. The explanation of this apparent paradox is that the varied requirements of modern industry call for many sorts of steel, and no country produces them all. Without international trade full advantage could not be taken of improved technique; poor countries would not be much affected, since they consume little in the way of elaborate products, but rich ones would suffer considerably.

(II) On the other hand there is the well-known fact that as a country's real income rises, so the proportion of its people engaged in services of all kinds steadily increases. This is really another consequence of the different ways in which the national incomes of rich and poor countries are spent. The proportion spent on food and simple manufactures progressively diminishes, whereas the proportion spent on entertainment, travel, education and other "services" increases, and a much more elaborate system of distribution is required.

Now apart from special cases, notably the international tourist trade, services are almost necessarily an internal affair. No matter how good the people of some other country might be at retail selling, an increased demand for retailing must mean an expansion of the local trade. Hence the view that as standards rise, so the importance of international trade decreases.

Since we expect the average real income to rise in future, partly as a result of the population trend, we want to know what the truth of this matter really is. Fortunately, there is no great difficulty in reconciling the two views, for the confusion is a purely verbal one: the first analysis was concerned with the absolute amount of a country's trade, the second with its size in relation, say, to the national income. There is nothing inconsistent in saying firstly that a rich country will do more trade, and would, therefore, lose more through its abolition or restriction, and secondly that this trade will represent a smaller proportion of its total economic activity. The important point about the first argument was that it showed another reason why a country may find increased trade advantageous as its real income rises, apart from the obvious one of wanting more of the old imports. There may be no very obvious reason why any one of the specialities should be made in one country rather than in another, but if each country supplied all its own wants, then many industries would be too small to be efficient.

So far we have been discussing what changes might be expected in the absence of further governmental interference with trade; we have been examining, if you like, the probable changes in the basic material on which the governments can work. We have also been concerned with the fundamental or long-term factors which make an international division of labour advantageous, rather than with the disturbing influence of business fluctuations or cycles.

Before we go on to consider questions of politics, however, we must make one important point—perhaps the most important in our whole study of international trade. We have seen that the absence of population increase will certainly make our demand for imports smaller absolutely than it otherwise would have become. (It will probably be smaller even when reckoned per head of population; this would reinforce the argument, but is not necessary to it.) This means, of course, that the total gain which the country will derive from the existence of foreign trade will be smaller than it would otherwise have become. But it does *not* mean that we shall be in a worse position to conduct our trade on a basis advantageous to ourselves; far from it. Our position will be stronger on account of our smaller numbers.

Perhaps this can best be seen by putting the first proposition the other way round. The loss which the country would sustain if foreign trade were rendered impossible will be smaller if it still has 40 million inhabitants than if the number had grown to 45 or 50—the reason being simply that there would be more trade to lose and more difficulty in satisfying the requirements of large numbers without it. But the very fact that our need for imports would be smaller improves the chance of our getting them on favourable terms. To put it crudely, the more mouths we have to feed, the more outlets for our exports we must find and the stronger the presumption that we shall have to lower the prices we charge.

This conclusion need not cause us any surprise. It is really only another application of the general principle which we met in Chapter VII[1] about the effects of an increase or decrease in the supply of a particular factor of production. From the point of view of the world economy, Englishmen may be regarded broadly as belonging to one specialized group who produce certain manufactured goods. If the number in this group decreases relatively to the numbers in other complementary groups, e.g. above all those which specialize in food production, then we can expect to trade on better terms.

The reason why this conclusion is of such great importance is that we might otherwise encounter very real difficulties in finding outlets for an adequate quantity of exports on terms even approximately as favourable as those we now enjoy. The population factor is not likely to put us in a better position than we are in now; it will rather be required as an offset to the forces which are tending to make that position worse. Even with its aid we must, I think, expect some deterioration.[2]

These unfavourable forces are, as we shall see in a moment, partly political. But even if we could banish considerations of economic nationalism and war economics, yet the factor of technical progress seems sufficient to establish our conclusion. The backward, and therefore low-wage, countries are especially likely to improve their efficiency in producing many of the goods which we now export, but in which our advantage has been based on little more than an early start; they will thus become ever more serious competitors. It would not matter much if they secured an all-round improvement and increased their production in all directions; but their natural course is into those markets where we sell,

[1] Cf. pages 155 and 164.

[2] There is one special way in which a smaller population is said to ease our "balance of payments" problem—the income from our overseas investments will cover a larger proportion of our imports. Up to a point this is doubtless true, but we must not forget that the income from some of these depends largely on the size of the British market.

rather than into those where we buy. In the past we have more or less maintained our position by always keeping one move ahead: if efficiency could not be further improved in the old industry, then we have developed a new one, or a new branch of the old. It would, however, be optimistic to assume that this process can be continued for ever; if Governments take steps to restrict trade, then our position is further endangered, if only because we are a leading example of a nation which must not merely "export or die," but export a great deal.

We may now proceed to deal briefly with the political reactions which may be expected to various economic developments. We shall say nothing about the very possible extension of policies aimed at greater self-sufficiency as a safeguard against war, beyond pointing out that this would reinforce our other conclusions. The magical word "defence" can be, and is, used to justify almost any form of economic lunacy, in addition to policies which really would bring enough extra security to outweigh the loss of real income. It is a trump card for all vested interests, because it may be held superior to all arguments based on such mundane things as calculation of costs. Or perhaps it ought to be called the joker, because it can be used on any occasion and wins against any opposition.

The reasons, apart from considerations of war economics, why we may expect restrictions on international trade to be increased, fall into three broad categories. As usual these overlap somewhat, but it is helpful to sort them out as far as possible. Each may be described as a more or less "natural" consequence of the changes in the underlying data which we have seen to be likely.

In the first place every slump is likely to produce a fresh crop of restrictions on imports, many of which will create vested interests and be retained even if prosperity returns.

Every Government will seek to improve the position of its particular country, to reduce its own unemployment problem, even if it thereby makes the position of others still more difficult. Clearly the world situation cannot be improved in this way, but in the absence of some international agreement the tragic game of beggar-my-neighbour is likely to be continued. Some countries will indeed have little option in the matter because of their lack of exchange reserves—if exports have fallen, then imports must be reduced somehow, and the alternative method of a violent deflation may quite rightly be considered most unattractive. This excuse will not be available to the richer countries, such as the United States or ourselves, but they may nevertheless seek to have a surplus of exports, visible and invisible, over imports, so as to reduce unemployment.[1] The most hopeful assumption from the point of view of international trade is that they will try to secure this by means of exchange depreciation, which would at least produce no net tendency in the direction of greater self-sufficiency, because it stimulates exports as much as it curtails imports. But apart from the manifest impossibility of its being used by all countries at the same time, it is likely to be supplemented by tariffs and other measures designed simply to limit imports.

If the above proposition is accepted (and it would surely be unreasoning optimism to dispute it), then restrictions are likely to grow with the mere passage of time, unless slumps are virtually eliminated. The fact that the risk of slumps is likely to be increased is not necessary to the argument, but may be thrown in for good measure.

It may, however, be argued that after a time a limit will be set to this process of progressively depriving consumers of more and more of the potential benefits that might be secured by an international division of labour. Individual countries may see that they gain little by way of employment

[1] Cf. the discussion on page 88, and the chapter on Beggar-my-Neighbour Remedies in J. Robinson: *Essays in Employment.*

from the mere *existence* of high tariffs, and seize the opportunity of a period of prosperity to surmount the transitional difficulties involved in a reduction. Or there may be some sort of international, or at least regional, convention to secure simultaneous reductions. At the worst there might be some agreement to refrain from further restrictions.

This possibility cannot be rejected out of hand, though the lessons of experience are not very encouraging. But there is also the possibility of a different reaction, leading to our second broad class of restrictions. Some nations, particularly those which feel they might be more successful than others at dealing with general unemployment, may deliberately decide that it would be better to forgo some of the advantages of international division of labour in order that they may have their destiny more within their own hands. "Of what use is it," they may say, "to concentrate on those industries for which we have a comparative advantage if the world market is so unstable? Admittedly, in years of good trade we enjoy larger real incomes as a result, but at any moment the foreign market for which we have organized our production may collapse, leaving us powerless to do anything about it; we are then simply dragged into the world slump."

We need not discuss how justified such an attitude would be—it clearly depends on how much more successful the nation would really be at avoiding general unemployment when it was rather less closely bound to the world economy, and on the sacrifice involved in its particular case in producing goods at home instead of securing them by means of trade. We are concerned only with the easier question of whether this policy of deliberate "disentanglement" will in fact be adopted; or rather, with the extent to which its application will spread, for the process has already been begun in several countries.[1] And we must surely conclude

[1] The motives which lead a country to seek greater self-sufficiency are so mixed that it is hard to attribute any one case to any particular

that the desire to increase the nation's security by "reducing its dependence on the vagaries of world markets" will, rightly or wrongly, exert a growing influence.

Our third category of restrictions also springs from the desire for increased security. Changing circumstances, particularly those connected with technical progress, frequently change the answer to the question of which industries it is most advantageous for each country to have. If the transition is effected, then the nation as a whole will be better off, but particular sets of producers (both workers and capitalists) will suffer in the process. They are very likely, therefore, to bring pressure to bear on the Government to grant them protection against this "flood of cheap imports"; and, especially if they can argue that their industry would be valuable in time of war, then they are likely to succeed.

There is, of course, nothing new in this, but it may well be more important in future. In the first place the mere passage of time will generally mean that restrictions accumulate, for the old ones are seldom repealed (though they sometimes become ineffective or unnecessary). In the second the general attitude, both of governments and of public opinion, has become far more sympathetic towards the attempts of producers to increase their security, even if it does involve some cost to the consumer. In the third the whole problem of overcoming frictions and making adjustments is aggravated when the trend of population is no longer upwards—more adjustments are likely to be necessary, and it will be more difficult to make them smoothly.[1] And finally the interests concerned will often be able to make out a more plausible case.

The reasons for this last statement are partly implicit in what has gone before—if adjustments are harder to make, then there is more case for a tariff which would render them

cause. Thus Germany's policy may aim more at security against trade interruptions due to war than against those due to world slumps, but the latter element is important. Perhaps the Irish Free State would serve as an illustration, or New Zealand's "insulation" policy.

[1] Cf. Chapter II, passim.

unnecessary. But we must also remember that there will be a larger volume of trade in luxuries and things of which each consumer buys very little. The cry of "dear rubber dolls" or "dear calendars" is hardly likely to rally the opposition so effectively as that of "dear food." The people of a rich country may, as we have seen, stand to lose more in the aggregate by not taking advantage of the possibilities of international trade, but they can better afford to do so and the loss in each single case may be very small. Moreover, it may often be the case with these luxury goods that there really is very little to be gained by buying the imported article rather than the home product; the reasons why it is advantageous for us to import wheat are very strong, but with manufactured luxuries there may be "very little in it," so that the producers' security involves only a small cost to the consumer. Even where this is not really the case, price comparisons may be difficult because the two articles are not identical, and the producers may argue that the burden will be very small "once the consumer learns to appreciate the merits of the domestic product; but they must, however, have a high tariff so as to be sure of securing the market."[1]

The above is by no means an exhaustive catalogue of the reasons why we must expect restrictions on international trade to increase. On the other side we shall doubtless find some increase in the efforts of various governments to foster exports. But this is seldom as easy as replacing imports by home production and generally involves the payment of subsidies, which are unpopular, even if they inflict no greater burden on the population than protective tariffs; the net effect of governmental interference will undoubtedly be to reduce the volume of trade below the level which it would otherwise have attained. It would not be surprising if the

[1] The question is not, of course, whether the arguments are sound, but whether the particular interest concerned will get away with it.

volume became actually smaller than it now is, at least in the case of those countries whose population has ceased to expand at all rapidly. In most cases, including our own, it is almost certain to decline relatively to the national income.

In conclusion, it is worth noting how vulnerable our own exports are to the probable growth of restrictions. Many of our staple lines consist of commodities such as textiles which could be produced without great difficulty elsewhere. They are likely to attract the attention of governments seeking suitable "infant industries" to protect as part of a policy designed to secure "a more balanced economy" by increasing the degree of the country's industrialization. Or local production may be stimulated simply "to relieve unemployment" or "to preserve foreign exchange." The governments may be acting quite sensibly from their own point of view—once the local industry is established the loss of real income involved in producing such goods at home rather than importing them may be quite small, particularly where our advantage is mainly due to an early start; at any rate it may be smaller than the loss involved in replacing some other import. But the truth of this is really immaterial. The real question is whether the foreign Government will act on this assumption; and here the fact that these goods obviously *could* be produced locally may well be decisive.

On the other hand if we develop new exports which are largely of the luxury class, then these are particularly likely to suffer virtual prohibition whenever a country becomes anxious about its balance of payments. The years since 1930 have furnished one example after another of policies designed to curtail "non-essential imports." Our own introduction of tariffs in 1931 was supported with arguments to the effect that it would "direct our foreign purchasing power into the channels where it was most necessary."[1] We stand to lose

[1] Those familiar with Bernard Shaw's play, *The Apple Cart*, may remember the statement by Magnus: "At a pinch, I think they could do without the Christmas crackers."

almost more than any other nation from policies of this sort, because our imports are so largely "essentials" and our exports largely "non-essentials"—finished products as such are liable to be considered suspect when restrictions are being imposed, and our exports mostly fall into this category.

Is there a moral in all this? Can we draw any conclusions as to the policy which Great Britain should follow?

In general terms it is clear that we should seek with all our power to prevent this gradual throttling of world trade. We must attack the practice whereby each nation seems to regard the international field as a sort of dumping-ground for its domestic difficulties, sacrificing the benefits of international trade to the supposed alleviation of some maladjustment. We must try to show that this practice all too often creates worse maladjustments than those it seeks to cure; and not only this, but that as a rule they come home to roost eventually in the country where they originated (if only as a result of reprisals), so that the policy does not pay in any sense.

The difficulty is, however, to devise machinery whereby this principle (which would be accepted by many countries) can be translated into a programme of action. This is a subject for the diplomatist rather than the economist, who cannot as such be expected to say much about the rival merits of world economic conferences, direct conversations between leading statesmen, and so on. We can, however, make a few brief comments, especially on the negative side. Thus it is clear that our position is too vulnerable for us to risk playing with fire. We must resist the temptation to try to snatch minor advantages for ourselves by joining in the game of restrictions. There must, above all, be no repetition of such penny-wise practices as the quota on cotton goods imported into the Crown Colonies—a measure which not only forfeited us our right to take a high moral line about "trusteeship," but also caused more ill-feeling in proportion to the trade secured than almost any other device which might have been adopted.

On the positive side our greatest[1] single contribution would be to maintain a high level of employment by internal measures. This would not only ensure a large market for other countries' exports, and so remove one of the strongest forces making for restrictions, but might inspire them to do likewise. As always, slumps are our greatest enemy.

In the field of international trade proper we must be prepared to vary our tactics to suit the special circumstances of each case. Our greatest strength is undoubtedly derived from our enormous buying power, but we should use this bargaining counter with discretion. We can reasonably insist on fair treatment for our exports in a wider sense than the formal requirements of the most-favoured-nation clause would dictate, i.e. we can insist on its being observed in the spirit as well as in the letter; when dealing with countries in which trade is closely controlled by the Government this will probably mean that some stipulation about the amount of their purchases will have to be included. We can also try to persuade other countries not to foster local industries which would be particularly damaging to our trade. But we should not use our bargaining power to make other countries break the spirit of their most-favoured-nation agreements with third parties—once more for the simple reason that we have far too much to lose (including the interest on our oversea investments) for us to risk provoking retaliation.

The new situation calls for action by private enterprise as well as by the Government. Naturally our exporters must strive to be efficient, and above all study the requirements of all potential customers. But the matter does not stop at that point. There are a number of methods by which goods

[1] Greatest, that is, in the economic field. It would be still more valuable if we could appreciably reduce the general fear of war, which is an unrivalled breeder of restrictive policies.

can be marketed, for example, in such a way that the trade is likely to be welcomed by the foreign country, rather than regarded as something to be restricted. The reader will find a number of suggestions of this kind in the P.E.P.[1] Report on International Trade, together with others for political action. None of them are sensational, but they are not to be rejected on that account. There can be no royal road to success when the forces making for greater restrictions are so powerful and so varied. We must be thankful for small mercies, and for the fact that our problem will not be intensified by a growing population.

[1] *Political and Economic Planning.* See especially pages 11–35.

CHAPTER XI

SOME GENERAL CONCLUSIONS

POPULATION trends affect other aspects of our economic life besides those discussed in the preceding chapters; indeed, it would be hard to name one which will *not* be affected to some extent. But we have surveyed the main fields which are of general interest and can leave the investigation of particular problems, such as the effect on individual industries, to those more intimately concerned. We must now review our conclusions about the wider consequences.

We have dealt mainly, it must be remembered, with the comparatively near future, in which the population will decline only slightly, the leading features being rather a great change in age-composition and the absence of the customary *increase* in numbers. The change-over from an increasing to a stationary population has effects which are in many ways similar to those of the subsequent change to a decline, but the distinction should nevertheless be borne in mind.

However this may be, for the period under discussion the economic outlook must be regarded as at least potentially favourable. Provided we can learn how to take advantage of it, the new situation should enable us to raise our standard of living at least as rapidly as in the past. If that is so, then we can look with comparative unconcern on such things as the headaches which future Chancellors of the Exchequer may have to endure. A high standard of living is an end in itself, a satisfactory budget only a means to that end.

We must, however, emphasize once more the overriding proviso to which this optimistic conclusion is subject. The nation must become better at tackling the essentially man-made problem of general unemployment. The risk of our being overtaken by this disease will actually be greater, perhaps even considerably greater. Unless we become better at applying the necessary remedies at the right times and in proper proportions, then our potentially greater plenty will be nothing but a mockery to us. Or rather (and this is perhaps worse) some people will enjoy it, if only precariously, and their good fortune will serve as a contrast to aggravate the lot of the unemployed and other unfortunates. Inequality for which there is no rational or equitable basis is a major evil in itself, and even if this were mitigated by generous payments to the unemployed, there would still be the demoralizing effect of being without an occupation for years at a time. One may very reasonably say that the whole framework of society will be endangered if slumps are allowed to become more severe and more persistent.[1]

The methods which should be adopted to deal with this major problem have been set out at some length in Chapter V, and we need not go over all the ground again. All I would like to repeat is that the problem is not one of scarcity in any sense (except that of scarcity of initiative in high places and of understanding generally), and that unless at least a partial solution is found, then many other problems will be both very difficult and hardly worth solving.

The last point is distinctly important, for it would be quite a mistake to imagine that the new situation will only raise problems in this one direction, the solution of which would cause all manner of other blessings to fall into our lap without any effort on our part. In almost every chapter we have found at least one difficulty which must be faced if we are really to make full use of our opportunities. Measures must be taken to avert the growth of frictional unemployment; to check the monopolistic and restrictionist practices of vested interests, which are likely to be more dangerous when one of the forces making for an expanding economy has disappeared, and which might deprive us of much of the potential rise in our standard of living; to reduce the

[1] Whether the upheaval might lead ultimately to a better social structure is a question which I can only mention.

great inequality of incomes, particularly where it is based mainly on unequal opportunity or inheritance; to put our public finances and international trade on a satisfactory basis; and so on. These problems are subsidiary in the sense of being less important than the main one, and a failure to solve them satisfactorily could hardly prevent *some* advance being made. But if our aim is, as it should be, the greatest possible increase in welfare, then they constitute an important challenge to our social ingenuity.

The above remarks cannot, as they stand, be used as a basis for any judgment about whether or not the fall in the birth-rate is "economically a good thing." All our conclusions have been influenced by other factors besides the trend of population, because the analysis would otherwise have been so unrealistic. If, however, we roughly disentangle the influence of population trends from that of capital accumulation and technical progress, then we find that the conclusions in many respects are surprisingly little affected, except in degree.

As an example we may take the important question of general unemployment. We argued that the difficulty of avoiding heavy general unemployment would be greater in the future than in the past, mainly for the following reasons:

(I) Per head of population, the stock of material capital in existence at any time would be greater, both as a result of accumulation in the meantime and (at least in the later years), because of a fall in population; this would reduce the number of obvious openings for capital outlay.

(II) The average income would be larger, both because of the increased amount of capital per head and because improvements would have been made in technique; this would make for greater fickleness or instability in demand, and also (though this is rather doubtful over long periods) for more saving.

(III) The trend of population would be downwards, further reducing the openings for capital outlay, and making those that remained risky and very much dependent on "confidence" (perhaps "courage" would be a better word); they would appear unattractive except in periods of good trade, whatever the rate of interest might be.[1]

It is clear that the population factor makes a very substantial contribution to these arguments, but the case certainly does not rest on it alone; the problem is in part simply a consequence of increasing national wealth.

The reader can easily take other examples for himself, which will show that most of the developments which we have shown to be likely would take place as the result of the population factor alone, but on a smaller scale. The danger of increased frictional unemployment was very largely due to it, and so, of course, was the rise in the pension bill and in the yield of death-duties; it played a smaller, but still important, part in the combination of forces making for a higher real income per head. Perhaps the most significant case where we find population acting in isolation is in connection with international trade; we have to thank the declining trend of population, and nothing much else, for a most welcome alleviation of our task in finding adequate outlets for our exports.

If there is to be an "economic verdict," then, on the population changes which we are to expect in the next twenty-five or thirty years, it must be couched in much the same terms as those used for the outlook as a whole. They put us collectively on our mettle. If we can show sufficient social resourcefulness and adaptability to solve various problems of adjustment, then they will give us a good reward;

[1] Cf. pages 116 et seq.

if we cannot, then they will prove a curse instead of a blessing.

At the same time it is only right to point out that the verdict ought to include a clause to the effect that the economic importance of population changes is often grossly exaggerated. Whatever might be the case in the year 2035 if fertility continued to decline, for this period they are seldom likely to dominate the situation.[1] Thus even in the case of unemployment, whether general or particular, they certainly render the task of keeping this down to a satisfactory level more difficult; but this would not be nearly so important if the task were not already arduous enough, and liable to become increasingly so for other reasons besides the changed trend of population. Similarly, our discussion of public finance showed that population changes would exert a material influence on certain items, each one of which was large enough to affect the whole budget to a significant extent; but, partly because these effects tended to cancel out, our final conclusions were that other factors would (or at least might) be decidedly more important.

It is especially necessary to emphasize the above point if we are considering the advisability of trying to influence the trend of population. Few people, I imagine, would want to advocate measures aimed at a further reduction of the birth-rate, on the strength of the advantages which a declining trend in our population brings at least potentially within our reach. But many believers in "safety first" might want to raise it so as to avert the increased danger of unemployment, preferring to forgo a potential addition to real incomes for the sake of the increased security of those we now enjoy. In assessing the merits of such a policy it is essential both to investigate the possibility of averting this danger by other means and to realize that the problem of unemployment would not be *eliminated* even if the birth-rate were doubled.

[1] As exceptions we might note the cost of education and old-age pensions, and the probable rise in juvenile wage-rates.

It is also important to realize that some of the less pleasant consequences of our coming population changes cannot be removed, and can be only very slightly mitigated, by anything we may do to the birth-rate. The pension bogey, for example, derives most of what frightfulness it really possesses from the increased *number* of old people who will be alive in future years as a result of the fall in mortality-rates. Presumably nobody would want to adopt a deliberate policy of shortening the lives of these people, or of compelling them to emigrate; but these are the only ways of affecting their number. An increase in the birth-rate would certainly do something to reduce the rise in the *proportion* of old people, though it could not possibly prevent it; but this would be of singularly little help to the active population, because it would also raise the proportion of dependent children.

This question has given rise to so much loose thinking and talking that we may usefully quote a few simple statistics to show what the real position is. In 1935, the base year for Dr. Charles's estimates, the proportion of people aged 65 or over was 8 per cent. Her first estimate, which assumed no change in fertility or mortality from the 1933 levels, shows a rise to 12·7 per cent by 1965, and the figure finally settles down at 16–17 per cent after 1985. In a static population the proportion would be rather over 12 per cent (on the basis of these mortality-rates). Hence almost the whole rise in the proportion before 1965, and about half of the total rise, represented the removal of an existing anomaly, not the creation of a new one. Even if fertility had never fallen below the level needed to keep the net reproductive rate at unity—that is, even if the question of an ultimate fall in numbers had never arisen—yet this part of the rise would have taken place; the most that we can say is that the process would have been slower.

Nevertheless, if this were the whole story, a rise in the birth-rate might still be considered desirable on the ground that it would at least avert the second part of the rise. But though this would undoubtedly reduce the burden of pensions, yet we must also consider the other side of the medal. In 1935 the proportion of people aged 14 or under was 23·3 per cent, or rather more than the 22·2 per cent appropriate to a static population; for 1965 Dr. Charles's first estimate gives 17·6 per cent, and the figure later settles down at 16·5 per cent. We may construct a rough measure of the proportion of dependants, young and old, by adding together the percentages for this class and for the previous one. The resulting index of the burden on the active population shows no very great variations, as we may see from this table:—

	Per cent
1935	31·3
1965	30·3
After 1985 .. .. about	33
Static population	34·5

The significant point is that the figure for the static population is the highest. In other words, if we raised fertility so as to make the net reproductive rate unity, we should increase the proportion of dependants above both the present percentage and that which would prevail if fertility remained constant at the 1933 level; this effect would not be confined to the initial years (when obviously the extra people would all be children), but would apply throughout. The difference is not very great, and for purely budgetary purposes we have seen that a child is less of a problem than a pensioner; but raising the birth-rate clearly cannot be justified on the grounds that we must maintain the proportion of active people.[1]

So far our analysis has suggested a rather negative attitude towards measures designed to influence the birth-rate,

[1] A similar calculation shows that the increased danger of particular unemployment owing to the rising proportion of elderly workers can only partially be averted by raising fertility.

whether upwards or downwards.[1] Those who consider the possible advantages to be derived from a downward trend in population to outweigh the difficulties which it causes should, nevertheless, admit that the balance is not decisive enough to justify opposition to measures which were otherwise desirable, merely because they would tend to increase fertility. On the other hand, those who reckon the increased danger of unemployment or monopolistic exploitation to be the more important factor should correspondingly admit that these problems not only *can* be tackled by methods other than a raising of the birth-rate, but will require such treatment whatever the rate may be, so that measures to raise it should not be undertaken if there are serious objections to them on other grounds. We should all agree, so it seems, to do nothing about it, or at least very little.

Such a conclusion would very possibly be welcomed by our harassed politicians, who would thereby be assured that there was really no (economic) reason why they need go to all the trouble of devising a population policy, getting it accepted, and putting it into execution. To some people it may appear rather a small mouse to have emerged as the result of so much economic labour. This verdict would, however, be fallacious. Quite apart from any feeling of well-doing which may spring from the thought of relieving the politicians' minds, the economic fraternity need experience no sense of shame about presenting such a completely negative conclusion, provided it is firmly established. It may somehow seem more satisfying if one's analysis leads to results which cry aloud for immediate action, but a definite negative is really just as useful.

On closer investigation, however, this attitude of total indifference seems to be based on a rather short-sighted view. Nothing that we have said so far needs to be withdrawn, but we must remember the following points:—

[1] We are, of course, confining our attention to the economic consequences.

(I) *The rate of decline.*—We have argued that the change from an increasing to a more or less constant population is economically not unwelcome, or at least that its consequences do not justify active steps to raise the birth-rate. We may legitimately extend this argument to cover the further change to a slow decline in the second period, the two developments being both due to the same fall in fertility and being analytically more or less the same. As yet, however, we have not attempted to discuss what rate of decline would give the most favourable results, nor what policy, if any, is needed to adjust fertility accordingly. Clearly there is no guarantee that the rate which happens to be established will be the best.

I do not see how one could possibly calculate with any degree of exactness which figure would be the optimum. Apart from other difficulties, opinions may very reasonably differ about the values of the things to be compared (roughly speaking, "higher incomes" and "less need for adjustment"). But if we contemplate the effects of a further substantial fall in fertility, leading to a more rapid decline, it is tolerably clear that the difficulties of adjustment increase far more steeply than the potential benefits. We can see this in an extreme form by considering the nightmare conditions which would prevail in 2035 if Dr. Charles's second estimate were fulfilled—conditions which we have refused to analyse on the grounds that society simply must prevent their existence.

Now the present level of fertility would ultimately establish a rate of decline of about 1 per cent per annum. Such a rate seems quite fast enough to produce most of the potential benefits—one might plausibly argue that it would be uncomfortably rapid. But even ignoring the last possibility, there is no solid reason for supposing that the persistent downward trend in fertility has yet been arrested; if nothing is done, therefore, we may ultimately find ourselves faced with a very awkward situation—"ultimately" probably meaning within the next thirty or forty years. Strictly speaking, this does not require immediate action, but if still smaller families once become fashionable it may be far more difficult to raise the average again than it would have been to maintain it. A very reasonable caution suggests that we should begin to take action, or at least to devise a policy, *now*; even if the effect were actually to raise fertility somewhat, we shall have lost very little, if anything.

(II) *The period of decline.*—The above conclusion is reinforced by another consideration, though this applies to a still more distant future. As our population grows smaller, so the arguments in favour of a further decline will grow weaker, and the arguments against it grow stronger.[1] Whatever the rate of decline, we should, therefore, like it eventually to taper off, leaving the population more or less constant at a lower level. The necessary rise in the net reproductive rate would, however, be most difficult to secure if it once fell far below unity. It is now under 0·8, and the inevitable slowness with which results appear in the population field suggests that we should at the very least try to prevent a further decline.

If we take a longer view then, there is a reasonable economic case for a positive population policy as a sort of insurance against future difficulties. We must not exaggerate its strength—our previous conclusion still represents the greater part of the truth—but "the effect on fertility" may reasonably be used as an additional argument in support of measures which would also be desirable on other grounds. The case would be greatly strengthened if fertility showed definite signs of falling further; if the fall were serious, then we might have to resort to measures which would otherwise be objectionable.

The question of how (if at all) we can raise fertility is a large and somewhat speculative one, which really lies outside

[1] This is not true of all the arguments, but as leading examples we may take the difficulty of finding adequate export markets on the one hand and the possible loss of the economies of mass production on the other.

the scope of this book. A thorough treatment of it would have to begin with a study of the reasons why fertility has fallen so greatly, not only in this country but throughout the Western world. Any number of reasons have been advanced to account for this phenomenon, such as the spread of contraceptive knowledge; increased fear of war; greater insecurity of employment; increased urbanization; housing difficulties; desire by the parents for a higher standard of living; desire to give a small family a good start in life; the increased tempo of modern life; the incompatibility of a large family and modern entertainments; increased openings for women in trade and industry; and so on. Nearly all of these seem to me to have had *some* influence, and a combination of two or more may easily secure results where one would have been powerless. If our aim were to secure the maximum effect on the birth-rate from a very small number of measures, we should have to assess the importance of each cause with great care and choose our policy accordingly. This investigation should indeed be carried out,[1] but it cannot be attempted here. The answer is by no means clear-cut, and it is not really essential for our purpose; for our conclusion was not that a large rise in fertility should be regarded as a primary objective, but simply that a limited rise would be welcome if it came as a by-product of schemes which were also desirable for other reasons. Even those who would favour a larger rise should remember that no action ought to be omitted (provided it is not in itself objectionable) merely because it would not solve the whole problem.

With this preface we may now proceed to a very brief examination of various measures which might be taken to raise fertility. They fall into two main classes, which we may call "measures of encouragement" and "measures of coercion."[2] Broadly speaking, the former category are all

[1] The question of fertility and attempts to influence it will be dealt with from many aspects, including the historical, in a forthcoming work by Mr. D. V. Glass.

[2] "Blackmail" might be a better word.

desirable in themselves and should be adopted as soon as the detailed arrangements can be completed. They include:

(*a*) *Family Allowances.*—The case for these is discussed in Appendix A. They represent a direct encouragement to parents to have larger families, which may be important in influencing a number of borderline decisions; it is no "proof" of their inefficacy to say that 5s. a week is a quite inadequate inducement to child-bearing. Nevertheless the case for their adoption rests mainly on their social desirability rather than their effect on the birth-rate. For a relatively small outlay the community can do a great deal in this way to reduce poverty and malnutrition and to improve the physique of the next generation; it can also remove the anomaly whereby an unskilled worker with a large family is often better off when unemployed than when he is at work. It seems hardly necessary to add a further reason for supporting such a measure, but so far as it goes the population argument is certainly favourable; and it is not beyond the bounds of political possibility that this relatively weak argument may finally prove decisive.

(*b*) *Increased Income-Tax Allowances.*—The family man who is liable to pay income-tax does receive a sort of family allowance, because in computing his liability he is entitled to deduct £60 from his income for each dependent child. If this amount would otherwise have borne tax at the full rate (5s. 6d. at the moment of writing), he is, therefore, left with £16 10s. more spendable income than his childless neighbour. It is not difficult to make out a case for increasing the amount of this relief, but clearly it must rest more on our ideas of social justice than on its efficacy in raising the birth-rate. Again, however, the population argument is favourable—for what it is worth.

(*c*) *Improved Maternity Services.*—The case for these need not be argued at length. They may encourage child-bearing by making it appear less of an ordeal; they may reduce maternal and infantile mortality, and so avoid the need for so much child-bearing; and they are thoroughly desirable in themselves.

(*d*) *Crèches and Nursery Schools.*—Once more these are desirable quite apart from any effect they may have on fertility, and they may ease the population problem by reducing mortality-rates. But they may well prove surprisingly effective as a stimulus to child-bearing if, as we are frequently told, the deterrents to this lie rather in the *inconvenience* of a family rather than its cost.

(*e*) *Housing Policy.*—One of the deterrents to a large family is undoubtedly the difficulty of securing a house which will be considered adequate by modern standards at a rental which the parents are prepared to pay. A concealed but effective form of family allowance may be granted through governmental provision of such houses, preference being given in the selection of tenants to people with large families.

Once again such a policy can easily be justified by its effect on social welfare, quite apart from any influence it may have on the birth-rate. Indeed, it has already been put into practice to some extent in municipal housing schemes, and the process of favouring the family man is sometimes carried much further by a system of rent rebates which takes account of family responsibilities. To mitigate the inconvenience which children must cause to their parents, housing estates should be provided with adequate playgrounds, if not with crèches.

The objection will probably be raised against this and the previous suggestions that they are doubtless very desirable, but must be strictly limited on the grounds of cost. Actually this cost is not really very large, and should probably be accepted in any case by a truly democratic community for the sake of the increase in welfare alone. We saw, however, in Chapter V that increased redistribution of the national income is desirable as part of our campaign against unemployment. We may temper the wind to the shorn taxpayer by saying that these services should be used as the principal channels for disposing of the money. Population policy should not, of course, be the only guide in the selection of the services to be expanded; but when other things are nearly equal it may be used to tip the scale.

(*f*) *Marriage Loans.*—These and other devices for encouraging early marriages are more debatable proposals. In some cases they will doubtless accelerate the wedding, and this will somewhat increase the probability of a large family. But "boy and girl" marriages will be deplored by many as socially undesirable, and so will the foundation of a home on the basis of debt. If the loans serve to keep young couples out of the hands of the less scrupulous hire-purchase traders, they will be socially beneficial, but will not much affect the date of the marriage, and direct measures might be preferable.

It may be more important to review the bans on marriage at present imposed by various banks and other institutions. Where these apply to the woman's employment we are in rather a dilemma: if the wife could retain her job, we might have more early marriages but fewer children. However, raising the birth-rate is not our major objective, so that if the policy is considered desirable in itself this risk must be run.

(*g*) *Cheapening of Education.*—Middle-class parents are particularly likely to restrict their families in order that they may give each child the conventional and very expensive form of education. It is at least arguable that our public school system causes the cost of this item to rise quite disproportionately to the real educational value of the service supplied. The "value" of such an education is far too largely a "snob value."

This subject is far too large to discuss here, but its social importance is obvious. If some policy were adopted which would reduce the cost of this "conventional necessity," then it might have a notable effect on the fertility of a class traditionally regarded as particularly valuable to the community. It would also be highly beneficial in itself.

(*h*) *Increase of Social Security.*—This is placed last, not because it is the least important, but because it is necessarily rather vague and general, and obviously desirable in itself. A feeling of insecurity may do more to make life seem "not worth living" than a low income—more especially if the risks are ones which the victim feels to be quite unfair and outside his control. The bearing and rearing of children is essentially a long-term affair, which is liable to appear unattractive if the parents feel their position to be insecure—whether owing to the fear of war, or unemployment, or indeed anything. Measures designed to minimize these risks, whether by reducing the danger of the catastrophe occurring or by mitigating its consequences, may bring an increase in the birth-rate as one of their minor blessings.[1]

Amongst the measures of coercion we may mention:—

(*a*) *Heavy Taxation of Bachelors.*—This is not very different in principle from tax-relief for family men, but there may be important differences in degree. Thus the reliefs amount to very little where the taxpayer is only liable at a reduced rate, and only a minority pay any income-tax at all; the mere difference in name and spirit may be of significance. Logically the system should be extended to include taxation of married couples who have not had a specified number of children within a specified time, and if we want to do the thing thoroughly we could have provisions for exemption on the strength of a medical certificate.

[1] We might perhaps produce a greater effect on fertility if insecurity were only reduced in the case of married men. This would not justify a refusal to improve the lot of the others as well, if that were possible; but clearly it may not be. Thus the ideal policy would be to avoid slumps; but if one does overtake us, then preference can be given to married men (other things equal) in deciding whom not to dismiss. There is a great deal to be said for such arrangements, quite apart from any effect on the birth-rate.

(*b*) *Occupational Restrictions.*—It could be made a condition for the holding of various posts in the public service that the employee should be married by a certain age and have a certain number of children within a certain time. The regulations could also be extended to other occupations with the aid of a licensing system. Once again exemption might be granted on the strength of a medical certificate.

(*c*) *Restrictions on Women's Employment.*—There seems to be a definite correlation between the level of fertility in a district and the scarcity of openings for women to secure paid employment.[1] This suggests that a policy of excluding women from such employment would help to raise fertility. Of course, there can be no guarantee that a woman will have children merely because she is compelled by economic pressure to regard her place as being in the home; but there will probably be some results.

(*d*) *Restrictions on the Sale of Contraceptives.*—The main effect of these would probably be to establish a bootlegging trade and to stimulate the use of methods which require no appliances, and at least reduce greatly the chance of conception. There might, however, be some rise in the birth-rate, if only as a result of mistakes.

(*e*) *Propaganda.*—This ought perhaps to be put on a neutral list; it all depends on the spirit in which the propaganda is carried on. If it is based on nationalistic or racial pride, with military considerations and "patriotic duty" playing a large part, then it is to be condemned as coercive. On the other hand it might be largely educational, emphasizing especially the long-term advantages of a larger family. Human beings are only too liable to overestimate the importance of immediate effects; and clearly child-bearing involves a very considerable loss of freedom in the early stages, quite apart from the question of expense. People may legitimately be reminded of the part which children play in making life more interesting for their parents in years to come.

[1] Cf. *Political Arithmetic*, page 205.

The line is not easy to draw, but propaganda which honestly aims at explaining the true facts and then leaves individuals to make their own decision is desirable; propaganda which seeks to establish a duty to the State is coercive.

There seems little question that the State *could* influence the birth-rate very considerably if it were really determined to do so. Measures of encouragement might not have very much effect unless they were conducted on such a scale as to be wildly expensive; they should, however, be applied whenever there is a good case for them on other grounds as well. Coercive measures, however, can be tightened up to the extent of making life almost impossible for people who do not have the required number of children—notably by occupational restrictions. Whether a community which had to resort to such measures to secure its survival really deserves to survive is a question which as yet does not arise. For whatever may be the proper course in other fields, this is surely one in which a democracy should try voluntary methods first.

APPENDIX A

THE CASE FOR FAMILY ENDOWMENT[1]

I

EVERYBODY agrees that the State must use its powers of compulsion to influence the distribution of the national dividend; at the very least the destitute must be prevented from starving, and few would support the complete abolition of State education.

The advocate of a new extension of this practice has, therefore, no lack of precedents. He does not need to justify the principle of taxing to provide social services. Rather does the abundance of precedents constitute an embarrassment; for he must demonstrate that the merits of the proposal outweigh its disadvantages, and the latter are seriously increased by the amount of taxation needed for existing services.

In suggesting a reconsideration of the case for extending the social services to include some form of family endowment I do not claim that the matter can be settled on strictly "economic" grounds alone. Inevitably one's judgment is affected by one's social philosophy, if not by one's private interest. But the question is one which can very properly be argued by economists, even if the final conclusion may be, to quote Professor Pigou, largely "a confession of faith." And I hope to show that the economic case for a minimum scheme is very strong indeed.

II

It is a useful preliminary to consider the position as it now exists in Britain. We find an excellent example of how social arrangements develop in practice. The principle of child endowment has never been accepted, yet a system has developed piecemeal which does in fact subsidize family men in several ways. It is not based on any consistent theory of the rights of parents, children, and the State; but at each stage it has seemed reasonable to those in control to use State powers to modify the distribution of income which would otherwise have prevailed.

Let us start with some cases where an advantage is given to

[1] Reproduced by kind permission from the author's article, "Family Endowment Reconsidered," in *The Review of Economic Studies*, February 1938.

the family man *as of right*, which improves his position relatively to that of his childless, but otherwise similar, neighbour. The clearest case is the income-tax allowances. Under the present scales the father is allowed to deduct £60 from his taxable income for every child who is dependent on him. Provided that his income would otherwise have been large enough for this sum to be taxed at the standard rate, his payment is therefore reduced by £16 10s. The State thus ensures that he has about 6s. 4d. per week more spendable income than his neighbour, though the exchange values of the services which they have marketed (which would determine their position under pure *laisser-faire*) were identical.[1]

A second case arises out of the system of unemployment insurance. A man with dependants pays no higher contribution on that account, and his liability to unemployment is not vastly different. Yet he draws, as a matter of right, an additional benefit of 3s. a week for each child.

A third illustration is the provision of free education to all who like to take advantage of the offer. The parents, and even the children, may perhaps discount this benefit somewhat on the grounds that they would have preferred an equivalent amount of money. But it certainly constitutes *some* discrimination in favour of the family man, and in many cases leaves him free to spend money which he would otherwise have paid for his children's schooling.

If we abandon the stipulation that the benefit must be payable as of right, we can easily add to the list. Nearly all forms of relief are granted on a basis of household needs, and, therefore, increase with the number of dependent children. (This is notably the case with the U.A.B., where the extra amount is virtually a "right.") And there are many indirect subsidies to family men, such as preference in the allotment of council houses.

In short, there are a great many arrangements already in existence whereby various classes of family men are given some help in meeting the cost of bringing up their children. They certainly do not follow any logical principle, as we may see from the following results:—

1. The family man and the bachelor who do the same work receive the same income so long as they are in employment;

[1] At the same time it is interesting to note that the income-tax provisions penalise the married couple as against two single people. The State thus encourages parenthood whilst discouraging marriage.

but if they are unemployed then the former draws 3s. extra benefit for every child.

2. The family man receives (again as of right) a subsidy of 6s. 4d. a week for each child in reduced income tax, provided his income is *above* a certain figure; the subsidy rapidly diminishing as income falls.
3. The State offers to bear one of the costs of parenthood (education), but not others which may be equally important, such as food and clothing.

We should not, however, condemn the present arrangements out of hand merely because they are not based on a consistent theory of the relationship between the individual and the State. Every scheme of redistribution requires that the State shall extract from its citizens part of the income which they consider to be their rightful property. A realistic judgment of any proposal must, therefore, take account of their attitude and prejudices, even if these are somewhat irrational. After all, this is far from being the only sphere in which consumers ignore the dictates of pure reason in spending their income, either privately or collectively. The proper role of the economist is to examine the system which results from the present social prejudices, comparing it with the one at which he would like to aim; if he finds it unsatisfactory he must then try to educate public opinion to demand a change.

III

On what grounds, then, do we want the State to influence the distribution of incomes in favour of the family man? Why should he not simply receive whatever amounts he can induce somebody to pay him for the services of himself and his property, in the same way as the bachelor?

The most important argument is the one which finds popular expression in such statements as: "£2 a week[1] may be all right for a single man, but it is not enough for anybody with a family to support." In more sophisticated language the economist may talk of redistribution in favour of those to whom the marginal utility of income is high.

As a corollary or extension of the above we may take the arguments which elaborate various consequences of distributing

[1] In other ranks of society we may hear the same about a salary of £200 a year or a dole of 17s. a week.

incomes with little regard to family needs. Thus we do not simply deplore the general loss of possible welfare which such a system entails; we consider particularly its effect on such things as health, nutrition, housing, and the environment in which the next generation is growing up.

Some people will also support schemes of redistribution because of their alleged effect on the size, and perhaps the heredity, of future generations. This is a matter in which the arguments are by no means all on one side; it has been dealt with at length by other writers[1] and I shall, therefore, say little about it.

Finally, as with all schemes of redistribution, we must consider the probable effects on the size of the national dividend, and the reaction on the economic system generally.

IV

The first argument clearly supports not only the present measures of redistribution but far more comprehensive ones, unless they were such as to reduce the national dividend substantially. If a given income is to be divided amongst a given population it will yield more satisfaction if the basis takes account of family responsibilities than if it ignores such matters—provided that we do not give so much weight to them as to leave the bachelor worse off than the family man. Of course, family endowment has no monopoly of this virtue; the same claim can be made for proposals to redistribute income on other bases. But most people's ideal system would include some measure of differentiation in favour of the family; and we must not reject a proposal to remedy one defect merely because it leaves others untouched.

All schemes of redistribution, however, have to face the problem of devising social machinery which will effect a smooth transfer. The present arrangements do at least mitigate the worst instances of mal-distribution, and a supporter might claim that on the whole they directed the money available to the families whose need is greatest (notably the unemployed); moreover, in the cases where this is most doubtful (such as the income-tax allowances) they have the great advantage of being widely accepted as reasonable by the people who pay the bill. In other words,

[1] See in particular E. Rathbone, *The Disinherited Family*, pages 235 ff. (London: George Allen & Unwin).

whilst we may look forward to a time when public opinion will demand bold and comprehensive measures (and agree to the necessary taxation), yet in the present age of rearmament we must present a very strong case for any extension which will further strain the taxing machinery.

We can best judge the strength of the case for further redistribution to increase the welfare of families by following the second argument. The investigations of Sir John Orr, S. Rowntree, and others suggest that the problem of the family man earning a wage insufficient to provide a decent minimum is of very considerable importance, and in many cases becomes acute where there are more than two children. The larger the family the larger the house should be, but the larger also the requirements for food; and in many cases the result is that one or both is inadequate. In these families, therefore, the next generation is being brought up in an unsuitable environment, and the evil is intensified because the proportion of children who belong to these families is so much larger than the proportion of families which fall in this class.

These investigations are too familiar to call for reproduction of their results. But it is worth emphasizing that in the case of children inadequate incomes and large families are so strongly correlated that any attempt to remedy the former by measures which treated all households as equal units would be fantastically expensive. If we want to eliminate malnutrition, for example, the available resources must be distributed in a manner which gives more to the large family than to the small. For this particular problem we can ensure the maximum results from a very small expenditure by such devices as free milk for children and nursing mothers; by distribution in kind we ensure the wise use of the funds and prevent the recipients (to put it crudely) from wasting the money on beer. But it is impossible to carry these measures very far without making them rather ridiculous—it is ludicrous to picture a benevolent Government distributing wholesale a variety of foods officially considered good for the recipients. Quite apart from the very serious administrative difficulties of greatly extending these services, a democracy cannot be perpetually denying the ability of large numbers of its members to spend their income wisely. And, actually, Mr. Booker has shown[1] that expenditure on food per head responds very faithfully to changes in income available; if families are given cash allowances some

[1] *Economica*, November 1937.

may be wasted on beer, but most will fulfil its purpose of improving nutrition, housing, and clothing.

In brief, I find it hard to believe that anyone who reads these and similar works carefully will deny that the case for including some form of family endowment in our system of income redistribution is very strong. Mr. Rowntree modestly suggests 5s. a week for each child after the third, which he estimates will cost not more than £6 millions a year, even without an income limit and without allowing for any off-sets. Such a provision would add greatly to welfare in proportion to its cost; but there seems a great deal to be said for including the third child, and we may even look forward to a time when society decides to make some collective provision for *every* child, just as it now offers each one free education.

V

Nobody will suggest that such a measure would let loose the Malthusian bogy. The future of the birth-rate is a subject which has all too often confounded the prophets. I personally doubt whether a moderate subsidy would have a significant *lasting* effect, though the reduced financial strain might lead some parents to complete their families more quickly, and there might be fewer early deaths. It is certainly not one of the objects of this article to suggest that such a measure will banish the fear of a declining population.

As for the heredity of the next generation, there seems little reason to fear that this would suffer through a differential stimulus to parenthood in poor families. Child-rearing is not going to become a profitable pursuit (at least so far as immediate income is concerned); and the stimulus (if any) may act most strongly on the lower middle and artisan classes who approach the matter in a greater spirit of prudence than the labourer, whose position is in any case so insecure that forethought is almost a mockery.[1] The community seeks in any case to prevent starvation, however improvident the parents may have been, and so largely removes Nature's check on "excessive breeding by the poor."

The conclusion must surely be that the effect on the size of the population will be comparatively unimportant, and that the effect on its quality will be felt mainly in the change of environment. I repeat that this improved environment is important

[1] For fuller treatment the reader is referred to Miss Rathbone's work, cited above.

because such a high percentage of children come from large families whose income is inadequate.

VI

If we approach the problem of family endowment along the lines of this article, it is natural to prefer a single national scheme to a multitude of occupational pools. If income is to be deliberately redistributed so as to favour the family man, then the policy should be carried out on a national basis. The single scheme has the additional advantage that it can be made to cover independent workers and small employers who would be very difficult to fit into the "pool" system based on wage bills. And, clearly, their claim to inclusion is just as great as that of wage-earners—the need for family endowment arises out of the inadequacy of *incomes*, however they may have been earned.

We shall, therefore, discuss the effects on the national dividend of paying allowances of 5s. a week in respect of each child after the third (or the second, if we become more ambitious) until it leaves school. We shall argue the point later as to whether there should be an income limit, but in any case the funds are to be raised by general taxation.

Such a redistribution of income does not in itself affect the size of the national dividend. Apart from administrative costs no real resources have been used up in the way that rearmament uses them up in producing instruments of destruction. But it does present a very real fiscal problem—how to raise the money without promoting evasion or discouraging enterprise. If I do no more than mention this point it is not because I consider it unimportant (though every increase in taxation has been regarded as the last straw, yet the camel survives) but because the effect of taxation has been adequately discussed by other writers. Clearly, however, the budgetary problem cannot be a serious impediment to Mr. Rowntree's modest scheme.

As against this possible loss of incentive we have an advantage whose importance may well be growing. At present we (in effect) give a man family endowment when he is out of work but not when he is employed. Where the family is even moderately large the difference between a man's income when he is in work and his unemployment benefit may be very small, perhaps insufficient to off-set the additional expenditure on food, clothes, fares, etc., which employment entails. The danger of thus undermining the incentive to work became apparent when the Advisory Committee recommended that the allowance for children should be raised from 2s. to 3s.; they suggested a maximum benefit of 41s. so as to reduce the chance of its exceeding the earnings of an unskilled man. But the Government refused to accept this advice, with the result that a man with six dependent children suffers a considerable loss of income if he obtains unskilled work.

It is not easy to judge how important this factor is in actual practice. On the whole, most family men seem to have retained a strong desire to work and be independent, and the trouble is rather with the younger ones who have grown up in the atmosphere of depression and the dole. But there must be *some* demoralization on this account, and in any case it will soon be the turn of the latter group to find their wages little higher than their benefits (assuming they have families). One does not need much imagination to foresee what will happen then; at the very least there will be a strong temptation to take a temporary holiday on the dole.

In any case, it is most unsatisfactory that a family should be worse off when the breadwinner obtains work than when he is idle. Yet a reduction of benefits is a political impossibility—they represent the minimum which any party is prepared to consider adequate for the household's needs. Similarly, there is no solution to be found in a general raising of unskilled wages. If industry is to be run by private enterprise, or, indeed, by any system which tries to be economical, these must depend on value of service (i.e. on marginal net product). In a world of imperfect mobility, imperfect adjustment, and imperfect competition we may squeeze the capitalist or the consumer of luxury goods somewhat in favour of the workmen, or the skilled in favour of the unskilled; and, of course, we can give concessions to favoured groups of highly sheltered workers, such as municipal employees. But trade boards and the popular sentiment in favour of a minimum "living wage" have probably done about as much as can be secured in the first way, and the second offers no general solution; to wait and hope that greater efficiency will come to the rescue is a policy of optimistic despair.

The only real way out is to recognize the simple facts that the dilemma is due to our policy of giving family allowances only to the unemployed; that we cannot retreat from this practice; and that therefore we must press on and grant family allowances to the employed as well. Only in this way can we avert the "collision" between wages, based on value of service, and benefit or relief, based on household needs. This argument might not be sufficient in itself if the system of family allowances were considered undesirable *per se*—we might prefer to rely on men's sense of independence, plus a strict test of willingness to work. But where the case for family allowances is already strong the preservation of the incentive to work constitutes a further reason for granting them. It seems probable that its beneficial influence will outweigh the effect on the national dividend of higher taxation.

There are other effects on the national dividend which I will do little more than mention, since they are subjects of greater controversy than the axiom that work should yield a larger income than idleness. They are not very important if the scheme is restricted to families with more than three children, because then the sums involved will not be large. But if we look forward to subsequent and more ambitious developments, then they will become highly relevant.

A system of family allowances will redistribute income in favour of people who are extremely likely to spend it. (Indeed, the main case for the proposal was that the recipients cannot buy what we regard as the minimum requirements for a decent standard of living.) It will, therefore, undoubtedly raise the propensity to consume, to an extent which depends on the kind of taxation used. (Even if there is little vertical redistribution between income groups, the transfer within the group will be in favour of spenders.) Those who consider such a development to be a useful means of securing that potential (relative) plenty which is so elusive, will, therefore, welcome it on this ground, as well as on the ground that our actual income is in any case likely to require careful distribution if nobody is to go short.

Family allowances will also help to maintain a high level of employment by their effect on the character of demand, and hence on the amount of industrial adjustment needed. Normally a considerable proportion of the higher incomes made possible by greater productivity or emergence from a slump is spent on novelties and comparative luxuries; not only does this require a reduction in the relative size of the staple industries, but the new ones are themselves unstable, because of the fickleness of such demand. Whereas if the increased income is largely distributed to those families where expenditure per head was low, then the extra demand will be for further amounts of the familiar products.

Both the above consequences are independent of any possible

effect on the birth-rate. Should this be appreciable they will both be reinforced, and there will also be an increase in the inducement to invest.

VII

The object of this article is to deal with principles rather than details of administration. But it is clear that the latter do not afford any great difficulties if we adopt a single national scheme.

The main question to be decided is whether the scheme should apply to all families, or whether there should be an income limit. In New South Wales allowances of 5s. a week are paid by the State in respect of every child after the first, but a low income limit is imposed—the total family income, plus endowment, must not exceed the basic wage, plus 5s. for each child. The difficulties of administration have been surprisingly small, considering that it is not restricted to wage-earners but also applies to small farmers, independent workers, and so on. Perhaps a similar system could be applied here, though it is to be hoped that the whole amount of older children's earnings would not be included in computing family income.

But there are two serious objections. In the first place a means test is objectionable in itself if it can possibly be avoided; it would be far preferable to regard the allowances as an act of deliberate policy to improve the position of all family men, relatively to that of their childless counterparts, whatever their income. In the second, the saving to the Exchequer will not be very great unless the income limit is placed undesirably low—here the analogy with New South Wales is deceptive, because of the higher real income of its unskilled workers. If we confine the scheme to families in excess of three the whole cost is in any case small, and the saving might be little bigger than the expense of administering the test. If we include the third child, then the matter is more serious, but still the number of children excluded would be comparatively small unless the limit were placed very low; the absolute number of large families is certainly greater amongst the poor, even if the same cannot now be so confidently asserted about the proportion.

We might perhaps compromise by saying that income-tax deductions could not be claimed in respect of a child who had received endowment in that year. This would involve no additional income determination and would to some extent reduce the strain on the Exchequer.

If there is to be no income limit, then the administration is simple. When the proud father applies for his third birth certificate (assuming that we include third children) he would be given the juvenile equivalent of a pension book. If we wish payment to continue until the child leaves school irrespective of the fact that in the last few years his elder brothers will not still be dependent children, then that is all. If we wish the payments to cease as soon as he ceases to be the third dependent child, then the ages of the older ones will be noted in the book, and enquiry made about them annually when new books are issued. The same system enables us to apply any other test that may be considered desirable, such as the older ones reaching 18.

On the whole it seems reasonable to insist that children who have left school shall cease to count. How much, then, would our scheme actually cost if the allowance were fixed at 5s. per week? There is no official data which will permit of an exact answer. The census does not record the number of dependent children in each family, so that we cannot tell how many of the ten million or so "possibles" will be in families with three or more. But it is essential to have some indication, so I have made a rough estimate ("guess" might be a more truthful word) by trying to fit them in with the number of married people, and by analogies with Australia, where the requisite data are available. This suggests that about one and a half millions would actually receive allowances, at a cost, therefore, of about £20 millions a year. From this would have to be deducted the saving in the benefits and allowances to children of the unemployed (since the same child would not qualify for these and for endowment), some reduction in income-tax concessions, and probably some on poor relief and miscellaneous social services. To be on the safe side, however, we might neglect these.

This estimate may seem surprisingly low, though actually I think it is more likely to be high. The explanation (apart from the small size of the average family) is that a great number of the children under 15 at any one time are first or second children in families which may subsequently be large enough, but are not yet so; whilst another large proportion consists of later children whose elder brothers have already left school and, therefore, ceased to count. It is only for a comparatively short period that a family of four will draw endowment for *both* the younger ones, and, of course, the two elder ones will never qualify. At the same time they will *benefit* from the scheme because the family income will be enlarged just in the years when need is greatest.

I think it may safely be concluded that the budgetary cost is not prohibitive, and (unlike pensions) it seems likely to fall rather than rise. In return we should effect, with the minimum administrative difficulty and very little "stigma," a really beneficent redistribution of incomes. We should also remove, almost completely, the anomaly of men receiving more for being unemployed than for working. For what other proposal can greater claims be made?

APPENDIX B

UNEMPLOYMENT POLICY

THE object of this appendix is to discuss at rather greater length four of the proposals which were put forward in Chapter V for reducing general unemployment. We shall not be able to give an exhaustive treatment, but shall try to bring out the more important points.

MONETARY POLICY

Here it is mainly a question of discussing the limits to the effectiveness of a cheap money policy. There is little more to be said about the first and third points mentioned in the text,[1] namely, that both the central bank and the ordinary banks can only operate directly on the markets for relatively secure loans, and that in bad years little private outlay would be stimulated even by very low rates. We must not exaggerate their importance—the banks may have an appreciable *indirect* effect on other markets, if, for example, they buy Government securities from a private investor who then subscribes to a new issue of shares; whilst the prospects for some forms of capital outlay, e.g. housing, do not deteriorate so drastically in a slump, because certain classes of people may actually find their real incomes increased. Nevertheless they do suggest that "cheap money," though obviously desirable, should not be regarded as a panacea. It would be more effective if banks took a less limited view of the assets which they consider eligible—thus their direct influence on long-term capital market is at present exercised solely through purchase and sale of trustee securities. They might be prepared to invest a part of their funds in direct loans to industry for long periods; they might even make the interest to be paid on these loans vary with the company's profits, thus assuming a part of the risks of the enterprise. This would reduce our present dependence on the effective transmission of the stimulus from the gilt-edged market to that for new issues.

There is more to be said about the obstacles which may be encountered in an endeavour to establish low rates. We may

[1] Page 122.

perhaps neglect the possibility that people will be induced to transfer their funds abroad; recent experience has shown that such a course involves many dangers, e.g. exchange control and default by foreign borrowers, which more than outweigh the advantage of a rather higher interest rate. Double taxation is also a deterrent, which could be increased if necessary, but in any case the countries which might appear attractive will probably be in a similar position.

A more serious difficulty is the possible opposition of vested interests, especially banks. Low interest rates would directly reduce their income from loans, yet clearly the co-operation of the banks is essential. Without admitting that the present level of their profits is to be considered sacrosanct, we may suggest that a way out of this dilemma should be found through the development of an alternative source of income. Instead of trying to attract depositors from each other by rendering all sorts of services for them at low charges, the banks should combine to insist on adequate payment. The clearing of cheques and other current account facilities are so valuable to their clients that a united stand, based on the very reasonable argument that low interest rates make the use of the client's balance less valuable as an off-set, could hardly fail to succeed.[1]

Political pressure by other capitalists to secure a reversal of the cheap money policy must, of course, be simply resisted. There is, however, the danger of a sort of "passive resistance" on their part. As interest rates fall, so more and more people may prefer to keep their wealth in very "liquid" form—either as money (including bank deposits), or at best in very short-term loans. This is by no means unreasonable from their point of view, for bonds would be yielding only a small income, whilst they expose their holder to the risk of suffering heavy capital depreciation if rates subsequently rise;[2] money, on the other hand, cannot depreciate in terms of itself, and has the advantage of being always available for use, without any payments for brokerage or the like. Clearly, so long as wealth can be held in the form of money without any "carrying costs," there must be a minimum,

[1] In the depression of 1930–34 the banks tacitly combined to maintain overdraft rates instead; this is the reverse of what is wanted.

[2] As an illustration of the dangers of buying long-term bonds, the price of 2½ per cent Consols touched 94 in January 1935, but fell to 80 in September; in 1938 it went down to 64, at a time when we were still officially enjoying cheap money.

well above zero, to the rate of interest at which people will subscribe for long-term bonds.

In judging the seriousness of this obstacle we must distinguish sharply between a policy designed to secure a low level of rates in "normal" years, and one designed to secure still lower rates as an additional stimulus in years of depression. In the former case we should be able to secure results in the end, even if there is an appreciable time-lag. Thus the banking system might not at first be able to push the gilt-edged rate below, say, 2½ per cent except by purchasing a vast amount of securities. But with the passing of time some at least of the people from whom they had bought would grow weary of holding their wealth in liquid form. They would, indeed, have little reason for expecting rates to rise again, since we have assumed that, with the diminished number of openings for capital outlay, lower rates will be needed merely to maintain activity at its present level, i.e. times would be as "normal" as they ever are. So they would dismiss their fears and return to the market, forcing rates down towards the minimum. It may be a slow process, but the authorities should be able to secure an average level of rates considerably lower than anything we have experienced in the past.

The lower the average rate, however, the more difficult it will be to secure an appreciable extra stimulus by means of "still cheaper money" in bad years. There will be less distance for the rate to fall, and as it approaches the minimum, so people will become more and more suspicious of the continuance of such rates. Logically speaking, if they believed in the lessons of history, this should lead holders to sell their bonds and wait for the end of the slump, when they would be repurchased at much lower prices. If everyone reacted in this way then the authorities' purchases would have a negligible effect on the price. But even if people's hopes (or fears) are not definite enough to induce them to sell out wholesale, yet they may be chary about adding to their holdings. Inertia may help the authorities to secure a fall in rates, but new issues at these rates may meet with a poor reception, even though they appear to conform to the market. The extra stimulus to capital outlay will thus melt away as soon as borrowers attempt to respond. To produce effective results the authorities will have to support the market further, e.g. by subscribing for the new issues themselves.

In view of this discussion and of the points mentioned at the beginning, we may conclude that a monetary policy designed to stimulate capital outlay is not sufficient in itself. Its most effective function will be to sustain somewhat the amount of private outlay in "normal" and "good" years, and to facilitate the financing of additional public works in bad ones. For the latter purpose the banks' concentration on gilt-edged securities is an advantage and not a disadvantage.

TAXING MONEY

The nature of this proposal is explained in the text. In judging its efficacy we must remember that if the tax is made too large it will bear hardly on people and firms who are holding money for purposes of active circulation. We do not want to interfere with legitimate trade, but only to discourage the holding of large sums "on capital account." In practice this would presumably mean a low rate of tax, e.g. ¼d. in the £ per month, and a moderate exemption limit, say £500.

Let us first consider its effectiveness in establishing a lower interest rate as the normal thing. By making money, at least in its most convenient form, bear a carrying cost we should certainly be able to reduce the otherwise irreducible minimum quite substantially; indeed, if we are prepared to tackle the difficulty of making notes subject to the tax also, then a larger tax might even lead capitalists to accept negative rates of interest, at least on short-term loans, for the sake of an assured repayment of their capital. Without considering these extreme possibilities we may conclude that the proposal, if given a fair trial, would make a valuable contribution to the solution of our problem. Even if there is scope for evasion (notably by hoarding notes if these are not taxed) yet the inconvenience, not to say indignity, of such a proceeding may deter many capitalists; it might even be pronounced illegal.[1]

It might appear that increases in the rate of tax would also supply a valuable extra stimulus in bad times by lowering interest rates still further. Nobody should speak dogmatically about a proposal which has never been tried, but I doubt whether the effect would be as large as might seem likely at first sight. We have already seen that the capital losses incurred in buying bonds when interest rates are temporarily low are very substantial; if the ordinary working of the tax has reduced the "normal"

[1] The whole problem is treated at length in A. Dahlberg: *When Capital Goes on Strike.*

level of rates, then there is, in any case, not much scope for further reductions, and people will be even more apprehensive about a subsequent recovery from what would seem a ridiculously low figure. Thus, if people had come to regard "about $1\frac{1}{2}$ per cent" as the "normal" rate, then they would be very reluctant to subscribe to a long-term loan at 1 per cent unless they thought the depression would last a long time—and it would need a very heavy tax to overcome this reluctance. Quite a small tax takes away the attraction of holding money if there is no particular reason for expecting interest rates to rise in the future, but quite a large one may have no effect on a person who is convinced that the present rate is abnormally low.

This conclusion is greatly strengthened by the fact that the "funds awaiting investment," of which one hears so much in a depression, can be kept liquid by other means than holding a bank deposit. They may be invested in treasury bills or call-loans to the money market—the rates on these may descend to zero, or even become slightly negative, but they will still be more attractive than bank deposits. To some extent this process merely passes on the problem without solving it—somebody else will be left seeking an outlet for *their* funds. But the pressure on long-term interest rates will be at least temporarily relieved, and if the upshot is that they are used to repay bank loans,[1] then it will disappear altogether unless the banks expand deposits again by buying securities themselves. As a special case of this we may consider the people who normally like to finance a portfolio of long-term securities with bank loans; for them, "funds awaiting investment" may simply mean unused overdraft facilities.

Once again, this does not mean that we should reject the idea of increasing the tax in bad times—it might even be made to vary automatically with the percentage of unemployment. Such a proposal would at least bring in additional revenue, at a time when it would be badly needed, without appreciably reducing effective demand; and it might stimulate some people actively to seek out some way of using their capital, for example, in house-building. If so, then we should not mind about its failure to reduce the rate of interest, for the object of that reduction (an increase in capital outlay) would have been attained directly.

[1] This result is inevitable if the rate on call loans becomes negative, for the banks will have no incentive to quote such rates. Similarly their holding of bills will fall rapidly if the return on these becomes negative, causing a further fall in the total of deposits.

TAXATION

If we wish to redistribute the national income by taxing the rich and expanding the social services it seems natural to think primarily in terms of raising the rates of income-tax and sur-tax; this is the direct way of "getting at" the large incomes, from which much saving is done. Such a policy, however, entails a considerable risk of reducing capital outlay. Heavy taxes on income tend to raise the rate of interest even on gilt-edged bonds, because they reduce the net income which the holder will receive, and which must provide the incentive to him to forgo the advantages (safety from depreciation and immediate availability) which he could secure by holding cash; unless something is done, e.g. by credit expansion, to offset this factor, then some capital outlay will be prevented. Their most damaging effect, however, is to take away part of the rewards which a risky enterprise will bring if successful, without providing any mitigation of the capital loss which failure would entail; a potential entrepreneur who appreciates this fact may well decide in favour of safety. Moreover, the progressive element in our taxes means that this factor will weigh most heavily with very rich people who might otherwise be most prepared to take the risks which any form of capital outlay must involve.

The above argument does not mean that we must abandon the use of taxes on income—such a course would clearly be impossible, and all taxes have some disadvantages. But it does mean that we should try to find some alternative, which would be less open to this objection, rather than rely on them alone for our increased revenue. The danger of a serious fall in capital outlay increases considerably as the rate of tax is increased.

Perhaps the best theoretical tax from this point of view is an annual levy of say 1 per cent on private holdings of capital of all kinds, including money.[1] Even with a provision for exempting small fortunes such a tax would yield a very substantial sum—there is roughly £10,000 millions of capital held by people with fortunes over £5,000,[2] so that a flat levy of 1 per cent would realize about £100 millions a year.

The advantage of such a tax over an income-tax yielding a

[1] Cf. Section 4 of an article by M. Kalecki in the *Economic Journal* for September 1937.

[2] Cf. Daniels and Campion: *The Distribution of the National Capital*, page 51.

similar sum is not that it will be paid "out of capital," and, therefore, more effectively reduce the gap between the community's income and its expenditure on consumption; it may do this or it may not—the natural presumption is that although it would be *assessed* on the basis of a man's capital, yet, being a recurrent charge, it would be *paid* out of his income. The important point is that it makes the millionaire pay the same amount, whatever the form in which he keeps his million. Unlike the income-tax, it does not increase the advantages of cash over bonds, or of safe investments over risky ones. Indeed, it may even drive people to stifle their fears of capital depreciation and buy securities in order to have some income out of which to pay the tax; if so it will actually stimulate capital outlay.

The difficulties involved in applying this proposal are, firstly, administrative—especially in the first year it would be very hard to make the necessary assessments—and, secondly, political or psychological—public opinion, particularly amongst the influential property-owning class, must be made to accept the innovation. Neither obstacle seems to be insurmountable, and research might very usefully be devoted to finding out their seriousness.

We do already have a levy on capital of a rather different kind, in the shape of death-duties. (Here the administrative problem has been rendered soluble by reducing greatly the number of assessments to be made each year, whilst the idea of taxing the amount which people inherit is socially much more acceptable than taxing, annually, what they own.) It should be clear that the arguments used above in favour of a levy on capital apply very largely to the case of death-duties also, but there is a further advantage to be considered. Especially in the case of large estates, death-duties are far too heavy to be paid out of income, even out of the income (itself heavily taxed) cf several years. From the point of view of the individual there are only two alternatives—either the amount must be accumulated over a long period, or part, at least, must be paid "out of capital." In practice the second alternative will almost certainly be adopted in many cases, so that part of the savings of the rest of the community will be off-set by the negative savings of those paying death-duties. We may conclude, therefore, that to raise £80 millions by means of death-duties instead of raising it by means of income-tax will not only be less deterrent to capital outlay, but will also be more successful in narrowing the gap between the community's income and its expenditure on consumption. And we may add, as it were in parenthesis, that it will be politically possible to raise larger amounts from the rich by adopting both devices than by relying solely on one.

If death-duties were not already in existence, we should clearly place their introduction high amongst our proposed "remedies," especially as there is so much to be said for them on social grounds in a world where inheritance is one of the great causes of unequal opportunities. But it is doubtful whether we can expect very much help even from a proposal to raise the rates—at least unless we extend their application to cover gifts *inter vivos*. We certainly should not reject this proposal, but we should not expect too much from it unless public opinion can be educated to accept the higher rates as socially desirable, and the administrative problem of preventing evasion solved.

A minor method of "taxing capital" is, perhaps, worth mentioning. We already have various taxes on the transfer of capital from one ownership to another. Even more than death-duties these are probably paid "out of capital"—a man will not restrict his consumption expenditure because he has paid taxes in the process of changing his investments, even though these might amount to a considerable sum. Some of the taxes may have a hampering effect on capital outlay, by adding to the cost of buying real estate or raising finance. But it should not be beyond the wit of man to devise a system of taxes which will minimize this effect, whilst levying a considerable toll on the rich man's game of playing around with his investments.

In conclusion, we may make the general remark that, from this point of view, the taxes to avoid as far as possible are those which automatically rise in amount if a man, by accepting some of the risks which must be borne if capital outlay is to continue, succeeds in adding to his receipts. This principle applies to other parts of our tax system besides those designed primarily to fall on the rich. Thus the levying of local rates on the present basis means that the sum demanded increases automatically if new construction is undertaken; this must be more deterrent to capital outlay than a system in which site value was the basis of assessment.

In using the above principle it is important to take account of psychological considerations. If a rich man would spend any extra income, which he might secure as the result of his venture, on cigars and champagne, then the Exchequer would "automatically" take a very large part of it in the form of extra customs and excise. Yet clearly this fact would not exercise such a deterrent effect as the increased payments in the form of direct taxes.

INFLATION

I shall confine my treatment of this topic to a discussion of the general issues involved. I shall not attempt to examine the details of any particular proposal or to compare the merits of different ones. There are certain questions which affect all of them, and these need to be dealt with first.

Briefly, then, it is clear that the "sound money" men are quite right when they say that we cannot make ourselves any better off *merely* by printing notes or making entries in bank ledgers. If all, or almost all, of the community's productive resources are fully employed, then a policy of "increasing demand" in such ways cannot even *lead to* an increase in the real national income. Even under such conditions the Government can use this device to enable it to purchase goods and services in the market, but it gains only by reducing the real value of the incomes of individuals, or by inducing them to dispose of existing stocks of goods. Broadly speaking, this was the position in Germany in 1923, and under such circumstances the continuance of rapid inflation can only lead to wildly rising prices.

Such a state of affairs, however, is the exception rather than the rule; it is vastly different from the situation which prevails in a slump, or even that which is likely to be our normal fate unless we tackle the problem of general unemployment. When there is a considerable margin of unemployed resources the main effect of giving each of us a nice new pound note would be to increase output, not prices. The printing of the notes would not make us any better off, but the resulting increase in employment would.

There need be no great mystery about this. It is not a completely different type of remedy, nor is it one about which we need rely on theoretical reasoning unsupported by any appeal to facts. Admittedly, money has never been distributed to every citizen in just the way visualized above. But special sections of the population have received what amounted to the same thing in plenty of countries. Thus in Australia in 1931–32 a bounty was paid to all wheat-growers, the money for which was "created" by the Government's borrowing it from the central bank. This procedure has just the same (material) effect as printing notes for the purpose, since the farmers would have paid their bounty money into their bank accounts, whether it came in the form of notes or a cheque on the central bank, and the trading banks would in either case have been free to hold their extra cash either in notes or as a balance with the central bank.[1]

In essentials these proposals amount to little more than a direct method of attaining what would otherwise be attained indirectly. Thus if the central bank creates new money by means of open market purchase of securities (a highly respectable process), and this is reinforced by the creation of more money by the trading banks through further purchases of securities (again a highly respectable process), then what we are hoping for is that somebody will set this new money into active circulation. If it is used for building a house, then the otherwise unemployed bricklayers will have more money to spend, just as the Australian farmers did or the recipients of our hypothetical pound notes would; and the stimulating effect of their purchases will be welcomed by all. It may be better (it is certainly "safer") for the new money only to go into circulation through these respectable channels. But the effect on prices will not be appreciably different—the fact that the house is being built in the second case may help to keep down rents in future, but is of no immediate significance.

In short, then, consumers' dividends and the like could be a valuable weapon if wisely administered and if the public were educated to appreciate the true nature of the process. But this latter task is not going to be a very easy one. We do not want to see a reaction from a state where the mention of the word "inflation" is enough to start a scare, to one where no limits will be admitted to the benefits to be secured from larger and larger doses. As a first step, let all readers now study Mr. Meade's book on the subject, and make their friends do likewise.

[1] The incident does, however, show the need for taking account of "confidence," or, to put it more accurately, of remembering that the public is, as yet, uneducated about monetary matters. For when the Labour Government had proposed to pay just such a bounty with notes the public became thoroughly alarmed, partly because Labour's opponents let loose a spate of stories about "the fallacies of inflation," illustrated by pictures of German billion-mark notes.

INDEX

For Product Safety Concerns and Information please contact our EU representative GPSR@taylorandfrancis.com
Taylor & Francis Verlag GmbH, Kaufingerstraße 24, 80331 München, Germany

www.ingramcontent.com/pod-product-compliance
Lightning Source LLC
LaVergne TN
LVHW011121300926
849160LV00008B/460

* 9 7 8 1 1 3 8 8 7 8 6 4 8 *